THE MOOSE that ROARED

IRONBARK PRESS

THE MOOSE that ROARED

REX MOSSOP

**WITH
LARRY WRITER**

IRONBARK PRESS

Published in 1991 by IRONBARK PRESS
Level 1, 175 Alison Road, Randwick, NSW.

© Rex Mossop

National Library of Australia
Cataloguing-in-Publication

 Writer, Larry

 The Moose That Roared — Rex Mossop

 ISBN 1 875471 07 3

 1. Mossop, Rex. 2. Sportscasters — New South Wales — Biography. 3. Rugby
League football — New South Wales — Biography. I. Writer, Larry. II. Title.

 070.449796092

Design concept: John Collins
Front cover photography: Ern McQuillan
Editor: Norman Tasker
Production: Jennie Fairs
Research: Geoff Armstrong
Finished art: Kylie Prats
Typesetting: Photoset Computer Services and Hippopotamus Dreams
Printed by: Globe Press

DEDICATION

After long deliberation, I dedicate this book to a policeman who passed away some years ago. Superintendent Ron Walden was the man who started it all for me. He was Manly rugby union club's first grade coach who saw me playing in the local juniors and pitched me straight into first grade. Ron was my coach in those formative years. He bobbed up again as manager-coach of the 1949 Wallabies to New Zealand, my first trip abroad in Australian colours. My boxing bouts with Ron, over a period of many years in the ring at North Steyne Surf Club, had the desired effect of toughening me up and teaching me plenty about life.

To the "Ger", who always had time to explain, this book is dedicated.

ABOUT THE AUTHOR

Larry Writer is the author of the critically-acclaimed *Winning — Face To Face With Australian Sporting Legends, Australia — The Moments That Mattered,* and *Five Star Brandy — Greg Alexander And The Rise Of The Penrith Panthers.* He is also the editor of *Local Hero — The Wayne Pearce Story, Someone Else's Daughter — The Life And Death Of Anita Cobby, The Story Of Australian Rugby League, 200 Years Of Australian Sport, The Kangaroos — The Saga Of Rugby League's Great Tours, Sterlo! Story Of A Champion, Backpage Of Sport, Backpage Of Cricket, Border's Heroes, Ron Casey — Confessions Of A Larrikin, Big Mal — The Mal Meninga Story* and *March Of The Dragons — The Story Of St George RLFC.*

Before forming Ironbark Press with Deborah Wood and Ian Heads, he was a senior writer and editor with Australian Consolidated Press and for some years was that company's European Editor and London Bureau Chief.

CONTENTS

AUTHOR'S ACKNOWLEDGEMENTS

The interviews on which this book is based were conducted between myself and Rex Mossop at his home in Sydney. My thanks to Rex for all his patience and interest throughout the lengthy and often gruelling interview sessions and for speaking with such candour and honesty about his football and media careers and his private life.

My thanks, too, to Ken Arthurson, Alan Clarkson, Noel Kelly, Terry Fearnley, George Daldry and Warwick Ritchie for their valuable insights into the Rex Mossop story. Extra special thanks to Joan Mossop for making me welcome and for allowing me access to the family photographs, press clippings, letters and other paraphernalia that have accumulated over more than 60 years.

Of great assistance, too, in telling the story of Rex's long and colourful life was the marvellous research work done by sports historian Geoff Armstrong. *The Sunday Telegraph*, *The Sun-Herald*, *The Daily Mirror*, *The Sun*, *The Telegraph Mirror*, *The Sydney Morning Herald* and *Rugby League Week* were valuable sources of background information.

Thanks to News Ltd, John Fairfax and Sons, and the Mossop family for allowing me to use photographs from their files and albums.

Not for the first time, I thank Ian Heads and Norman Tasker for casting their knowledgable eye over the manuscript. I am grateful for their comments and suggestions. I also appreciate the support of my colleagues at Ironbark Press, Deborah Wood, Jennie Fairs, Ian Heads and Terry Fearnley — and, especially, of my wife Carol — throughout the writing of this book.

— **Larry Writer**

FOREWORD

By Ken Arthurson

R ex Mossop is a true Australian original whose turbulent and eventful life has made him one of the giants of sport and television for as long as most of us can remember.

The Moose has lived his life fearlessly, always speaking his mind regardless of the consequences. Men of high principles can't help stomping on other people's toes occasionally, and Rex has accumulated his share of enemies in both media and sporting circles over the years. As he says in his book, a man without foes has led an inconsequential life. He's dished out plenty, but he's copped plenty, too.

I believe Rex is the best and most authoritative commentator on the game of rugby league this country has seen. He knows league inside out — everybody acknowledges that — but the qualities that led to him becoming a legend as a football caller are the exact qualities that made him special as a player — and make him special as a man. Qualities such as integrity, bravery and the ability to give his best even when hurt. He is a man of great moral courage. If Rex Mossop has ever taken a backward step, I don't know about it.

As his coach in his playing days and today as chairman of the ARL, I have often disagreed with Rex — but I have never stopped respecting or liking him. His colourful ways, his controversial style, his heartfelt criticisms, have played their part in making rugby league the thriving sport it is today. Now and in the future, no matter how well the code is travelling, it will always need blokes like Rex Mossop. I am proud and delighted to contribute this foreword to Rex's story. His is a life well worth reading about.

PREFACE

By Noel Kelly

B y asking me to write the introduction to his book, Rex Mossop is probably hoping I'll forget he owes me a beer for saving his life. Rex is a loyal mate and an excellent companion, but even his best friends will tell you he's not a bloke to splash his money around. Still, I reckon he owes me one for getting him out of a spot of bother at Pratten Park one day. He was 36 then, in the last year of his long and illustrious rugby league career — and he was getting old and cranky. He decided to declare war on my Wests teammates that day and as the game wore on there were quite a few Magpies out to settle a score with the Moose.

Near the end of the game all hell broke loose. Two blokes held Rex down while half a dozen others got stuck into him. He'd asked for it, but he was going to get murdered. When I stopped laughing at his predicament, I made my blokes back off, then I pulled Rex to his feet and whispered in his ear, "For God's sake, Moose, calm down or you're going to get yourself killed." Was he grateful to me for saving his skin? Not likely. His reply to me was unprintable and he threw himself back into the fray.

Rex Mossop would always have a go. Whether he was representing Australia in a Test against the Poms, compering Controversy Corner or *Beauty And The Beast*, or ripping in during one of his TV or radio league commentaries, Rex would never pull his punches. He wouldn't know *how* to pull his punches. I've never seen him give less than his very best — as a player, as a commentator, or as a mate — in the 32 years he's been my friend.

I had plenty of chances to get to admire Rex Mossop. We first locked horns when he represented NSW against my Queensland side in 1959, and we opposed each other many times in the Sydney competition after I came down to play with Wests. We went away together on the 1959 Kangaroo tour and were roommates on the '60 World Cup campaign in England. When our playing days were over and Rex made the big switch to TV, I was a regular panellist on his much-missed Controversy Corner segment on *Sports World*. These days we still see each other. Not every week, or even every month, but we're good pals and whenever we get the chance to sit down and have a yarn there's always plenty to talk about.

Rex Mossop: First grade rugby star at 16, rugby Tests against the All Blacks and the Lions, three and half years playing rugby league with Leigh when the English competition was the best in the world, eight seasons with Manly league team during which time he became one of the greatest forwards in the game — skilled, tireless, durable and ruthless. In those years he played 10 Tests and three World Cup games for his country, numerous matches for NSW and two grand finals. Then, when he hung up his boots, he began his spectacular TV career — 28 years as the most respected, authoritative — and controversial — commentator in the game. I don't know of anybody else who has achieved so much in his chosen fields.

Of all the wonderful memories I have of the Moose, three stand out. I remember him in a Test against England, battered and bleeding, but still throwing everything at Vince Karalius and company long after many of his teammates were looking for somewhere to lie down. I remember hilarious times and heated arguments on Controversy Corner, discussing "pertinent league matters". And I recall him chasing me, with murder on his mind, after I crept up behind him one freezing morning on England's Ilkley Moors on the '59 Roo tour and gave one of his cauliflower ears a good, hard crack.

Mossop was always a good bite. He was a few years older than me, well into his 30s, when we toured with the Kangaroos in 1959 and I'd be forever having a go at him about his ears or his age. "Well," he got back at me one night, "if *you're* still being picked to play against the Poms when you're 32 you'll be doing alright. But I really doubt that you've got what it takes." In 1967 when I was selected for my third Kangaroo tour — aged 33 —

Rex remembered his words of eight years before and shook my hand. That's the sort of man he is.

I reckon Rex is the ultimate Australian Tall Poppy, and like all Tall Poppies, he's attracted critics. But I reckon a lot of people have got him wrong. He can be abrasive and appear over-confident with lots of noisy opinions. He's a perfectionist and doesn't suffer fools gladly. But anyone who's had a bit to do with him over the years knows what a wonderful, kind and considerate bloke he really is and what a lot of fun he can be. He's the sort of man that, if ever you were in any trouble, you'd turn to the Moose first. He mightn't give you any money — but he'd certainly help you out.

Rex's story covers a lot of territory. As a sportsman, media star and family man, he's packed more into his years than just about anybody else I know. I believe Rex Mossop has led one of the great Australian lives.

1

LIVING BY
THE CODE

The bloke scurrying up my street from the beach was in his mid-20s, nondescript in every way — except one. He was as naked as the day he was born. Moments before, I'd been lazing beside my pool on that hot November day back in 1976 when a neighbour telephoned with the alarming news that there was a nude man parading up our road. We'd had problems ever since the Labor State Government of the time took it upon itself to change nearby Reef Beach — for decades a quiet family swimming and picnicking spot near Manly — into a nude beach that attracted a rogue's gallery of perverts and exhibitionists. But this was Beatty Street's first streaker, no risk.

I raced out the front door and saw this galoot making for a parked car about 250 metres away. A quick sprint and I was on him just as he reached the vehicle. I grabbed him by the shoulder, but he shrugged my arm off and dived into the car where three of his mates waited with his clothes. I reached in and pulled him right out again. He didn't know whether to swing a punch at me or cover his privates. "You bloody idiot!" I roared. "Why the hell are you in the nude?"

"I did it for a bet," he blathered.

"Well, that makes you an even bigger bloody idiot! You stay right where you are. I'm making a citizen's arrest. No, leave your clothes in the car! I want the police to see you in all your glory!"

At this, his three mates climbed out of the car. I said to them, slowly and deliberately, "If any of you bastards interferes I'll knock you out." They took the tip and backed off.

By now a fairly large crowd had gathered. I yelled out to somebody to call the cops and about three minutes later a police car arrived. Can you imagine the bizarre scene: a middle-aged man holding at bay three young hoons and a trembling naked fellow trying in vain to conceal his manhood with a clump of leaves. God spare me days! The police hauled the poor fool away and charged him with wilful and obscene exposure. He was fined $75 in the Manly Court of Petty Sessions.

The incident attracted a fair bit of publicity at the time and my comment to one TV interviewer that the Government's arbitrary introduction of nude bathing was a disgrace because nobody wanted male genitals shoved down their throat has gone into folklore. I was lauded as a suburban hero for making the citizen's arrest, but the truth was I was not nearly so confident as I appeared. Four young men against one aging TV commentator are idiot's odds and I could have ended up badly hurt. But that's the way it's always been with me. For as long as I can remember, I have acted first and considered the consequences later.

I've never been a spectator in the game of life. I don't want to sound pompous but having the courage of your convictions, to act when others shrug their shoulders and walk away, to speak up when others remain silent, is a central part of a code I've tried to stick to ever since I was a kid, through my rugby and rugby league days and my TV and radio careers, up to the present time.

All the achievements, controversies, fiascos and feuds that have punctuated my 63 eventful years on Earth can best be understood in the light of my trying — not always successfully, I might add — to follow what I call the "Mossop Code". The code is nothing more than a set of guidelines about the way I live my life. Rules that were drummed into me by my parents so many years ago and rules that I learned in such hard knock schools as Depression-era Sydney, the engine-room of 10,000 scrums and the piranha pit that is the Australian media.

Yes, I've had failures and embarrassments galore. I've done enough dumb things to fill three books. I'm no Simon Pure, believe me. At times I've let myself and my family down badly. But I've always believed that if you try to be courageous, steadfast, loyal and generous, to be chivalrous to women and kind to animals, to stick up for a little bloke who's being belted by a big bloke, and at least have a shot at doing the best you can, then you are not going to go too far wrong in this world.

Critics have attacked me all my life for holding simplistic, black and white views. But that's the way it is. Chop a man's head off or don't chop it off; but never leave the poor bastard languishing in irons. I'll give a subject plenty of thought before reaching an opinion on it, but once I've made up my mind, that's it. I won't vacillate. I won't be swayed by contrary opinions. I don't believe in compromise, I believe in what I consider is right. This is a simple philosophy but it's the Mossop way.

I have never worried about making enemies. A man without foes has led an inconsequential life. I have never cared what people think of me. I know damn well that there are many out there who consider Rex Mossop to be an aggressive, overbearing, intimidating, intolerant, pig-headed monster. So be it, I'll never apologise for trampling on people's toes when I believe they deserve it. After all, mooses are not known as timid beasts.

Like when I made the citizen's arrest at Reef Beach, I can't help wading in when the occasion demands. Often I've copped a hiding for my trouble, but a bloody nose never hurt anybody. While combing through the old scrapbooks gathering material for this book, the newspaper headlines leapt up at me: "Mossop Sent Off — Again!","Rex Arrests Nude Bather", "Mossop Apprehends Can Thrower", "Rex Slams Newspaper Chiefs", "Mossop Takes Law Into His Own Hands", "Death Threat To TV Star", "Rex Hits At League Wimps", "Street Thugs Flee Mossop", "Moose Wins Ratings War", "Mossop Almost Drowned In Surf Rescue", "Rex Erupts!", "Mossop Sacked!" Just isolated incidents in what's been a colourful existence. My life has been one lived in the public eye. Wherever I went, whatever I did, trouble — and headlines — seemed to follow. Today, aged 63, I'm just beginning to make some sense of it all.

When I was young, my father gave me some valuable advice. "Never let the bastards know you're hurt," he'd say, He was talking about my football opponents, but I also took onboard his advice when dealing with critics who struck at my family or took cheap personal shots at me. I have always made a point of never responding to below-the-belt criticism. I've gladly taken, and just as gladly dealt out, criticism of a professional nature. It was my job to criticise the game of rugby league, players, administrators and so on. And when I've blundered or performed below standard, I've never held a grudge against a bloke who's taken me to task. But attacks motivated by jealousy or malice are something else again, and I have followed Dad's words to the letter. In my long TV career I copped more flak than just about any other personality ever has but I take pride today in never once stooping to the level of those detractors who fired personal abuse at me by exposing *their* mistakes.

When critics sneered and said that a battered old, rough and ready ex-footballer with a nasal voice could never make it in TV, I ignored their derision and buckled down to do the best I could in my own way. When trendy journalists and blokes such as Alex Buzo hauled me over the coals for speaking in tautologies, I didn't run to the grammar books, I kept on commentating the best way I knew — and the fans stayed with me. When the press unfairly hounded me about so-called mistakes I was making in my calls, when they knocked on my door at all hours of the night to grill me about some serious family problems that were nobody's business but mine, I maintained a steely and, I hope, dignified, silence.

After I suffered a stroke on camera in 1987 I claimed it was a middle-ear infection that had laid me low, while my detractors chuckled in the press about how I was over the hill and had scrambled names in my call that night. I could have called off the dogs by admitting I had suffered a stroke but, as Dad said, never let the bastards know you're hurt. So I didn't.

Throughout the infighting, double-crossing and conspiracy campaigns that marked my years at Channel TEN and culminated in my humiliating sacking in 1991, I never once slung mud back at those who were destroying a career I had worked hard and long for 28 years to build. Today, aged 63, mellow and happy with the bad old days far behind me, I'm glad I didn't give my enemies, the ones who indulged in personal and jealous abuse, the satisfaction of seeing me bite back — but I will try to throw some light on all the major dramas of my life in the pages that follow.

Those people who have turned having a go at Rex Mossop into a cottage industry will laugh, but all my life I have strived for perfection. Because I'm always going on about biffo today, many have the impression that I was an ordinary forward, a willing hard-nut and not much more. Well, the truth is that I *could* play a bit. I had few natural talents, but I made it to the pinnacle in both rugby codes because I trained and practised harder than anybody else in my day to make the very best of what skills I had. Likewise in television, I was a workaholic who did his homework. I learned all about the complex and highly-technical TV industry from the bottom up. I learned how to command attention in front of the camera, and I knew everything that was going on *behind* the camera. Apart from my rugby league calls on Channels 7 and TEN, in my TV career I was host of *The Club Show* for five years, of *Beauty And The Beast* for a couple, I fronted telethons, compered soccer games, fights, surfing contests, presented a nightly sports segment in the news, and on-air coverage of three Olympic Games. I was a sportscaster, variety host, newsreader, compere, scriptwriter and producer, and on more than a few occasions I even took the chance to sing on camera! And throughout all that time in TV — 28 years — I prided myself on my professionalism — and my consistent good ratings.

Another important part of the Mossop Code is loyalty. I'm an extremely loyal bloke to those who are loyal to me. Joan and I have been married for over 40 years, my best mates are blokes I've known since childhood. I've remained loyal to the Manly rugby league team even though at times people have told me I needed my head examined. I stuck solid to Channel 7 in good times and bad for 23 years.

However, when people turn on me, I don't forget. It hurts me when those I've considered to be friends kick me in the teeth, and there's no shortage of people guilty of that — many of them very high-profile people in sport, radio, newspapers and TV. So although I'll never lower myself to get involved in a public slanging match with them, there are quite a few people whose actions have ensured that they will have an implacable enemy in me for the rest of their days. I'll get to them later in this book.

There was a journalist a couple of years ago. We were good mates. I'd spent a couple of years writing my autobiography, just putting on paper all the things that had happened to me in my life, and I gave the manuscript to this bloke to read. He lost it. His carelessness with something that meant so much to me brought me undone. I have not spoken to him since, and I never will. I can never forgive, either, the hatchet job done on me by the Fairfax newspapers when my sons found themselves in trouble with the law. Receivership is a fitting reward for that mob. And there were the pygmies at Channel TEN and their lackeys in the press who, I believe, conspired to have me removed from TV. You know who you are.

It was ironic that the sea once almost took my life, when I was attempting to rescue a lifesaver in mountainous waves at South Steyne — because I have always loved the water. I'm a keen swimmer, surfer, skier and boating man. The ocean and the waterways are part of an Australian way of life that I believe is worth preserving at all costs. I've travelled extensively in Great Britain, the Continent, America, South East Asia — you name it — and while I always enjoy being away I never fail to return more convinced than ever that Australia is the land for me. It's all here. The sunshine, the sport, the open spaces, the superb food, the tolerance and inherent decency of the average Aussie.

My blood boils when this way of life comes under attack. And I believe it is under attack right now, from permissiveness, the drug culture, a breakdown in moral values and a reversal of the traditional roles of men and women. I know my conservative stance does not appeal to everybody, but appealing to everybody has never been what I'm about. I believe men should be men: strong and fit, masculine, protective and reliable characters who keep their emotions under control. I have no time for politicians who cry on TV or cricketers who hug and kiss or homosexuals who dress in chains and drag and parade up and down Oxford Street screeching to be noticed. I've cried, yes, but in private, and a handshake is about as demonstrative as I ever got when congratulating a teammate for good work on the field. I have friends who are homosexual, but they don't expect a tickertape parade because of their sexual preference.

The increase in crime — theft, drug abuse, sexual assaults, murder — indicates that as a nation we are dicing with disaster. Many of the offenders are young. Obviously parents and schools are falling down on the job. Many of the idols kids look up to have feet of clay. It is the responsibility of successful people in the public eye to set a good example for children to aspire to.

Every time the obnoxious John McEnroe or the bloke I call "the unmade bed", Andre Agassi, smash their racquet in rage at a bad line call, a similar sordid scene is soon after enacted on junior tennis courts across the country by kids who have seen how their heroes behave on TV and rush to follow their lead. Wally Lewis argues with a referee and hundreds of little Wallys do the same. I recently blasted Lewis on radio about his poor on-field behaviour and, I'm glad to say, I once took the chance to upbraid McEnroe, who is a pet hate of mine. He'd just put on one of his trademark tantrums during a match at Sydney's Hordern Pavilion, breaking his racquet and slamming a ball into the crowd. I could not contain myself. "You're a real bloody mug, McEnroe!" I shouted from my seat near where the American was standing. He swung around and glared at me and I continued, "Yes, and if you want to come over here I'll call you a mug again!"

There has been a definite change in the psyche of the Australian male over the last 30 or so years. I'm sad to say that many of the values that shaped our national identity — strength, courage, good manners, a willingness to put your body on the line for what you believe in — are for many men out of date.

Conservative political parties will always get my vote, I have no time for the left-wingers and socialists of Labor. I am devoted to the free enterprise system — but most politicians I wouldn't piss on if they were burning to death. They treat the public like idiots. I hate hypocrisy and politicians are past masters of the art. They would do and say anything to catch a vote, to be popular. In my experience, it is a rare politician who is motivated by doing something for the public good and not by naked self-interest. I've been asked whether I'd be interested in standing for office, but there's no way you'd get me into a committee room with all those wimps. I'd get so frustrated I'd feel like breaking heads.

Australians are too highly taxed. This destroys the incentive to work harder and encourages a welfare state, handout-obsessed society where everyone wants something for nothing. I'm bloody proud of the fact that I started work at 15, and without much of a formal education have achieved happiness, success and security. And, what's more, I have not asked the Government for a single thing in all my 63 years. There's no substitute for independence.

Sport has been good to me. In what has been a very physical life I have played union and league for my country, I've been a keen but scratchy golfer, I've sailed, surfed, skied and cruised, and I've boxed and wrestled enthusiastically and determinedly, if with little finesse. Sport has made me well known and opened opportunities that I have seized. It has given me financial security.

My main sporting love, and this will surprise nobody, is rugby league, a sport which has become in the past decade a multi-million dollar super-sport but which, in so doing, has lost its way. In order to sanitise this great game to make it palatable to its new followers and sponsors, the powers-that-be have sacrificed many of the features that made league the greatest game of all — like biffo! My view that a face-to-face punch-up between two men is part and parcel of the game is well-known. I indulged in plenty of stand-up stoushes in my time and consider myself a better man for it. Rugby league is a violent contact sport and tempers will flare and scores will be settled. The ban on biffo has brought the back-alley merchants out of the woodwork with their snide elbows and knees in the back of a tackled player. Likewise, the replacement and interchange rules have destroyed two more of league's grand traditions, traditions I'm proud to say were part of the Mossop Code in my playing days — endurance, and the need to keep playing even though you're hurt.

My wife Joan says that rugby league has been her main rival for my affections throughout our marriage. She's right. A bad back, aches and pains and creaking joints are just some of the legacies I carry from a long, long football career of 20 seasons. But even today, when I'm watching a game or commentating from the stands, it's all I can do to stop myself from throwing on a jersey, leaping the fence and packing down again in the front row!

Keeping fit is also part of the Mossop Code. I have worked out virtually every day for the past 53 years of my life. I couldn't live without my daily run, swim, game of touch footy or weight lifting routine. For all our pretensions to being a tanned, lean and physically fit race, too many Australian men are pathetic specimens: short of wind, flabby, beer-gutted and, most of them, too weak to knock a sick girl off a toilet. Mostly their condition is caused by laziness. You don't have to bench-press 200 kilos or run 30 kilometres a day to keep fit: a half hour's jog or a brisk walk is usually enough to keep you healthy, and live longer more happily. A lot of my friends can't understand why fitness is so important to me, and of course there are the idiots who call out to me when they see me running in the street or park. "Why are you running, you silly old bugger?" they shout. "Because I don't want to look like you!" is my usual reply. But really, I stay fit because I love life. I love my wife and my family, my dogs, my sport, my country. I want to be around a long time to enjoy them.

Well, that's the Mossop Code. That's where I stand on the things that are important to me. You know enough about me now to make some kind of sense of all that follows. Let's get on with the rest of my life — a life that took me from the carefree, knockabout beaches of Manly in the '30s and '40s to rugby Tests against the All Blacks and the Lions, three wild and woolly seasons playing rugby league in England, eight more eventful years with Manly, years of Tests, grand finals, Kangaroo tours, send-offs and controversies. Then, when I hung up my boots, it was out of the frying pan and into the fierce glare of the TV spotlight for 28 colourful and controversial years as commentator, host, compere and rabble-rouser.

It's been a good life. Some of it's been magic, some of it tragic . . . but let's get the show on the road. We'll start at the beginning.

2

A FAMILY
OF SCRAPPERS

My great, great grandfather was one of the few people to be held up by Captain Starlight and escape with both his money and his life. It happened outside Bathurst and it's family lore how the notorious bushranger was flabbergasted by the old man's fast talking and turned him loose rather than suffer a prolonged earbashing. I believe my 19th century ancestor would be pleased to know that following generations of Mossops have upheld his garrulous tradition.

Mossops have always loved to talk, sing and fight. In all these things I am my father's son. Norman Eric Mossop was born in Woolloongabba, Queensland, not far from the famous 'Gabba cricket ground, of Scottish, Irish and Cumbrian stock. He came to Sydney as a young man in the early years of this century and rapidly won for himself a reputation as a dandy. Wearing a cream panama hat and a white suit studded with stick-pins, my father became a familiar figure at sporting events. Dad was a fight manager who could handle himself when the need arose, and in the company he kept it arose often. He was also a very good rugby league fullback for Wests.

The First World War put a brutal stop to Dad's gallavanting lifestyle. Without a thought he signed up and was shipped to the frozen, knee-deep-mud battlefields of France where he was badly wounded in the ferocious battle of Paschendale. Dad was in the horse-drawn artillery. His job was to come charging in on his mount to about 150 metres behind the front line, disentangle the guns, fire at the enemy and get the hell out of there before the Germans could return the compliment. His mob was known as the "Shoot, Shit and Scatter Brigade".

Well, on this occasion Dad didn't scatter fast enough and a German shellburst left him bleeding profusely in the mud. They wanted to take his leg off right then and there, but Dad simply refused to let them do it. He was carried to a casualty clearing station. He lay there in intense pain for two days while the battle raged around him. Finally they repatriated him to Paris where he remained in hospital for eight months before being transported to England for two years of further treatment. He didn't arrive back in Australia until 1919.

Dad never told us much about the war. It's funny, but blokes who endured the worst of the fighting rarely brag about their exploits. He was very badly hurt — too badly ever to play sport again — but he never told us how he caught it. Everything the family learned about the horrors he endured came from army sources. He carried a long, deep scar on his forehead for the rest of his life, but whenever I'd ask him what had happened he'd laugh and tell me he'd been hit by a flying bottle in a French cafe. Until the day he died my father would sit in his chair at night, gingerly rubbing one leg against the other. We'd say, "Are you having a bit of trouble, Dad?" and he'd just grumble, "Oh, the bastard of a thing." His body — legs, stomach, head — was full of shrapnel. Some pieces were the size of a nail, and they'd move around inside him and cause a fair bit of discomfort. Dad was a hard, hard man.

On his return to Australia after the War, my father was admitted to Randwick Hospital for further treatment of his wounds, and there he met the love of his life. Nellie Thelma Kirkpatrick was a Bathurst girl who worked at the hospital as a volunteer aid, nursing the blokes who'd come home in bad shape. Norman Mossop — she called him "Mossy" — swept her off her feet.

I remember Mum as a typical woman of her time. She had a statuesque physique, a big bust and hips which she kept tightly corseted. She was loving, soft-hearted and generous and usually paid deference to my Dad. "Mossy," she'd say, "would it be alright if we did this? Do you think it would be alright if we did that?" I have memories of lying in my bed at night — almost 60 years ago — and hearing them laughing softly together in the adjoining bedroom. All their lives they loved being together, they enjoyed each other.

When Dad was discharged from Randwick Hospital, Mum returned to Bathurst, but the courtship continued long-distance, with Dad driving to Bathurst to be with Nellie as often as he could. On one of these trips he had a bad car accident and only drove again when absolutely necessary. This backlashed badly on me. As soon as I got my driving licence I became Dad's chauffeur. He'd say, "Son, take me to the club", then when he'd had enough to drink, he'd say, "Son, take me home!" I'd be spending all this time in pubs and clubs but my alcohol ration was always limited to a single bottle of Resch's Dinner Ale. I'd make up for lost time later.

Norman and Nellie were married and lived at Haberfield in the western suburbs of Sydney for a short time before moving to nearby Five Dock. That small house in Newcastle Street was my first home. I was brought roaring and kicking into the world on February 18, 1928, just five years after my brother Kirk. It was Kirk who persuaded my parents to call me Rex. He'd seen the name underneath King George's head on a coin and thought it sounded impressive.

My first memory, I'm sorry to say, is of being a guinea pig to a bunch of sexually sophisticated little girls who lived in our street. I was only a toddler at this stage but these girls would play doctors and nurses and mothers and fathers with me and generally have their curious way with the only little boy in the neighbourhood unwitting enough to drop his pants when ordered to.

Kirk was the ideal big brother. It's not that we played together all that much. Kirk was older and a lot more serious than me, preferring to busy himself with books and hobbies rather than running and booting balls and swimming. But one thing he'd religiously do would be to give me my pocket money each week from his own stash. Even if we'd had a blinding argument or free-for-all fight, at the end of every week I'd put out my hand and Kirk would drop one shilling and sixpence into it.

Notwithstanding his generosity, Kirk and I had regular barneys all through our growing up years. He was stocky and very strong and Dad had taught us both the rudiments of boxing. Whenever fraternal hostilities would erupt Dad would say, "OK, you pair, get over here!" Then he'd march to the hall stand where he kept two pairs of boxing gloves. "Now put these on and get into it!" Kirk and I would whale away at each other with Dad refereeing until the fight ended in a TKO or an honourable draw. I guess it was Dad who taught me that a good right hand was as effective a way as any to settle an argument.

In manhood Kirk and I still had our differences. My politics are somewhere to the right of Genghis Khan's, whereas Kirk became a supporter of the far left. The boxing gloves stayed locked away as we grew older but we'd argue politics hammer and tong for hours on end. His politics aside, I had great respect for Kirk. He went on to a fine career as an hydraulic draughtsman and late in his life became an excellent and very successful artist. Many of his paintings are on the walls of my home.

I will always hold myself partly responsible for my brother's death. As we entered middle age I tried to instil in Kirk my love of fitness, even going to the extreme of buying him a pair of running shoes to encourage him to take up jogging. Reluctantly he'd put them on and go for a gallop around the neighbourhood. One morning I received a call from a friend who told me Kirk had taken a bad turn while running. I jumped into the car and tore off to lend what assistance I could. I arrived at the spot and saw an ambulance and a group of paramedics. "What's going on? Where's Kirk?" I demanded. They seemed unsure of how to answer. It was then that I noticed that the back doors of the ambulance were open and a pair of feet were protruding through. On the feet were running shoes. I identified them immediately as the ones I had bought for Kirk. "There was nothing we could do," said a doctor then. "He suffered a massive heart attack and died where he fell." He was only 57 and had had a heart con-

A FAMILY OF SCRAPPERS

dition for years without telling anyone.

Our childhood in Five Dock was a rich and happy one. Dad's first job after the war was as a hardware buyer at Grace Bros department store. He then joined Anthony Horderns where he ran their hardware section for 32 years until his retirement. He never earned a big wage, but my father was a wonderful provider for us all right through the Depression. He worked hard to make sure we didn't go without shelter, food and essential clothing. I was in awe of his strong personality and I remember wanting to grow up to be just like him and marry someone exactly like Mum.

Times are tough in the Australia of the 1990s but I can assure you they were a whole lot worse in the '30s. The Depression hit the country hard and affected everyone. I didn't have a decent pair of shoes until I was nine and any clothing I did have was a hand-me-down from Kirk. By the time they got to me, my school trousers were so thin you could see through the serge.

Dad taught me right from wrong, not that this stopped me from being one of the wilder kids in the neighbourhood throughout my childhood and teenage years. He drummed into me that I should always try to be honest, brave and chivalrous to women. "Open the door for your mother . . . take your mother's arm on the street . . . don't forget Mum's birthday". That sort of thing.

Anthony Horderns in those days was *the* department store in an era of great department stores, a wonderland for any child. Going in there was a day's outing. Anything you ever wanted, you could buy at Anthony Horderns. Employees there took pride in the place and enjoyed a great camaraderie that extended outside working hours. The store would hold concerts for staff and Dad would be the MC. He was a marvellous entertainer and would have the audience eating out of his hand. He'd get up on stage at the start of a show and clown around, tell a few jokes, then say, "Welcome to the Hordernian concert of 1935. We have a wonderful evening's entertainment for you all tonight, but before I introduce Peter Dawson, the world-famous baritone, I'd like to sing a little song for you . . . 'If you were the only girl in the world . . .'" This would start a chorus of good-natured booing. Dad could strike up an instant rapport with any crowd, he was a marvellous ad-libber and completely without nerves when performing. I've never been intimidated in front of an audience either, and I reckon I inherited that from Dad.

Norman Mossop loved to sing and in fact had an excellent voice. The great Peter Dawson was one of his closest friends, and the pair of them would perform duets around the piano at home. Kirk and I would give Peter a terrible time. There we were, aged about six and 11, with one of the finest singers of all time performing for us in our living room, and whenever Peter would hit one of those wonderful notes we'd screw up our faces, cover our ears and go, "Aaaaarrgghhh!"

Once when I was six, Mum took me on a trip. We caught the tram from Five Dock to Circular Quay, a ferry to Manly, a bus from Manly Wharf to Sydney Road, Balgowlah, then walked half a mile down Condamine Street hill until we reached a pleasant bungalow on the corner of Condamine and Clarence Streets. It was about the longest trip I'd ever taken in my short life. Mum went inside to talk to the owner while I sat in the gutter and waited for her. Soon enough she emerged and we made the long trip via foot, bus, ferry and tram home to Five Dock. Somewhere on that return journey I asked Mum what was going on and she replied, "You've just seen the place where we're going to live."

When Dad arrived home that night Mum announced, "Mossy, I've rented a home in Balgowlah and we're committed to moving in there in a fortnight." Dad exploded, "Oh my God, Nellie, you've ruined me!" But no amount of waving his arms in the air and protesting would sway Mum this night. It was so rare for her to stand up to him but she had made up her mind. Exactly 14 days later I was a Manly boy. Eventually we bought the house and my parents lived there for as long as they lived.

3

ONE THOUSAND MILES FROM CARE

The beaches, waves and wide open spaces of the Manly of the 1930s were a revelation to me. The thriving high-rise metropolis of today was then a small village. Living around Manly and Balgowlah was like being on holidays all year round. "Seven Miles From Sydney — And A Thousand Miles From Care" was Manly's motto, and it certainly rang true for me. I was immediately hooked on the seaside life and have remained a devotee of the great outdoors ever since. My first sporting love was surfing. I was, and still am, a strong swimmer. Dad had me coached by Harry Hay, a former Olympian, and bodysurfing came naturally to me.

Old Harry used to train me in the Manly baths, and actually had hopes that I'd be an Olympic swimmer, but I couldn't hack the training. Endlessly pounding up and down the pool bored me to death, and it was inevitable that the excitement of the surf would lure me away. But Dad had spent a lot of money that he couldn't really afford on my still-water swimming tuition and I wasn't game enough to break the news to him that I'd given Harry Hay the flick. My father kept forking out the two bob a week to Harry, who needed the money himself and chose not to tell my father that his budding Johnny Weissmuller had moved on months ago. Eventually, of course, Dad found me out and gave me a sound belting for my deceitfulness. I deserved every lump.

Soon I progressed to board riding. Kirk made me a succession of surfboards, solid wood, no fin, and not quite two metres long. They weighed 20 kilos so it was a physical feat just to get them into the water. At that stage there was only me and three or four other blokes riding boards between South Steyne and Palm Beach. It was typical of my brother that he'd spend hours fashioning these terrific boards for me, but didn't have the slightest interest in learning to ride himself.

I joined Manly Surf Club and have remained a member all my life. I became a lifesaver and a proficient reel and belt man. My lifesaving and board riding days are now over, but I'm still a keen body surfer and whenever I've nothing much to do I'll take my dogs for a run down to the clubhouse where I happily while away a couple of hours with mates from the old days.

Until I turned nine or 10 I was a soft little fat guy. Then all of a sudden my physique changed. Maybe it was the good clean air and active lifestyle that made me turn almost overnight into a tall, lean, strapping young fellow. Dad bought me my first set of weights and by the time I was 12 I was bigger and stronger than most of the kids at school in my age group. At about this time I decided to give footy a go and tried out for the Balgowlah Church Of England Boys Society rugby union team. They played at Keirle Park, not far from our house. I didn't make the side because I had no skills at all. The other guys in the team had been playing footy for three or four years by then and there I was, 12 years old and clueless. But one quality I did not lack was enthusiasm. All I wanted to do was get picked in the side. Once on the field I knew I could show that coach the error of his ways.

For half a season I would turn up at the ground and be overlooked. Then, as the year drew on and the days grew colder, a few of the boys began finding excuses not to show up. So finally the coach had no option but to give me a run. Because I was a lump of a lad, he told me to stick my head in the scrum. I had no idea of the finer points; I couldn't pass properly, draw a man, kick or even understand most of the rules. But what I could do was chase and tackle. Nobody in an opposition jersey was safe. I'd dive at everything that moved. Even when a bloke had passed the ball, if he was near me I'd cream him as hard as I could. I loved this game.

I knew I was not cut out for confounding the opposition with dazzling footwork and running in length-of-the-field tries, so I built my game on strength, power and a killer attitude. Nobody ever taught me to be aggressive on the football field. It was a natural thing to me that from the opening whistle, the opposition was the enemy, and I had no interest in taking prisoners. Rugby union for me was a game of getting over the top, by fair means or foul, of the bloke playing opposite me. I carefully set out each week, even in the under-12s, to violently dominate my opponent, to make him fear me. Gradually as I grew older I learned that rugby was more than just a brawl with rules and a referee and I managed to acquire a few basic skills, but whatever I achieved in my rugby union career I achieved by tackling and running ferociously, always being where the ball was, and never taking a backward step. It wasn't until I played rugby league in England and came under the coaching of the astute old Pommie hooker Joe Egan that I learned how to distribute the ball intelligently and appreciate the tactical side of football.

In my second year of rugby I was selected in a junior district representative side to play against Hawkesbury Agricultural College. I went out there with my usual tactic of trying to monster the opposition and was rewarded by a line in *The Manly Daily*. In its report of the game, the paper said, ". . . and Rex Mossop did well." I carried that cutting around with me in my wallet, showing it to whoever would stop to look, until it just wore away and fell apart. To me, it simply backed up what I had known all along: that one day I would play for Australia.

I believe the seed of my ambition was planted many years before by my Mum's father, Grandfather Kirkpatrick. He'd been a wonderful rugby union player of the late 1800s and had represented NSW against the fabled Great Britain side of that era that was captained by the Reverend M. Mullineux. Had there been a legitimate Australian team in those days, my grandfather would have been in it. Mum, Dad, Kirk and I would visit my grandfather and grandmother in Bathurst at Christmas and Grandpa made a huge impression on me. He was a big man, not fat at all, just massively-framed. He had iron-grey hair cropped in a severe crewcut. The local postmaster in Bathurst for many years, he was a stern man, not given to excessive emotion. He would never cuddle or kiss my brother or me — but he was fond of us and inspired in me a severe case of hero worship. I was still only a child when Grandpa died. I have a lasting memory of him lying dead on his bed. As was the custom of the time, he'd been made-up and dressed in his best clothes so relatives could file by his bed and pay their last respects. The old fellow looked terrific. So good, in fact, that I was certain that he wasn't dead at all, just having a sleep. "Hey, come on Grandpa, wake up!" I recall yelling out to him before Mum gently led me from his bedside and explained to me that Grandpa was gone.

Another wonderful inspiration to me was a bloke named Ken Merritt, captain of the Manly rugby union team when I was 14 or 15. He was a back, but I admired him anyway. I'd watch him play every chance I got. He was by no means a player out of the top draw, but something about his tradesmanlike displays and the way he'd get along on his bandy legs appealed to me. One day I jumped onto the local bus, not looking where I was going as usual, and in my haste I knocked someone's bag from the luggage rack. It fell down the stairs and onto the road. To my horror, the man who had to get out of the bus and walk 300 metres back up the hill to retrieve his bag was none other than my hero, Ken Merritt. In a panic I jumped out of the bus and caught up to Ken. "I'm really sorry, Mr Merritt. I didn't mean to knock your bag out of the bus, honest!" I wailed. "Don't worry about it, son," he assured me, "it's alright."

There were two other blokes who made deep impressions on me when I was in my mid-teen years. One was Bill McRitchie, a rugby league star of the day who worked for my first employer. I was just a messenger boy, but I loved being in the company of big Bill, one of nature's gentleman. McRitchie was involved in one of league's biggest controversies when, playing for St

George against Newtown, he reeled from a scrum holding onto what was left of his ear. Veteran Newtown forward and legendary cop Bumper Farrell was charged with biting part of Bill's ear off. Bumper beat the charge when he claimed he could not have been the culprit because he took his false teeth out whenever he played. All through the furore McRitchie kept his silence, refusing to dob Farrell in. I learned a great lesson from him: never squeal.

Another league star of the day, "Changa" Schultz, taught me all about dealing out summary justice when I was bailer boy in his crack 18-footer sailing boat. We'd race regularly on the Harbour and Changa took it very seriously indeed. Any of his crew who incurred his wrath would be belted hard with his bailer, a baking dish bolted to a big lump of wood.

I was a keen sailor. In the early '40s I was a regular crewman in 16ft skiff races. These craft were the fastest skiffs on Sydney Harbour. Ours was called *Rival*. I remember one day we set out with four people on board — the skipper, the for'd hand, a sheet-hand and the bailer boy, me — with our biggest sails up. There was a steady 20-knot nor-easter blowing and we were all looking forward to a good day's racing. Sometime in the afternoon our skipper became concerned by a single straight line of clouds low on the horizon in the southern sky. He said it looked like a bad squall on the way. Within an hour we were nearly blasted out of the water by a 50-knot southerly. We made for the safety of Store Beach, but before we reached the sheltered cove we were pitched into the water where we waited to be rescued. Capsized alongside us was one of the best skiffs on the Harbour, *Escapade*, skippered by a man named Russell Slade who would later make a name for himself captaining bigger craft. True to sailing tra-‚ dition, there was always plenty of rum onboard *Escapade* and Slade's crew was notorious for getting very drunk. They certainly were this day. I saw one paralytically-pissed sheet-hand attempt to swim to a rescue vessel. He swam no more than a few strokes before he sank straight to the bottom, nearly three metres down, where he calmly sat, peering curiously up at us through the depths. Talk about feeling no pain. Two sailors dived overboard and brought him to the surface.

My teen years were ones of simple pleasures: football, surfing, sailing, dances at the lifesaving club, nights spent listening to the radio serials with my family, fun with friends at the aquarium and sideshow alley on Manly Pier, endlessly riding around the beaches and parks on pushbikes. One day when I was 14 I was out riding when a particularly shapely pair of legs passed by. Such was their effect on me that I almost fell off my bike. As their owner walked by — I can picture this today — I noticed how her garters held up her long stockings, an accessory popular with young girls in those times. Being backward has never been a shortcoming of mine and I struck up a conversation at once with the girl, who told me her name was Joan Bell. The attractive lass with the even-then voluptuous figure — "Look at her!" Mum used to chuckle, "She gets around with her bosom thrust out like a pouter pidgeon!" — became my wife, and Joan and I have been married for more than 40 years.

In those first tentative years of getting to know each other we were no different to any other young couple of the time. Money was tight so we'd entertain ourselves by walking or riding about on bikes together, going to the occasional dance at the surf club or the rugby club, and taking in a movie at the local picture show on Saturday night. In the time-honoured tradition of surfers and their girlfriends, poor Joan was regularly left stranded on headlands for hours while I was out there cracking wave after wave. God, it must have been boring for her, but of course we guys didn't give our girls a second thought, being all wound up in our surfing. But Joan has always been able to take the mickey out of me, to deflate me when she thinks I'm getting a bit too pompous for my own good. In those days she was always on about me being a Manly "blow-in" — "Anyone who wasn't born here never really belongs," she'd tease, this girl who was born close enough to the beach to hear the breakers crashing on to the sand.

Please don't get the impression that it was all happily-ever-after for Joan and me. After seeing each other for a couple of years we broke up, sowed some wild oats with other people, then got back together again. Time apart convinced us we were right for each other and we finally tied the knot in October, 1951.

With all my sport and chasing after girls, school was little more than a time-wasting irritation in my life. I attended Manly Boys' High in Darley Road from 1940 to 1943. I can't remember doing a single night's homework in all the time I was there. Mum and Dad tried to make me buckle down and study but even they, after a while, realised you can't turn a sow's ear into a silk purse. In a newspaper article a few years ago a Mrs Mary Moore, who taught me at Manly, was reminiscing about the scholastic performance of Mossop R. "Rex was a pleasant, likeable young man with two interests in life, surfing and football. We tried our best to turn Rex into a scholar, but we didn't have much success." Many was the time I'd race out during the lunch break for a quick surf at Manly beach nearby, then throw my schoolclothes on over my sopping trunks just in time to take my place in the first afternoon class. Small pools of water would form on the floor under my seat. I escaped high school with a gentleman's pass in the Intermediate, scraping through in four subjects out of seven.

It always rankled me in later life when I compared the healthy TV commentator's salary I was being paid to my brother Kirk's modest wage. Here was I, an ignoramus who could play football and had the gift of the gab, being paid a small fortune, while Kirk, who was highly intelligent, did wonderfully well at school and later studied at technical college for five years to become a fine draughtsman, made only enough money to scrape by. It's a crazy system.

There was one young teacher at Manly Boys' High who taught me more than the rest. She'd been recently divorced from a prominent cricketer of the day and lived in a block of flats just behind the Manly Surf Club. She was a very beautiful woman and I was at that impressionable age, going through all the emotional changes that accompany the coming of manhood. I developed a mighty crush on her. Often she would invite me to her flat after school. She had a profound effect on me in many, many ways, not least of which was an initiation into the gentle art of sex.

Like most teenagers I was a lawless little bastard. I was a bit of a lair and didn't mind throwing my weight around once I shed my puppy fat. I can't deny that I had a reputation as a neighbourhood scrapper. Dad had taught me the rudiments of boxing — "straight left in fast and across with your right!" — and most of my blues didn't last long. The one major bust-up of my youth came when I was 14 years of age. A schoolmate and I were up to some sort of no good at school and we were caught and hauled before one of the masters. This other kid caved in and told lies to escape punishment and this offended my sense of what was right and what was wrong. I was caned and he wasn't, so I decided to square matters by exacting a little pain on him myself. I challenged him to a fist-fight. Off we trudged to the place where all such contretemps were decided in those days — the ballroom of the Manly Surf Club. There, surrounded by the mounted photographs of all the local sporting heroes, we shaped up. The gate numbered about 300 of our fellow students. No news spreads as fast around a schoolyard as word of an imminent dust-up: "There's going to be a fight! There's going to be a fight!"

We peeled off our shirts and I took my shoes off too, realising we'd be slipping around a bit on the highly polished dance floor. My opponent was taller and heavier than me, but he couldn't handle himself at all. So I just kept avoiding his bull-rushes and sniping away at him, throwing my left into his face until his nose and mouth were bleeding and his features were red-raw. At one stage I stopped the fight and said, "Listen, mate, you look to me as though you've had enough. Let's call it quits." But he was a courageous kid and refused to give in. "OK, then," I replied, "I'll give you some more!"

My closest mates then remain two of my dearest friends today. Clarrie Davis, who became one of the most elusive centres ever to play rugby for Australia and went on to be Australian manager of Scandinavian Air Services, and Warwick Ritchie, an excellent board rider who ended up having a distinguished career as advertising manager for Ampol. In our young days we were known as The Three Musketeers and it was widely agreed that none of us had any brains at all. We wound up doing all right for a trio of no-hopers.

The Musketeers always had plenty of scams on the boil. There was one we'd pull when we were short of money, which was just about all the time. There was a little corner shop that used to service our school where you could buy drinks, lunches, biscuits — that sort of thing. They had a policy that if you returned a biscuit tin they'd refund you one shilling. The shopkeeper would stack the tins in the rear of the shop, then when he got around to it he'd refill them with biscuits and sell them again. We found a way to gain access to this storage area. When we were skint, we'd climb in, swipe a tin, saunter around to the front of the shop, present it to the shopkeeper and gratefully accept our refund. This went on for six months and while I'm sure the poor bloke suspected something was up, we got away with it. Another ploy was to shake the slot machines in the fun arcade at Manly Pier. If you shook hard enough, there was always a chance that five or six penny coins would fall into your hands.

Warwick Ritchie came to Manly Boys' from Grammar and copped tons of abuse for having been to a private school. There was a tough bloke at school called Braine, whose roughnut mates were known as Brainey's Gang. These blokes made a point of terrorising other kids and Warwick was a special target. Braine and his mates would get their kicks shoving the third Musketeer around and calling him "Little Lord Fauntleroy". Our motto being "All for one and one for all", there was no way I could let this continue. Braine was a big kid and had a reputation of being able to handle himself, but if somebody didn't put a stop to his bullying, Warwick was going to be Braine's target for the rest of his school days. I declared Braine on — if I beat him he would have to leave Warwick alone, if he won, his reign of terror would continue. Braine eagerly accepted my challenge.

We met after school on the beach underneath the Manly Amusement Pier. It was low tide and the sand was hard-packed, a good surface for boxing. When I arrived, Braine and and his boys were already there, and so was Warwick and Clarrie Davis, and about 150 other kids. Braine was ready to fight, shadow boxing and making threats. I kicked my shoes off and stripped off my jumper and put it on a log. Braine rushed at me and launched four huge haymakers, all of which whistled harmlessly over my head. That was as good as Braine got. He'd given his best and he hadn't even connected. Suddenly he looked scared. I hit him twice and knocked him onto the sand. He did not even try to get up. Collecting my shoes, jumper and fellow Musketeers I left, leaving Brainey and his gang to the jeers of their schoolmates.

I had another pal called "Dooker" Dobson. This bloke was dangerous company. His specialty was stealing secateurs and other garden implements from people's sheds and selling them at second hand stores and pawn shops. I was his accomplice on two or three of these heists. Unbeknown to us, our activities had been noticed by householders and one day when we emerged from a hockshop divvying up our ill-gotten gains we were confronted by a huge policeman. "Now, you two young bastards have been observed stealing garden equipment for the past two or three weeks. I could have you up before a beak, but I'm going to let you off with a kick up the backside and if I ever catch you stealing again I promise you I'll put you behind bars!" He then was as good as his word and gave each of us a thundering boot up the bum and sent us on our way. That's the way it was back then. Sadly, nowadays, a cop like the one who put Dooker and me on the straight and narrow with the help of a size 10 boot would himself be up before a beak charged with police brutality.

In the 1940s the wireless set occupied pride of place in every Australian home. Radio then was good cheap entertainment and families would gather around after dinner each night for their diet of drama, comedy, quizzes, music and sport. I'd well and truly caught the fitness bug by my mid-teens and I remember it was my usual form to listen to my favourite serial, *The Search For The Golden Boomerang, Martin's Corner* or whatever, then tear off on a flat-out one-and-a-half-mile sprint around the neighbourhood before collapsing in front of the wireless to absorb another quarter hour of derring-do. I'd do this three or four times a night.

No-one in the family batted an eyelid at this routine. Dad, in fact, was always supportive of my obsession to be fitter and stronger than anybody else. There's no doubt that my fitness helped me climb peaks in my chosen sports I would never have reached had I merely relied on my natural ability.

The Mossop family would crowd around the radio to hear breathless descriptions of big football games, boxing from Sydney Stadium and wrestling matches from the arena at Leichhardt, but the sporting commentator who had the greatest impact on me was the great Alan McGilvray, whose cricket Test commentaries have become legendary. Alan would sit at the microphone at the ABC studios in Sydney in those late 1930s years and receive a series of telexes from The Oval, Lord's or wherever detailing the latest development from the Test. He would then describe the action as if it were happening before his very eyes, punctuating a good stroke with the click of a pencil on his desk that sounded for all the world like willow connecting with a six-stitcher and sending it through the covers for four.

Cricket is one sport I've never been able to master, even though I once entertained a fantasy that I would wear the baggy green cap of Australia. It's strange how people see Australians, though. When I was playing rugby league in the north of England, my club set up a Wednesday night social cricket match played in the long twilight. "Right, Mossop, you're opening batsman," they said. "But I can't play cricket!" I protested. "What?" they retorted, "you're an Australian, aren't you!"

Putting my dreams of sharing the new ball with Lindwall to one side, I knuckled down to rugby union. I continued riding roughshod over my opponents in a very un-Christian manner for the Church Of England Boys Club side on Saturdays and turned out midweek for Manly Boys' High. We played mainly house pick-up matches there because World War Two was in full swing and we were not allowed to catch the ferry to compete against schools on the other side of Sydney Harbour for fear that we'd be torpedoed by lurking enemy submarines.

By the time I was in my mid-teens I was playing in the second row, still belting blokes, powering forward, and rucking and tackling hard. I loved to tuck the ball under my arm and charge right into the opposition. Though it was my policy never to stray from the middle of the rucks and mauls in general play, I developed a ploy of standing just in front of the goal posts when our opponents had a shot at a penalty or a conversion. It's amazing the number of times the ball drops short. I'd grab it then take off upfield, running in the clear for 20 or 25 metres before confronting defenders.

In my last year of high school — I was 15 — I was picked for a junior rep team that was to play in the curtain raiser to a Manly first grade fixture against an RAAF side. War had disrupted the rugby competition badly, with most able-bodied men in the services and only able to turn out for their teams when they were home on leave. At some stage of our game, Ron Walden, coach of Manly firsts, walked onto the balcony outside the dressing rooms where the big guys were changing and saw this tall, wiry young forward mixing it on the field. From memory, ours was a fiery match and as usual I was in the thick of it. "Who's that young fellow?" he asked. Someone looked up the team list. "His name's Mossop." "We need willing blokes to make up the numbers in grade," he said. "I have a feeling he might go alright."

4

THE WALLABY ROAD

"Strike for the ball, son, and I'll kick your shins in!" The warning was my welcome to first grade rugby from "Wild Bill" Cerutti, St George's feared and experienced international front rower. I'd been pitched straight into Manly's top grade by coach Ron Walden and now, at just 16 years of age, found myself packing down against a grizzled hardnut 20 years older than me. Unfortunately there were many more scrums in rugby then than nowadays and Will Bill had numerous opportunities to back his threat with action. Before long his huge boots had cut my shins to pieces. My downy, beardless cheeks, too, were rubbed raw from the old bastard grinding his bristles into my face as we grappled and manoeuvred for supremacy in the front row. Wild Bill was a short man, but as wide as he was tall, and I was a lanky beanpole. I had not yet developed the strong neck and back muscles necessary to compete in rugby's engine room, and I was an easy mark for Cerutti's boring-in tactics and flailing boots. Nevertheless, in spite of my youth and inexperience I was a first grade front rower representing my district and I was determined not to let him know he had me very worried indeed. I continued to strike for the ball, and he continued to strike my shins.

Well into the second half I took my revenge. Wild Bill had the ball and he came at me head-on, intent on trampling me into the turf. As he slammed into me I used his rampaging momentum to lift him up, dump him on the ground then drive in hard on top of him with my shoulder and both elbows. He grunted with pain and the elation of finally getting even sent me over the top. "Ha, ha!" I bellowed, "Take that! I hate you, you bastard, I hate you!" After the game I was stretched out in the dressing sheds, a mass of bruises and cuts. Suddenly Wild Bill Cerutti was in the room and heading straight for me. "Oh, Christ!" I thought, "He's going to belt me." The legendary Wallaby stormed up, put out his hand and said, "Shake, son, you did well today." He then turned to my Dad who was tending to my injuries by offering me swigs from a bottle of icy cold DA, and told him, "That boy of yours is going places in this game." Suddenly my battered shins didn't ache quite so much.

After spotting me in that junior representative match at Manly Oval, Ron Walden, who as well as being Manly first grade coach was president of the North Steyne Surf Club and a high-ranking policeman, had approached my father. He told Dad that I looked a likely prospect and asked if he had any objections to my being plunged straight into first grade. Dad always subscribed to the theory that if you're good enough you're old enough and I found myself pitched from schoolboy football into Manly firsts' front row, where, thanks to boots 'n' all customers like Wild Bill Cerutti, I learned my trade quickly and well.

My selection in the top grade earned me a mention in the sports pages of the Sydney *Daily Telegraph* of April 18, 1944. Under the headline "'Human Block' In RU Team" the article went on to say, "R. Mossop, selected as front row forward for Manly's first grade rugby union team next Saturday, has jumped from junior ranks. He has been described as the 'human block' because of his build. Only 16 years of age, he is over six feet tall and weighs 13 stone 10." In the second round match against Easts, the *Telegraph* noted that "Mossop was the best forward on the ground. Always on the ball, he was a tireless rucker." I loved rugby and was always disappointed each week when the ref blew fulltime. I wanted each match to last forever.

Manly did poorly in the 1944 season, coming last after winning the premiership the year before, but for me my debut season was a time to learn. Rugby union in the '40s boasted a number of notorious hard men. It seemed every team had a scrapper whose sole aim in life was to intimidate me. To turn the other cheek to these guys would have been like waving a red rag to bull. In spite of my tender years I never backed off and was happy to punch it out with anybody. To me, punching had just as much place on the field as passing, tackling, kicking and packing into scrums. A whack to the jaw was to me a wonderfully appropriate way of letting my opposite number know who was boss. Even though I was not particularly good with my fists, as my amateur boxing record of four fights for two wins and two losses testifies — I genuinely loved to blue.

I copped many a hiding, but after a while the whackers of the game learned to leave me alone. I grew up fast. Rugby union when I was starting out was heaven sent for doing a little physical damage to your opponent. Rucks and mauls went on for ages then so if you wanted to get square with a bloke there were plenty of opportunities to do so.

My motto was "retaliate first". I learned early never to give an opponent who had wronged me a warning, never give them an inkling that I was about to hit them. If a player did something illegal to me I would not react at all. I would simply bide my time until a suitable opportunity presented itself, then go *whack* and that would be the end of the discussion. It's like bringing up children. If you keep warning them, saying, "Look, if you do that again, I'll smack you," they'll walk all over you. Act immediately, and rugby opponents, like little kids, will know exactly what the score is.

All through my football career — in union and league — I instinctively hated my opponents. I had no interest in shaking hands with them after a game, sharing a beer in the dressing room, or meeting their wife and kids. They had to be the enemy to me if I was to perform my job properly. I always worried that if I liked a bloke in the other team I might not be prepared to tackle him quite so hard. I ended up mates with opponents like Nick Shehadie, Norm Provan and Noel Kelly, but against my better judgement.

Over the next few years I became a prominent rugby second rower, without quite cracking major representative honours. My rugby style was pretty well set by the time I turned 20. I was a big, fit, aggressive bloke with the nickname "Moose" who made up for any deficiencies in skill with a willingness to do the hard forward slogging and always be where the ball was. I was becoming known, too, for my distinctive cauliflowered ears and the way I'd always roll my sleeves right up around my biceps. Justice Herron, the president of the Australian Rugby Union at the time, once commented when he saw me run onto the field, "Look at Mossop, he's always ready to fight. See the way he rolls his sleeves up." That was rubbish. I have always hated long sleeves. I find them restricting. Even when I'd wear a footy jumper to keep the cold out when surfing in winter, I'd cut the sleeves off at the shoulder.

I copped the nickname "Moose" because of the characteristic way I would lower my head and charge, arms and legs flying, into rucks like a wounded moose. It's not well known, but before I was "Moose" Mossop I was known as "Blossom"! I remember one day at Manly Oval when we were playing a game on a ground that was especially hard and dusty I dived at an opponent, hit him hard around the chest and the two of us skidded across the baked ground. A cloud of dirt flew up and a teammate, it was Jimmy Mantova, called out, "Look! Blossom's in the dust!"

I had my first cauliflower ear by the time I was 16, a result of my lug being constantly ground against the hips of front rowers when I packed into scrums. The wear and tear causes fluid to build up in your ears, making them painful, swollen and misshapen. You have to keep having them syringed then bandaged until the scar tissue grows hard. Even then, a knock on a cauliflowered ear can take a chip out of it. My first cauli came gradually, my second happened a lot more suddenly. We were playing Northern Suburbs at Manly Oval and I'd fielded the ball and was backing into a ruck when *smack*, Roger Cornforth, a huge Norths and Australian forward, flew into the ruck and his head collided with my ear. My head was ringing and the pain in my ear was excruciating. It was never the same again. I swore I'd have my ears fixed surgically when I retired from football, but by then they'd become a trademark and I'd grown quite fond of them. In my time I've entered "ugly ears" competitions — and won. But for mine the worst set of caulis belonged to the late and legendary Newtown forward "Bumper" Farrell. Bumper just pips my one-time deadly enemy and now good mate Harry Bath, who also sports a monstrous set.

Fitness, too, set me apart in an era when conditioning was not taken quite so seriously as it is today. For many footballers then, both union and league, a training session consisted of a few laps of the oval, some ball work, a game of touch then some serious elbow-bending at the local pub to round the evening off. As I'd always done, I ran and pumped iron on my own every day, in addition to team training. And I wouldn't touch a drop of alcohol throughout the week, though I loved getting stuck in on Saturday night after the match. I had a theory, too, about the treatment of muscular injuries. Rather than resting such injuries I would exercise them, work the muscles hard with running or lifting until the pain disappeared.

Manly won the wooden spoon in 1944 and 1945, and came third last in '46, but gradually we were getting a team together that would give the competition a shake in the last years of the decade. In 1946 I made the State 40, a squad of players from whom the NSW side would be picked. I was selected in the NSW second XV to play Southern States, and for NSW firsts in a match against Combined States, curtain raiser to an Australia versus The Rest selection trial for the upcoming Wallaby tour of New Zealand. The following year under the coaching of the former international Aub Hodgson, Manly, with Ron Walden now club president, were minor premiers, but we were thrashed in the grand final by Easts. In 1948 Aub was unseated as coach and Ron again took the reins and got us to the grand final where we were again beaten, this time by Randwick. That year I again made a State squad and also represented City.

On our run to the semis in 1948, we faced St George in a crucial round 15 game. Reported *The Daily Telegraph*: "An injury to St George winger Peter Knibbs enabled Manly to win 17-12 at Kogarah Oval yesterday . . . Knibbs was injured after he levelled the scores at 9-all with his third penalty goal. Manly forward Rex Mossop tackled Knibbs around the neck. Knibbs got his pass away but Mossop did not release him. Knibbs was pulled to the ground in a forward headlock and had his face rubbed in the dirt. After ambulance attention, Knibbs returned to the field but was in a daze. Campbell kicked a field goal to put St George ahead 12-9. Knibbs was staggering around the field when referee Tomalin saw him offside, and gave Manly a gift penalty almost under the posts. Knibbs then collapsed, and while he was being carried off the ground Charlie Eastes scored the winning try for Manly. Knibbs was taken to St George Hospital with concussion."

In the middle and late '40s we had a bloke at the club named Billy Simpson, a terrier-style of breakaway, a workaholic in the mould of Ray Price or Queensland's current star Jeff Miller. He had a good mate, Harry Stillwell, who was a Manly stalwart and knowledgable supporter of the game. One day the pair of them pulled me aside, and in the nicest possible way informed me that, in their opinion, I was at a crossroads in my career. They told me if I could channel my aggression into good, hard forward play I would go all the way in the game — and there was a Wallaby team off to New Zealand next year, 1949 — but if I continued as I had been, always in strife with referees and whacking opponents at every opportunity, I'd self-destruct and be rubbed out of the game. The truth was that I was becoming a thug. I'd go looking for trouble on the field and anybody who even looked sideways at me risked copping a Mossop right hand. People who know me will probably disagree, but I can take constructive criticism and I listened to what these two blokes had to say. There would be plenty of send-offs and punch-ups to come, notorious occasions when I reverted to my bad old ways, but from that day on I did at least try to clean up my act.

Ron Walden was the heart and soul of Manly rugby union club. A former international rugby player and Australian amateur heavyweight boxing champ, surfing stalwart, and a detective-sergeant in the police force, Ron was a bloke to be reckoned with. In my early years with Manly, he was convinced that I needed to improve my strength so he would send me off to North Steyne Surf Club to wrestle with a fellow called Mick Samios. Mick was a Greek milk bar owner who had been an Olympic wrestler. Being tossed all over the gym by this bloke worked wonders for my neck and back muscles, as well as providing Ron with a great source of amusement. The former boxing champ also liked to get me into the ring with him for a spar. Well, like any young smart arse would, I'd land a good one on him when the occasion arose. Then, just when I'd be feeling pleased with myself for shaking Ronny up, he'd go *bang* and knock me off my feet with a single punch. As he helped me up he'd say, "Now, that will teach you not to take liberties with your betters!" But I never learned, and Ron kept knocking me down. I could have made a fortune selling advertising space on the soles of my boxing boots.

My old Musketeer mate Clarrie Davis followed me into first grade and starred on the wing. He was lightning quick and very elusive, but was fragile and would get hurt a bit. Still inseparable mates, we were always trying to work moves with each other on the field. Once we were representing NSW against Queensland in Brisbane. The scores were close when Clarrie got the ball and sidestepped his way diagonally across the field and into the clear. While he was dancing and darting I set sail up the middle of the field and was in support when he was hemmed in by defenders right on the Queensland line. Without breaking stride Clarrie cross-kicked straight into my hands and I scored right beside the posts. Clarrie distinguished himself in Tests for Australia.

We had another international on the other wing in Charlie Eastes. Charlie today is my next-door neighbour. He was gifted, large, fast and very hard to tackle. He started the 1947 Wallaby tour of the UK like an express train, scoring five tries in his first couple of games. Then a broken arm ended his campaign. He would have come home a superstar, but that's football. My greatest recollection of this wonderful winger is of him starring for us in Australia's first-ever seven-a-side competition in 1946 at North Sydney Oval. He was irresistible that day and scored about 15 tries. We'd just win the scrum, pass to Charlie and he'd do the rest. Toward the end of the competition, I positioned Charlie and was about to pass him the ball when he gasped, "No, Moose, not me. I'm buggered, go on your own!"

There was a fearless goalkicking fullback in Billy Barry, in later years a headmaster in the Manly region; a fine international centre and winger in Alan "Scratchy" Walker who also played Test cricket for Australia; and excellent halves in Spencer "Spanner" Brown and Brian Cox, father of Mitchell and Phillip, who made their names in a later era. Brian was small, but quick and durable, and Spanner, the best attacking five eighth in Sydney for many years, was rewarded with a Wallaby trip to South Africa in 1953. He died tragically young of a heart attack while playing squash, his other great sporting love. Spanner's early death jolted me. He was a man who carried no excess weight and neither drank nor smoked.

In the forwards we had quick-striking hooker Wal Dawson, the tough-tackling lightweight breakaway Billy Simpson and Reg Morton, nicknamed "Fours" because he had very poor eyesight and wore glasses. He was hard and strong and his job was to give me protection when I leapt high for the ball in lineouts. Even though he was virtually flying blind on the field, he was extremely effective. He explained his credo to me one day: "If it's round and smooth, I pass it. If it has hair I belt it." How could we fail with a philosophy like that!

My father became senior vice president of the club and was well-liked by everyone. He was an approachable man and players were forever coming to him with their problems. He found jobs for many of them and was a major factor in the harmony that existed at Manly. We were a close knit bunch of blokes, all good mates, and they were great times. I drove a 1928 four-cylinder Chrysler with running boards. It was an old heap, but Kirk and I did it up and it went fairly well in spite of a distinctive *boom-boom-boom* noise that came from somewhere under the bonnet and would startle pedestrians and telegraph our approach minutes before we arrived. I could fit 14 passengers and a keg in that car, and frequently did.

When I left school I became a messenger boy and then an apprentice fitter and turner at Hallstrom's Refrigeration at Alexandria, but the pay was poor — 17 shillings and sixpence a week — and before long I left to become an office boy at Tooth & Co for not a whole lot more. A friend of Dad's then organised a position for me as a travelling salesman for Christie's Cosmetics where I earned five pounds a week, a fortune to me. Later I repped for a company called Fred Clark's Stainless Steel Sinks. I was well-suited to the life. I liked to talk and people liked talking to me. And being a high-profile footballer opened doors and closed sales.

Work, training and playing kept me busy, but Saturday night was party night. Rugby dances, social gatherings at the surf club, night clubs, restaurants, cabarets — and while alcohol was scarce so soon after the war I don't recall anybody ever dying of thirst. Joan and I were still having an on-again-off-again relationship and I'm glad to say she wasn't around one particular night when I made a total ass of myself. The football club put on a dance at the old Pacific Cabaret at Manly and, there being no beer available then, I was drinking wine and couldn't handle it at all. I was as drunk as a skunk. I remember sitting in the foyer of the club wondering where the hell I was and why I was feeling so crook when a bloke walked past and made a disparaging comment. I knocked him backwards and over a table on which was arranged an elaborate flower setting. This huge posy landed on the poor bugger who looked for all the world like he'd been laid out for an expensive funeral. I was blearily admiring my handiwork when the first grade coach, the formidable Aub Hodgson, emerged from the cabaret, grabbed me by the lapel and dragged me into the street. He walked me the length of Manly Corso, never releasing his grip on my lapel and, every 20 metres or so, delivering an almighty kick up my backside. He kicked me from the cabaret to the Corso to the ocean beach down to Manly harbour and onto a bus. The bus drove off, I passed out, and snored through my stop. I spent a cold, sick night stretched out on the back seat of the bus at its terminus at the Spit.

In 1947 the New Zealand All Blacks toured Australia and Manly club entertained them at a barbecue at, from memory, Mona Vale on Sydney's northern beaches. There were eight or 10 Maoris in the All Blacks and they spent most of the night in a huddle getting very drunk together. We suspected they were up to no good and our suspicions were confirmed when they grabbed our diminutive halfback Brian Cox, tied him to a paling they'd ripped off a nearby fence and suspended him over the open flames of the barbecue. At first we all laughed at Brian's predicament, but soon it became clear that things were getting out of hand and our halfback was being badly singed. I confronted the ringleader of the Kiwis and told him to release Brian. "Listen," I said, "I know you're just having fun, but you're hurting this man." The bloke suggested I piss off. "Look," I continued, "this is a good party and we're all having fun, but if you don't untie that man I'm going to take you out onto the street, bash you up, then drag you back here and *make* you untie him." For a moment the New Zealander's eyes lit up at the thought of a stoush, then, perhaps aware of the sensational headlines such a brawl would inevitably attract, he backed down and let Brian go, so averting an international incident.

At the end of the 1948 season, Eddie "Aga" Kann, rugby writer with the Sydney *Sun* summed up my career to date: "Young Mossop has certainly made plenty of enemies from all quarters over the past three years, but his dedicated attitude, allied with his fearless will to win, make it essential that he is selected for next year's Wallaby tour of New Zealand, where his style of play will be required by all 15 Australians to stand any chance of success against the All Blacks." The article made me feel very grown-up and responsible. Maybe, just maybe, I'd have the chance to renew acquaintances with my friend Sterling on his home turf.

I couldn't wait for the 1949 season to kick off. To make a Wallaby tour of New Zealand is the aim of every Australian player. The All Blacks were, and still are, at the very top of the rugby tree, the team everybody loves to beat. They had a fearsome reputation, and their forwards were noted for ruthless, powerhouse scrummaging and murderous ruck play. To my mind, playing a Test against them would be the closest you could come to being in a war.

My campaign to be a Wallaby got off to a good start when I was selected in the North Harbour side to take on South Harbour, the first rep game of the year; but all my plans nearly came to a shuddering halt when I had a set-to with the outstanding South Harbour breakaway and future Australian coach, Dave Brockhoff. "Brocko" was a terror and would run to tackle you swinging his arms in the air. This day he was giving our half-back Brian Moffatt a terrible time, harassing him at the back of the lineout. I warned Dave to desist but he kept it up. There was nothing else to do. I threw a sweet right hand that caught him flush on the jaw and knocked him down.

The ref was Lew Tomalin, a very senior and respected official. Tomalin and I had clashed before on many occasions and there was no love lost between us. He saw what I'd done, took in Brocko lying on the ground, and blew his whistle hard. If he sent me off I knew, the rugby hierarchy being a conservative and very pukka bunch, that my chances of being selected as a Wallaby were nil. For several seconds my fate hung in the balance as Tomalin deliberated. He then blew a penalty against my team and gave me a severe caution, obviously believing that Brockhoff had received his just desserts for monstering our half-back when he didn't have the ball.

I went on to make the City side and then the NSW team that thrashed Queensland two games straight and lost a match to the New Zealand Maoris. I was, however, overlooked when the selectors chose an Australian team to play the New Zealanders. NSW beat Queensland decisively twice more — I played for my State both times — and on the evening of the final interstate match in Sydney the Australian side to tour New Zealand was picked. On selection night the Manly boys gathered at the Sporting Union Rooms, a misleadingly upmarket moniker for an old shack behind Manly Oval, scene of innumerable rorts, grog parties and dances. A three piece group was competing with the hiss and fizz of many kegs of beer being tapped.

The beer was flowing, the pretty girls were dancing, and then suddenly the gaiety was broken when someone yelled, "Shut up, everyone, the side's being announced." There was a hush. I was gripped with a tension I'd never known, a tension that made me realise just how badly I wanted to realise my childhood ambition to play rugby for my country. The Wallabies' names were read out alphabetically. ". . . Allen . . . Blomley . . . Brockhoff . . . Cawsey . . . Cornforth . . . Cottrell . . ." They came to the Ds and I heard "Davis, Clarrie". A cheer rang loud. On through the alphabet the announcer droned. ". . . Garner . . . McCarthy . . . Mossop . . ."

Euphoria, total madness. I was ordered to chug-a-lug a large jug of beer then made to jump onto the stage and sing. No problem at all in the condition I was in. For some reason I warbled *I Want To Take You On A Slow Boat To China*. What a night, one to remember. I would be selected in many other touring teams before I hung up my boots, but the memory of hearing my name read out for that 1949 Wallaby tour of New Zealand will last long after the others have faded.

5

BEATING THE
ALL BLACKS

I f a Test series against the All Blacks was a war, then the Australian Rugby Union selected its troops well for our 1949 campaign in the Shaky Isles. The team managers were Ron Walden, who was almost a second father to me, and, of all people, my old nemesis Wild Bill Cerutti, whose dressing room prediction to my Dad all those years ago had come true. Captain was Trevor "Tubby" Allan, the Gordon skipper and by then a seasoned Wallaby. Neither of us knew it in 1949, but our lives would follow a bizarre parallel path: we were Wallabies together, both defected to play rugby league with the same club in the north of England then returned to sell cars with Stack and Company before becoming TV commentators — me with Channel 7, Tubby with the ABC.

Trevor was the son of the famous Gordon coach "Slab" Allan. He'd gone to Great Britain with the 1947-48 Australian side and at 21 became the youngest Wallaby captain in history when the tour skipper Bill McLean broke his leg and Tubby took over the team. Allan's incisive running and ferocious head-on tackling saw him hailed as one of the finest footballers to play in the British Isles this century. After a succession of bad knocks to the head, caused by his habit of running in and hurling himself at attackers, Allan always played in distinctive headgear. He was an intelligent, tactically astute and aristocratic centre who did rugby proud. He certainly did not deserve the callous treatment meted out to him by the New South Wales Rugby Union when he announced his intention to switch to league immediately after the 1950 grand final. The Union "named" him and publicly expelled him from his home club, Gordon. It was punishment without precedent.

But back in 1949 as we prepared for the All Black campaign in good spirits and with hopes high, everything in the rugby garden was rosy. Like all good touring teams, ours was a mix of experience and promise. Allan, breakaways Col Windon and Roger Cornforth, five eighth Nev Emery, fullback Brian Piper, half Cyril Burke and second rower Nick Shehadie were seasoned performers at the highest level who would guide the tyros, blokes like myself, Clarrie Davis, Dave Brockhoff, winger Ralph Garner, centre John Blomley and the wild young Gordon prop Bevan Wilson.

Many critics at the time tried to tell us that we would be playing a weakened All Black side. While it was true a number of their stars were engaged in a series against South Africa, the oredominantly Maori side they put in against us was one to be reckoned with and would have been the nucleus of the team to South Africa had the colour bar not been in force. It was led by the Maori centre Johnny Smith, who Trevor Allan swore was the best back he had ever opposed. The one-eighth islander had been barred from the recent Maori team to Australia because it was deemed he did not have enough Maori blood in his veins; and was banned from touring South Africa because he had too much! He was backed up by the flying Ben Couch and Vince Bevan, also Maoris who had been ruled ineligible for the South African tour on racial grounds. In the forwards was the awesome "Tiny" White, six feet five and a very mobile 17 stone. Tiny, then just starting an illustrious All Black career, gave me problems in that series and in years to come. He was a farmer, hard as nails, and my lineout opponent.

Tiny was the unlikely source of a remedy to ease my aching cauliflower ears. After a Test in which he'd done his level best to rip the things from my head, he pulled me aside and told me how he treated his own caulis. "You bathe them in hot milk several times a day," he confided. "Hot milk?" I said doubtfully. "Well, I'll try anything once." To my surprise, Tiny's treatment worked and eased the pain considerably. I made sure there was plenty of milk in my hotel room fridge for the rest of the tour. One day I returned to find about a dozen local cats helping themselves to the milk supply in my room. The moggies were planted there by my playful teammates.

Another good remedy for aches and pains were New Zealand's sulphur baths. Every chance I got I'd immerse myself in the bubbling liquid which worked wonders for my cuts and bruises. A few years ago when Joan and I visited New Zealand on holiday we made sure we had sulphur baths and they were as therapeutic as I remembered them to be.

Just how seriously they take rugby in New Zealand opened my eyes. In Australia I was used to rugby being adored by enthusiasts but ignored by just about everybody else. Over there it's a religion. All of our games were watched by huge, very parochial crowds. I remember in one provincial game many spectators in the record crowd were forced to perch in trees to get a view of the action. Another thing that astounded me was the depth of knowledge of the locals about the touring side. We'd be walking along the street and I'd hear some kid say, "Look, there goes Nick Shehadie. He's six foot two, weighs 16 stone and plays in the second row . . ."

No matter what the opposition, the opposing forward pack would always comprise eight hard men. I found the typical New Zealand forward very, very tough — but lacking a little in courage. They were very good at trampling you when you were caught at the bottom of a ruck, or clouting you when you were on the ground, but were curiously reluctant to slug it out one-on-one.

As the campaign wore on, the Aussies — strangers in a strange land — grew closer together and team spirit ran high. Much against my nature I found myself *almost* liking some of these blokes who'd been opponents back home. We partied hard after our matches and although New Zealand then was "dry" we had no trouble finding grog — we'd just go to the venues where the coppers gathered. So what's new?

After a big win early in the tour against Bay Of Plenty our post-match celebrations began at the team hotel, fuelled by lots of contraband booze. Groupies, pretty local girls keen to find romance with a Wallaby, followed us around, just as they have followed cricket and football teams since sporting tours began, and this night they were there in numbers. I'll own up to being in the thick of the action, but I was not alone.

Tubby Allan was never a big drinker but he'd played a blinder that day and he was determined to wipe himself out. His Gordon clubmate Bevan Wilson, a bitter on-field foe of mine back home, did what any good Highlander would do and supported his captain. Bevan was a playful, bear-like hulk who loved to wrestle and demolish furniture when pissed. At the height of proceedings Bevan leapt onto the window sill — we were two storeys up — and announced that he was going to climb down the drainpipe to ground level like a human fly. Thankfully we talked him out of it. Bevan was a funny fellow and now we're good mates. He's the only bloke who's ever bitten me on a football field. Bev was playing league in England at the same time as me and when our teams met we decided to settle a few differences that had originated on the rugby paddocks of Sydney. We got mixed up in a tackle and he bit me. I was, however, choking him at the time.

Fullback Brian Piper was not as lucky as Bevan that night after the Bay Of Plenty match. Somewhere around 2am, when most of us had either passed out or were in our room making love to the local lasses, a terrible moaning sound drifted up from the street below. Those of us in a condition to do so investigated and found Brian lying in a tangled heap on the footpath. Somehow he'd fallen eight metres from a ledge after climbing out of his hotel room window. He was taken to Bay Of Plenty Hospital. The concussion, compound fracture of the forearm and facial injuries he suffered in one moment of madness ended his tour.

One man with whom I struck up a firm friendship and who remains a good mate today was Nick Shehadie. Nick in those days was a happy, gentle giant whose nickname was "Loved-By-

All". No offence, Sir Nick, but way back then few would have picked you to turn into the outstanding Lord Mayor of Sydney, sporting and business leader that you became. Nick's father was a leader of the Lebanese community in Australia and high in the Church. Wherever Nick was playing in the world, his dad would find an excuse to be there on ecclesiastical business. I remember calling on Nick at his haberdashery shop at Coogee when I was a travelling salesman. Not much work got done. He'd brew up some of that wonderful Lebanese coffee and we'd sit and drink it and talk football for hours. A lovely bloke. Loved-By-All was a typical Randwick forward, expert at keeping the ball alive and running, running, running from kick-off to the final whistle. To my mind, his only shortcoming was that he was *too* lovely a bloke and lacked aggression. Being tackled by Nick was like being pounced on by a big, cuddly St Bernard dog.

As well as all the skylarking, we *did* play a bit of football on this tour. We won nine of our 10 games against provincial teams. Our only loss came against West Coast-Buller in a game of wild brawls and terrible refereeing. Roger Cornforth and I were repeatedly penalised by referee Pratt for punching but transgressions from the New Zealanders were ignored. Pratt also sent Bevan Wilson off, then allowed him to return to the field. In an astonishing display Pratt penalised us at a ratio of four-to-one and even though we scored five tries to their two we were beaten 17-15. At the official post-match function we were still seething at his display and when it came time for Tubby Allan to call us to our feet to toast the referee I led a group of players who refused to stand. At that, Ron Walden stormed over and said to us, "You men are part of a great Wallaby side and you will stand and drink to this referee." Sheepishly we did what we were told. I remembered that incident years later on the 1959 Kangaroo tour of Britain when we were called on to stand and toast an English referee who had caned us unfairly and unmercifully that afternoon in a game against Barrow. I was captain of the Kangaroos that day and, just as Ron Walden had got stuck into me in New Zealand, I came over and exhorted a group of angry and reluctant Aussies to get to their feet for the toast. Later I approached the referee to give him the chance to rationalise his atrocious display. I'll never forget his response. In his broad Cumbrian accent he told me, "Eh, laad, thee is 'ere today and gone tomorrow. I 'ave to live 'ere for the rest o' me days!"

Beating provincial teams is all well and good but our real mission was to win the two-Test series and become the first Wallaby side ever to win the Bledisloe Cup, the glittering prize of Trans-Tasman rivalry. The First Test at Athletic Park, Wellington was the debut Test for Clarrie Davis and me, and it ended in a resounding 11-6 win to the Wallabies.

The All Black tactics were to use their forwards and the boot of five eighth Couch to constantly turn us around, but Roy Cawsey, the second-string halfback thrown into the custodian's role after Brian Piper fell out of the window, kept flying high to catch Couch's kicks and send the ball soaring into New Zealand territory. Against Trevor Allan, the brilliant Johnny Smith didn't make a break all day. We dominated the first half of the dour match, scoring three tries to lead 11-0 at the break. In the second half we hung on against wave upon wave of desperate All Black attack. Our forwards, Shehadie, Brockhoff, Cottrell, Windon, Baxter, Wilson, Cross and Mossop, gave the well-drilled New Zealanders a lesson in tight-rucking rugby. Nick and I won the lineouts 36-19, no mean feat against an opponent like Tiny White.

I recall that game as a non-stop hurly burly in which I repeatedly threw my body into the rucks and mauls, belting anyone in a black jumper. Before the match I'd been sick with nerves, but afterwards I was accepted by teammates and opponents as a Test forward, and that's a feeling you just can't buy.

We wrapped up the series and captured the Bledisloe Cup with a victory in the second and final Test. In all the years since, only Alan Jones' 1986 Wallabies have won a Test series against the All Blacks in New Zealand. If anything, the Second Test was a harder game than the first. As we waited in our dressing room to run onto the field in front of 25,000 spectators at Auckland's Eden Park I noticed that I no longer felt that sheer terrifying nervousness that I had experienced before my Test debut. This time the adrenalin was pumping, but I was composed and focussed about what I was going to have to do in the game — such a beautiful, hyped-up feeling. We scored three tries to one and ran out victors 16-9. Once more the forwards' fierce domination of the rucks and mauls laid the foundation for bright attack from the backs. The game was close, and only made safe for Australia in the last minute when Nev Emery scored near the posts.

We all went wild when the final whistle was blown. Trevor Allan was hoisted high into the air and the prized trophy was presented to Ron Walden. I was over the moon. A radio announcer managed to pull me away from the celebrations long enough to ask me to send a cheerio to the listeners back home. I grabbed the mike. "Hi Dad, hi Mum, hi Kirk! We've beaten the bastards! You beauty!" I roared. Swearing on radio was just not done in those days and my exultant message was picked up in the press and drew frowns from a rugby establishment used to a little more restraint from their ambassadors overseas. The powers-that-be noted my words and filed them away for later.

Even then, these toffee-nosed Australian rugby administrators in their tweed jackets with patches on the sleeves were getting on my nerves. There's no doubt that many of the things I did in my career — my sendoffs, my aggressive play — embarrassed them. But I was my own man and could not have changed for anyone. One or two of them told me years later that I was always considered to have the attitude of a rugby league player. At that stage of my football career, however, I had no interest at all in league. I loved rugby, my teammates and all the fun we had together. An old mate, Ray Stehr, the former league great who had distinguished himself by being sent off twice in a three-match Test series against the Poms, was now acting as a talent scout for the English club sides Leeds and Leigh. He'd indicated that both clubs were interested in my joining them but each year when he'd make an offer I'd tell Ray "Thanks, but no thanks."

After a night of great revelry in Auckland we turned up at the airport the following day to catch our flight home. It was then that a complete stranger, a Mr A.H. Carmen, approached me and took me aside. Carmen introduced himself as the publisher of the *New Zealand Rugby Almanac*. The *Almanac* was the Bible of Kiwi football. He told me that three Australians had been named among the publication's five footballers of the year: Trevor Allan, Ralph Garner and Rex Mossop. This was the icing on what was a wonderful tour for me, and an honour I cherish to this day.

There was an almost-fatal postscript to the victorious 1949 Wallaby tour of New Zealand. When we arrived home we organised a reunion at Garie Beach, south of Sydney. Everything was going according to plan as the big day approached, until a beer strike threw a spanner in our works. Even in those far off days, it seemed that beer strikes were planned to cause the maximum inconvenience to drinkers. Clarrie Davis and I came up with a plan to freight some beer to Sydney from Western Australia by ship. The 12 dozen bottles departed Perth and finally arrived intact at the Sydney wharves via Adelaide and Melbourne. However when Clarrie turned up at the docks to collect it, the wharfies informed him that unless we gave them half our beer a little accident would be arranged and the whole lot would be smashed. He called me and I charged down and we pulled a few standover tactics of our own. I told these wharfies that if anything happened to even a single bottle of our beer I'd inform the police and then come down and take some bloody action myself. They speedily saw reason and I think we ended up giving them a dozen bottles just in case we ever needed their expertise again.

Anyway, the beer arrived at the reunion and was consumed in great quantities. We all got very drunk then sat in a stream and let the cool water flow over our bodies. It was then that Clarrie started to complain that he was feeling sick. He was not alone by that time, so we took little notice of our mate's grumbling. An hour or so later, well into the afternoon, we realised that he really was in a bad way so I put him in the back of my little Austin A40 utility and drove back to Sydney as fast as I could in my inebriated state over roads that were bumpy and pot-holed. I knew I shouldn't have driven, but Clarrie by now was desperately ill and I had to get him home. That night he was admitted to hospital and was diagnosed as having a burst appendix. He had nearly died back there at Garie Beach and the rough ride to Sydney in my ute nearly finished him off. But Clarrie pulled through and by the time the 1950 season rolled around he was jumping out of his skin to join the fray.

COLLISION COURSE

M anly were well-established as one of the leading clubs by 1950. In '49 we'd only just missed a place in the semis. We'd finished equal third with Randwick and Easts but were eliminated on percentages. By 1950 we were stronger and considered ourselves an excellent chance of winning our first premiership since 1943.

The other attraction of that year was a tour by the British Lions. I desperately wanted to cement my place in Australia's Test lineup so played like a man inspired in the club matches and rep fixtures leading up to the selection of the national side. Once again, my over-vigorous play threatened to bring me undone. Frank Tierney in the *Sunday Herald* attacked me for "breaching the offside rule almost as much as Dave Brockhoff" and *The Sydney Morning Herald*, the paper that would cause me so much grief later in life, weighed in with criticism of "illegalities" in my play. Nevertheless when the Test team was picked I was in it.

The British Isles were a splendid side. In my view they had three players who would have been greats in any era. Bleddyn Williams, the Welsh centre, was a champion. He was a short man, almost portly, with thick waist, chest and neck. His powerful, low-to-the-ground running could slash an opposing backline to pieces. Irish legend Jackie Kyle was a masterly five eighth, adept at setting up his supports, and in 19-year-old Lewis Jones the Lions boasted one of the all-time great fullbacks. Lewis was a wizard. He invented, then refined, the goosestep acceleration that current star David Campese uses so effectively.

You'd move in to tackle Jones, he'd kick out his foot to put you off balance, then accelerate past you and into open space so fast he'd make you look a fool. He eventually turned pro and our paths crossed again on the fields of northern England.

Both Tests, in Sydney and Brisbane, went convincingly to the British Isles, 19-6 and 24-3. The thrashing was a huge disappointment after all we'd achieved in New Zealand the year before. We forwards cancelled each other out but they ran us ragged in the backs. In the Sydney Test Bleddyn Williams was running at will and his opponent, the highly-skilled and highly-strung John Blomley, was powerless to stop him. At halftime Blomley was shedding tears of frustration. He held himself personally responsible for the big score the Lions had already posted against us. "For God's sake, Jack," I said, "there's no use crying about it, we've got to stop this Williams. Tell you what, try to grab him and hang onto him until I arrive. I'll discourage the bastard." Blomley did as he was told. He held Bleddyn in the tackle long enough for me to race in and punch him to the ground. Williams was carted off with concussion and Blomley, with no Williams to contend with, played a whole lot better. Australia bridged the gap, though not enough to win. What I did to Williams was rough justice, but a Test match is no place for shrinking violets. Williams knew that, too, and harboured no bad feelings. John Blomley went on to become a doctor and was another who died before his time. But I'll always remember his effusive thanks to me that day for services rendered.

It was not until the Lions' final game, against NSW at Newcastle, that we exacted revenge. A big, strong blues team was picked, but the turnaround in our fortunes was largely due to the selection as captain-coach of Basil "Jika" Travers, a 31-year-old who'd played for Oxford and appeared in six Tests for England between 1947 and '49. He was a Rhodes Scholar and became a long-serving headmaster at Sydney's Shore. Jika was a cultivated fellow but a hard, uncompromising man when it came to rugby. His coaching technique brooked no individual thought. We were all given little slips of paper on which were printed such morsels of rugby wisdom as "They can't run without legs", "Don't argue with the referee", "They can't score tries without the ball" and "Talk to your teammates all the time". Jika, despite receiving little affection from his team, in just five training sessions produced a XV that out-thought, out-scored and out-fought an international side that had rode roughshod over all opposition that winter. Nick Shehadie, Spanner Brown and Clarrie Davis were our best, with Nick and Clarrie each notching two tries. We all received pewter mugs to mark our 17-12 win, and were allowed to keep our jerseys.

Manly, too, kept on winning and met Gordon in the grand final at North Sydney Oval. The match is still remembered as the roughest club match ever played in Sydney. I was up against my Wallaby teammates Trevor Allan and Bevan Wilson, but good times in each other's company were forgotten as we ripped into each other. I once overheard my close mate Tubby exhorting his forwards to belt "that bastard Mossop" every chance they got. They did as they were told. As well as Wilson, Gordon sported a couple of true hard men in their pack: Hugh "Snow" Naughton, a hulking silent type who said little but hit hard, and Ian "Bomber" Miles, a NSW teammate of mine who sledged a lot and could back up his bad-mouthing with his fists.

Wrote Frank Tierney in *The Daily Telegraph* "This grand final was a sensational match, rarely equalled for rough play, which Manly won 21-15 . . . Use of every means of committing an illegality was adopted by some of the players, and the long sequence of rabbit killers, late tackling, kicking of men on the ground, was encouraged by the reluctance of referee Harold Tolhurst to take drastic action earlier. In fairness to the referee, it is necessary to state that he was fully occupied in following the ball. In the flurries of fists and legs in the rucks he was not able to see all that occurred. But one incident, in which two forwards stood a yard in front of him and headlocked each other then threw punches, while the crowd roared, cannot pass without comment." Those two forwards were me and Snow Naughton. While I was caught in Naughton's headlock, Bevan Wilson king-

Rex, the young woodworker, a study in concentration in the family garage.

Mother, father and brother in the late-1920s. Nellie and Norman Mossop with four-year-old Kirk at Five Dock.

Above: Rex, the teenage Manly surfer, riding the waves on his long board. Right: Rex's brother Kirk in his 20s. A keen photographer, he would roam the headlands for good photo opportunities.

Above: A dog lover then as now, the young Rex was snapped by his brother Kirk.
Right: Even into late middle age, Norman Mossop (far right) was the life of company cricket matches.

Left: The young rugby forward practices his punt in the family front yard at Condamine Street. Below: Proud reel man in the Manly Surf Club march past in the late '40s.

Above and below: Joan Bell, local beach beauty, and Rex Mossop, budding rugby star and man-about-Manly, in their courting days.

Top: Joan and Rex on their wedding day, 1951. Above: Nightclubbing at Sammy Lee's cabaret with fellow Musketeer Warwick Ritchie and wife Barbara.

Training with the NSW rugby union team at University Oval with young Nick Shehadie in 1946.

Opposite page: Rugby Mossop-style, for NSW (top) and Manly, over-vigorous and always on the ball. Right: With fellow Wallaby Nev Cottrell in New Zealand in 1949. Note the heavily taped ears. Below: The 1949 NSW rugby side. Trevor Allan is front row, third from left; John Blomley second row, second from left; Charlie Eastes second row, fifth from left; Clarrie Davis, the second Musketeer, third row, first on left; Rex Mossop and young Nick Shehadie, back row, first and second from left.

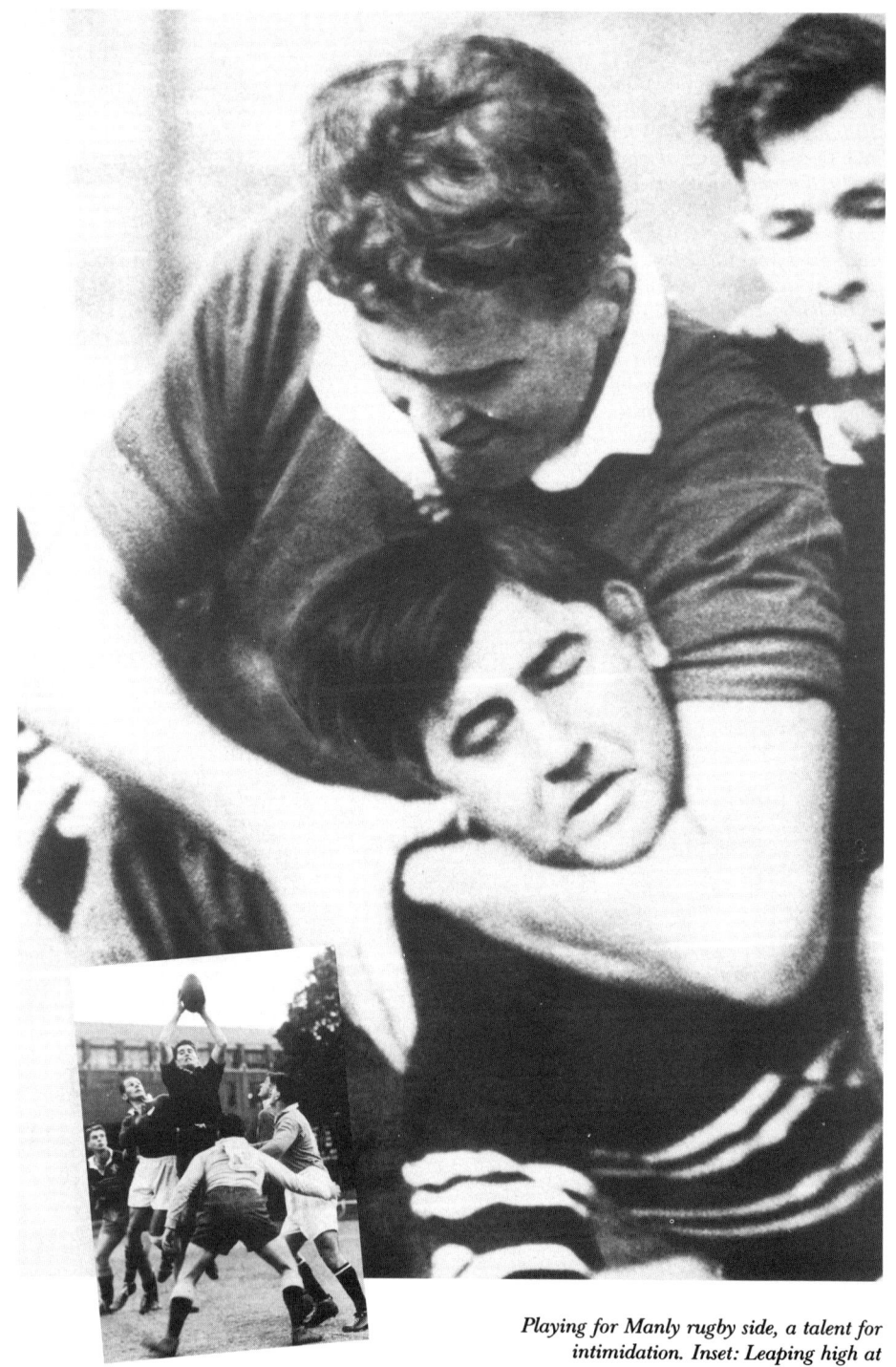

Playing for Manly rugby side, a talent for intimidation. Inset: Leaping high at lineout training.

Looking the part in his travelling salesman days in the late 1940s.

Rex celebrating his 21st birthday with friends around a football cake.

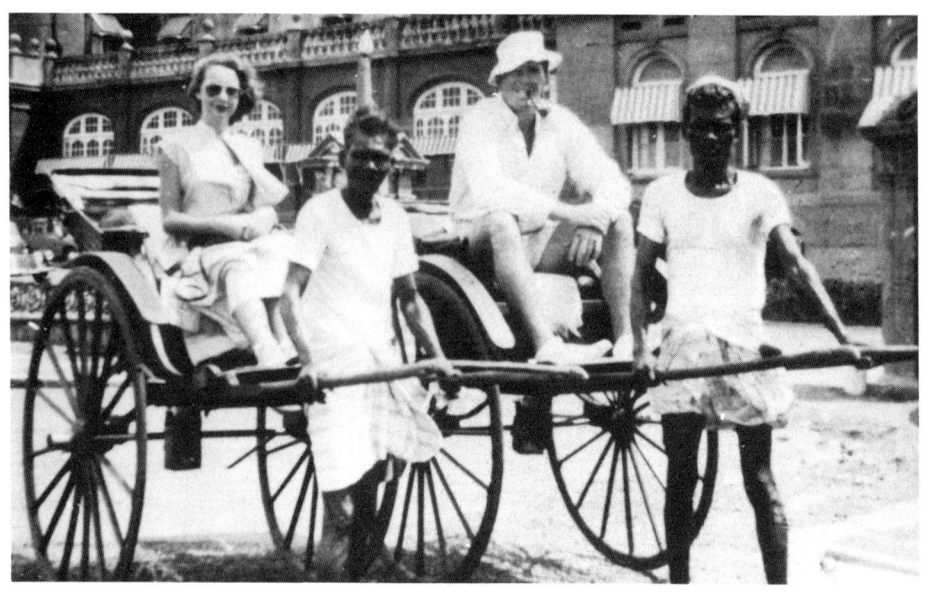

Above: Joan and Rex travel in style in Ceylon, en route to England and a brand new ball game, 1951. Left: Practising the skills of the professional code in the famous hooped jersey of Leigh. Opposite page, top: With new son Kirk in the backyard of the Mossops' home in Leigh, 1952. Right: Norman and Nellie Mossop, shortly before Nellie's death.

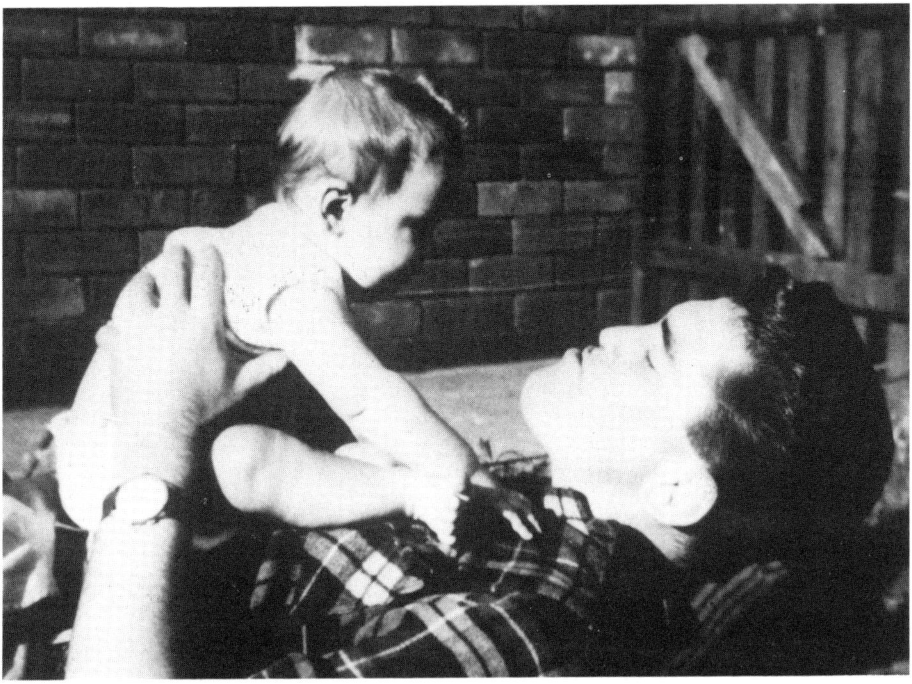

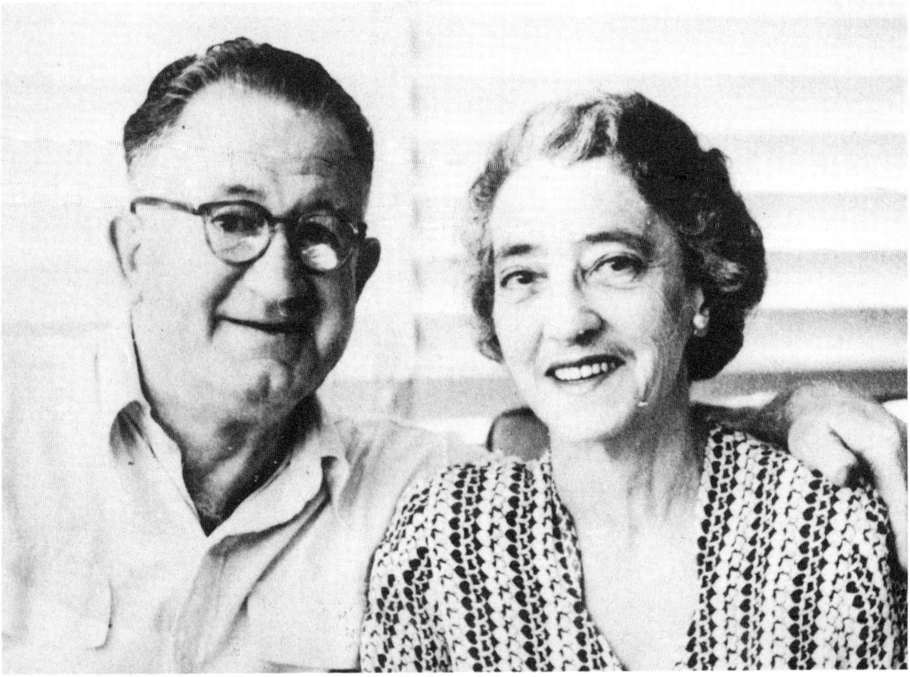

Left: No football today, as winter ice and snow make Kirkhall Road, Leigh's home ground, unplayable. Below: Rex accepts his Other Nationalities representative team cap from Leigh's Lord Mayor with club president Jimmy Hilton looking on.

Right: Newlyweds Joan and Rex at a football club function. Below: Christmas in Leigh with fellow Aussies Alan Walker, Nev Benson and Trevor Allan.

Training on Brookvale Oval in 1965 with sons Greg (left) and Kirk.

hit me, knocking me unconscious. When I regained my senses I was into it again, this time locking horns with Bomber Miles. We'd been belting each other all day and there was only eight minutes to go with Manly leading comfortably when we decided to forget the ball and get stuck into each other. We traded blows for about a minute while the referee frantically blew his whistle for peace. At last, he gave up on us and sent us both off. We filed off the field with the excited cheers of the crowd and referee Tolhurst's parting comment of "Silly big bastards!" ringing in our ears. As we reached the player's tunnel Bomber turned to me and winked.

As I slumped onto a bench in the dressing room Dad came up and offered me the customary bottle of DA. It was a ritual he repeated after every match. I was battered, bloodied and dazed so he said nothing, just sat beside me in the room, a silent supporter. No son ever had a better or more understanding father.

After the match I consoled Trevor Allan. The next day he confirmed what everybody suspected. He had accepted an offer to play rugby league with the Leigh club in England. Tubby was an ornament to the amateur code, captaining his club and country with style and success. His defection to "thugby league" was a body blow to the Rah-Rahs. So they made an example of him. Other star players had turned pro — Ken Kearney, Tony Paskins and Rupert Mudge among them — but he was the only one "named" and expelled from his club. What they did to Trevor Allan was a bloody disgrace. It sickened me to see these stuffed-shirt clowns in cravats criticising from a position of power and inherited wealth a young bloke whose only crime was that he'd taken the chance to become financially secure by turning pro. Not having the advantage of family wealth, Tubby made what for him was the right decision. He accepted the Leigh club's offer of a 6000 pounds sterling signing-on fee, married his sweetheart Judith, and departed for four years to establish himself in a wonderful new game, leaving far behind him the vitriolic crap slung about by the rugby hierarchy in that narrow-minded era.

Grand final victory celebrations raged around Manly for days, but my fun was interrupted by a trip to the tribunal. I was relieved to receive a severe caution on account of this being the first time I had ever been sent from the field. It would not be the last.

As I readied myself for the 1951 season — a year when Manly would be out to defend its premiership and Australia the Bledisloe Cup in a home series against New Zealand — I reflected that I had now been playing the amateur code for seven seasons and apart from a host of priceless memories had precious little to show for it. Joan and I had finally decided to get married, but making ends meet on my travelling salesman wage was hard. We wanted a home of our own and were keen to start a family but simply could not afford it. Ray Stehr kept trying to persuade me to follow Tubby Allan to Leigh. Their offer was still on the table, he said, "Four thousand pounds sterling, first class travel by boat for you and Joan, accommodation, a good winning bonus." My old friend was beginning to make sense, but weighing against the riches on offer from Leigh was my genuine love of rugby union and my keen desire to once more lock horns with Tiny White and his All Black mates in front of a home crowd. I had never even played rugby league. But there is no doubt that I was beginning to worry about my future, at 23 I was no longer a kid, and I'm afraid I took out my anxieties on my opponents.

What turned into a disaster season for me began brightly enough when in April I played my 100th game for Manly. *The Daily Telegraph* recorded the occasion: "Playing his 100th first grade match, international Rex Mossop starred for Manly against Drummoyne at Manly Oval. Before the match Manly club president Mr R. Walden presented Mossop with a miniature mounted silver football. Mossop received a great ovation from the large crowd. Mossop excelled in lineout play during the match. In the rucks he worked like a beaver and very often broke out in the open to start movements. He capped this fine performance by diving through a mass of Drummoyne forwards to score the last try of the day. And again the crowd cheered Mossop."

From then on it was all downhill. Playing for NSW against Queensland at North Sydney Oval just a few weeks later I became the first union player sent off in an interstate match in 20 years when I was given my marching orders for "rough play". The tribunal suspended me for two matches. In a pointed reference to my send-off in the 1950 grand final, ARU chief Justice Herron alluded to the need to clean up rugby following incidents the previous year that had "violated the traditions of the union code". It was clear to me that the union bosses had my number.

None of this, however, prevented my selection in the First Test against New Zealand. That Australian side, which included many Queenslanders whom I believe were blatant political selections, was no match for a brutal All Black outfit that beat us 8-0 on a Sydney Cricket Ground quagmire. Several of our best men were overlooked for that Test and replaced by Queenslanders who, quite simply, were not up to the occasion. There is political skulduggery in every sport, but no administrators were as adept at it as the rugby chiefs of the '50s.

Phil Tresidder in *The Sunday Telegraph* wrote that I played the game of my rugby career that day, but I copped a battering for my efforts. One of the All Black forwards was the New Zealand amateur boxing champion and he paid me special attention. I was knocked cold twice, kicked in the back, held in a ruck and belted, raked with sprigs, and badly cut about on my face and head.

My next game was a club fixture against Drummoyne. I should never have played as I was still a mess from the Test; I carried stitches in my face and was swathed in protective tape. I ran onto Drummoyne Oval in a dangerous mood. Just 25 seconds into the game a lineout formed, I jumped for the ball and was illegally interfered with by a Drummoyne forward. I snapped. Swinging around I punched the nearest bloke in a red jersey fair in the face. The poor guy's name was John Lord and he went down with his nose badly broken, a bleeding mess. The referee sent me off at once. It was my third send-off in 10 matches. I reckon my long, slow walk from the field was the low point of my sporting career. The tribunal heard my angry defence that I had been provoked and that I was sick of being a target for the game's bashers and wasn't going it cop it anymore. Then they suspended me for a month. The suspension cost me my place in the two remaining Tests, both of which were won by New Zealand.

I was totally disenchanted with the way rugby union was treating me but I returned to the domestic competition and continued to play my guts out for Manly. We reached the final that year but were beaten by Easts in a torrid match. The game was my swansong as a Rah-Rah. Weeks before I had decided to finally accept Leigh's offer to turn professional. I badly wanted to be selected for the 1953 Wallaby tour of South Africa — I was considered a certainty to go — but I had decided that once you reach a certain stage of your life your wife, the family that you're planning and establishing security, must take precedence over anything else.

While I was suspended I had long discussions with Joan, with Dad and Mum, and with my employer. They all said what I was wanting to hear, that going to Leigh was a chance to establish myself financially and see the world into the bargain. Dad, however, was sad to see me leave union and did not relish the prospect of my being overseas. He and Mum were both getting on a bit and Mum, especially, was in ill-health with angina, a heart condition. But the old man said to me, "Knocking back this money is like declining to pick up your lottery winnings. You'll never have this much money in your life — and you're going to be paid for doing something you love. You'll have no problem adjusting to league, believe me." As I said, no man ever had a better Dad. The day after Manly was eliminated from the semis I announced that I was switching codes.

In an official reaction from the ARU, Justice Herron sent me steely good wishes. "Rugby union has the greatest appreciation of Rex Mossop's qualities as a player and sportsman. It wishes him the best of luck in rugby league. Mossop was a great supporter of rugby union, which would have liked to retain him. Whether he is doing the right thing is a matter for Mossop himself to decide." A further ARU statement noted, "The Rugby Union will take no action against Mossop other than the automatic expulsion provided for in the laws of the game." The door had slammed.

Joan and I were married at St Matthews Church in Darley Road, Manly, on October 26, 1951. The rugby hierarchy were a whole lot more upset with me than my teammates, who all turned up at the wedding and made it a riotous affair. After the service, the goodwill and the grog flowed. I distinctly remember Scratchy Walker who, like me, laboured under the mistaken belief that he could sing a bit, trying to snatch the microphone from the suave French crooner I had hired to perform at the reception.

Very late that night after the reception, a group of us repaired to the Cellarette wine-tasting area of the South Steyne Hotel — Joan and I, Clarrie Davis and his girlfriend, Warwick Ritchie, and Manly union stalwart Aub Hodgson. In their cups, my friends attacked me in a good-natured way for not throwing a farewell party for them before Joan and I left for England. "Be buggered!" I protested, "I've spent a fortune on you freeloaders today, and you're not getting another penny out of me!" The grumbling about my supposed tightness with money continued until I'd had enough and challenged Aub, whose niggling had really got under my skin, to a fistfight on the beach outside the pub.

We flailed away at each other in our drunken stupor — some of our blows even landed — until a police car pulled up and the cops demanded to know what the problem was. "No problem at all," Aub and I chorused, suddenly mates again. The police departed, Aub went too and Joan and I were left to stagger home to our marital bed. I was very under the weather and I assure you there was very little action between the sheets on that particular night. At seven next morning there was a knock on the door and in walked Aub. He plonked himself on the end of our bed, knocked the top off a couple of cold bottles, and the party started all over again.

A couple of days later, still hungover but ecstatically happy, Joan and I left the warm Sydney spring of 1951 for the gathering gloom of a north of England winter. Waiting for us was a new way of life, a new country and a brand new ball game.

7

WILD COLONIAL BOY

O ur honeymoon on the high seas en route to England was the perfect remedy for the bruises, to my body and my pride, that I'd sustained in that last turbulent season of rugby union. As Joan and I lazed beside the *Orcades* swimming pool, rode a rickshaw in Ceylon and marvelled at a snake charmer in Aden we knew that this adventure marked an end and a beginning. It was goodbye to rugby. In spite of my problems with the tribunal and clashes with pig-headed officials, it was a game I had excelled in at the highest level, and loved for its mateship and the free-flowing, rough and ready way we played it at Manly. Farewell, too, to irresponsibility and my wild bachelor days. From now on I would be a husband and father playing football for money to provide food and shelter for Joan and the family we were keen to start.

We docked at London in November, 1951, tanned, relaxed and wide-eyed at the strange and wonderful sights we had seen on our four-week voyage. Eager Leigh officials were waiting to greet us when we berthed. They had made the long drive down from the north to show us the sights and have a good, first look at this wild colonial boy who was costing them so much money. My 5000 pounds signing-on fee was then the record sum ever paid by an English club for a forward.

London was the magical city we'd hoped it would be. Big Ben, Tower Bridge, Buckingham Palace, Trafalgar Square, the Houses of Parliament. Post-wartime rationing was still in force, and Londoners were doing it tough, but to us the city sparkled. The club had booked us in at the Regent's Palace, a beautiful old family hotel. Joan and I checked in and then it was off to the West End for a real treat. The American entertainer Mary Martin, whom I had lusted after from afar for years, was starring in the London production of *South Pacific*, the hit musical of the day. We had excellent seats in a box beside the stage. When Mary, a beautiful girl and a wonderful singer, launched into *I'm Gonna Wash That Man Right Out Of My Hair* she seemed to look right at me. I nearly leapt right out of our box to get to her. All of a sudden I was feeling a long, long way from Manly Oval.

Next morning we headed north to Leigh and reality. After the beaches, sunshine and wide-open spaces of Australia and the dizzying glamour of London this rain-washed, soot-encased industrial village in Lancashire with its narrow, winding streets of grimy factories and mean terrace houses brought me down to earth with the force of a Tiny White tackle. Joan and I both came down with a chronic case of homesickness and many times early on wondered to each other what the hell we had got ourselves into. But in spite of the cold, the damp, the snow and the clouds of black soot that billowed from thousands of coal fires to envelop the town and choke our lungs, we persevered and by the time we headed home three and a half years later Leigh and its people held a special place in our hearts.

Joan fell pregnant in quick time, Quick enough, in fact, to have her mother counting the months. Our first son Kirk was born in the English autumn of 1952.

The Leigh club could not have been kinder. In addition to my 5000 pounds record signing-on fee, with which I bought a block of land not far from Mum and Dad's place in Balgowlah, I was to receive 10 pounds for a win, eight pounds for a draw and six pounds for a loss — big money in 1951. Joan and I were also provided with a nice little two-storey house on the outskirts of Leigh, and I found a job selling the paper products manufactured by the company of the English League and Leigh president Jimmy Hilton. My partner in crime at Hilton's was none other than my old Aussie club adversary, Wallaby teammate and good friend Trevor Allan, who was the Leigh captain.

Trevor and his quiet, lovely wife Judith and Joan and I became inseparable. Tubby sold me his snappy MG TC and together we'd set out to explore the dramatic countryside of England's north, as well as heading south to London from time to time. Midway through the 1952 season, when the grounds of Lancashire were unplayable, so frosted up you couldn't get a pick into them, my old Manly teammate Neville Digby-Bennett, who was then captaining the very pukkah London rugby club Rosslyn Park, rang and said, "Rex, come down to London and I'll get you a game with us." That was fine by me. Of course neither Neville nor I let on that I was a league player. Had the officials found out, we both would have been in serious trouble and the club penalised for fielding a professional player. I ran on in a match against Cambridge University as "Alan Cameron", the bloke who had replaced me in the Australian rugby side. We won the game and afterwards the Rosslyn Park secretary approached me and said, "Well done, Cameron. When next you're in London, contact me and we'd be delighted to give you another run."

We had great times and met many new friends. A good number of old mates, too, turned up on our doorstep. You never appreciate your family and friends as much as when you're far away from them. We were always glad to accommodate the many travelling Aussies who dropped in during our stay in England. Letters and phone calls from home also gave our spirits a lift. From the beginning of our time away, Dad wrote regularly with news and kept me up to date on the Manly union side's fortunes. One report from home, however, alarmed us. Mum's angina problems had lately grown worse and were causing such concern that brother Kirk had taken a year off work just to look after her.

As soon as I arrived in Leigh I was introduced to my new teammates and did my best to learn all I could about rugby league. Nothing, however, could have prepared me for my first match, against Warrington at Wilderspool. That day I clashed with two men, both Australians, who would have a profound effect on me. As I ran onto the field I was aware that the Warrington forwards were staring hard in my direction. They were being stirred up by a heavyset, sandy-haired young bloke with prominent ears and a baby face. I knew Harry Bath only by reputation. He'd been a certainty for the Australian Test side in 1946 before injury ruled him out. He then moved to England where his brutal though crafty forward play and fine goal-kicking stamped him as one of the world's best. Now here he was, snarling at me and working his teammates into a frenzy. "Get this convict Australian bastard Mossop; belt this bloke!" he was telling them. I was badly pissed-off to hear such garbage coming from a fellow countryman. "Well, mate, I thought, if that's the way you want to play it, fine. And, by the way, what the hell are you, a Ugandan?"

There on that icy English pitch back in 1951 began one of rugby league's great feuds. Bath and I belted each other all afternoon and every time we met on the field for the rest of our careers we did our best to inflict serious damage on each other. Our unreasoning hatred — we just instinctively loathed each other — simmered away for years and finally exploded in the 1959 grand final between Manly and St George when Harry and I squared off for what is still remembered as the most vicious fight ever witnessed at the SCG. A series of nasty inci-dents in that classic match had brought us to flashpoint and we fought toe to toe until the referee sent us from the field.

Many years later, as often happens with fierce enemies, we became good friends, and remain so today. Recently I was on the Gold Coast, and, as I always try to do when I'm there, I dropped in on Harry at his newsagency. I told him I was writing this book and the old bloke, the only fellow alive with worse-looking ears than mine, chuckled, "I bet you won't print the whole story. I bet you won't tell them how you stomped on my head back in the '59 grand final!" Well, rest easy Harry, I have. But you deserved it, and I'll gladly go into the whole unsavoury incident in more detail in a later chapter!

On the wing for Warrington that day was the best attacking

player I have ever seen in any code of football. Brian Bevan was a balding, spindly, toothless Bondi boy who turned up in the north of England looking for a game of football after being shunned by Easts after the war. This man was lightning. And added to his blinding speed he could step and swerve without breaking stride. Bevan, known variously as "The Galloping Ghost", "The Bondi Streak" and "The Bony Ballet Dancer", scored the phenomenal tally of 796 tries for Warrington between 1946 and 1962. One of these is acknowledged as the best rugby league try ever scored. Bevan picked up the ball behind his own goalline and confronted and beat *every* bloke on the other team on his 110-yard swerving, ducking and weaving sprint to touch down between the posts at the other end of the field. There was never a drawcard like Brian Bevan. Thousands would turn up to the game just to see him play. When he was out injured, Warrington management would publish his name in the team list anyway, knowing the gate would be way down if word leaked out that the bandy-legged wing sensation was not able to play.

Brian, who died recently in his late 60s, looked like nobody's idea of a footballer. Virtually every centimetre of skin sported some kind of dressing; he'd turn up in the changing room before a match and his personal trainer would have all these strips of sticking plaster laid out on his bench, pre-cut to fit his knee, elbow, thigh, hand, whatever. He'd also routinely take the field wearing shoulder pads, elbow pads, reinforced jockstrap, hip pads, knee guards, shin guards and ankle guards. He looked like a bloody mechanical man. But could he play!

Bevan's frail physique was deceptive. He was durable and could withstand a battering. But before they could batter the little bastard, his opponents had to catch him — and that was easier said than done. I admit I couldn't wait to get my hands on him in that first game against Warrington, but the old campaigner made sure my league career got started on the wrong foot. Once in the game he was running with the ball, I lined him up and moved in to crunch him, then in a flash he stepped inside me. Despairingly I flung my arm out to grab his jersey and Brian ducked right into it. I'd necked him. His legs shot out in front of him and he crashed hard to the ground, landing flat on his back. There had been no malice in my tackle at all, it was purely a reflex action, but when the local hero hit the deck and stayed there crumpled in a heap, all hell broke loose. Bath and his boys made a beeline to belt me, and then the crowd decided to join in the fun. About 30 of them spilled over the fence and onto the field, fists clenched and baying for Aussie blood. Trevor Allan called for our teammates to form a protective circle around me. While all this pandemonium was raging around me, images raced through my head of Custer's Last Stand.

It took me a while to settle in to my new code. There were similarities between league and union: you stayed on the ball, you ran hard, you got over the top of your opponent. But there were many differences, too. In defence you had to put your man down every time, not just halt his progress and wait for a ruck to form. This meant leaving the ground to smash him before he could get the ball away to a support. And every time you ran with the ball you took your life in your hands. Running into the opposition was like running through a forest of coathangers; high stiff-arm tackling, aimed right at the attacker's head, was the order of the day. I remember sitting alongside Reg Gasnier on the plane taking the 1959 Kangaroo team to England and the young centre asked me what to expect from British defenders. Knowing Gasnier's superb running style, shoulders back, head held up high, I replied, "Reg, just remember to duck!"

The English game has always been based on attack; scoring tries has always been more important than stopping them. But when they do tackle, Poms like to go high. "Why go low, when you can take a bloke's head off with a stiffy and not even scrape your knees?" was their attitude, with few exceptions. We Aussies, on the other hand, loved to tackle hard and low, head-on or side-on, it was all the same to us. So at Leigh our English teammates sat back and let us do all the defensive work. Many would bludge on us, shirking their tackling, knowing full well that Allan or Mossop would make the tackle that they dogged. Finally we got jack of this and confronted our teammates. "You blokes are not pulling your weight in defence," we said. "Well," they replied, "you guys are fit and getting all the money, and you enjoy tackling, so we thought we'd leave you to it!" We told them that wasn't on and from then on things improved, but not much.

In my first year at Leigh I made the mistake that most union forwards make when they switch codes of always trying to be exactly where the ball is. So, every time a player was tackled and play broke down while he played the ball, I'd have to run backwards to get back on side, then run forwards again to keep on the ball. Apart from losing my momentum, all this to-ing and fro-ing meant that I was running about 10 miles a match further than anybody else. It wasn't until I'd played at least 20 games that the penny dropped and I learned to pace myself, to read a game so I could trail the action, select the moment to become involved and so make maximum impact.

I owe a huge debt to the man who took over the coaching of Leigh in my second season there. Joe Egan was a legendary English rake who hooked the ears off the best Australia could throw up against him in the Test series of the 1940s. It was Joe who taught me how to use the ball. I'd based my entire football career on tucking the leather under my arm and running hard into the opposition — very successfully, I might add — but when I was tackled the ball died too. Soon after he took over at Leigh, Joe Egan pulled me aside and said, "Run with the ball in your hands . . . like this" and he'd demonstrate. I learned that holding the ball in your hands while you run creates options. You can pass to the right or left, you can dummy to the left then pass to the right, you can draw a man's tackle then, with your hands free, pick up a teammate who is trailling you through the ruck and send him into the clear. I became adept at putting my opponents in two minds: "Is he going to pass or run?" I could see them thinking. Their indecision gave me the advantage. I was well-suited to a ball-playing role. I had good hands, mainly thanks to the years of passing and catching practice my old Manly rugby halfback Neville Digby-Bennett and I put ourselves through in our spare time at North Harbour Park.

Joe Egan honed my ball skills in seven-a-side midweek touch football matches. I'd never played touch football before and liked the game immediately. When I returned to Australia I introduced touch football to the Manly area and can proudly claim to be a pioneer in this country of what is now a booming sport. It is now played by thousands of men and women throughout NSW and Queensland and there are interstate and international matches on a regular basis.

Ball distributing forwards were unknown in Australian league at that time, but virtually every club in England boasted a number of men who could scheme and set up their supports. The prince of ball players was Brian McTigue of Wigan. Brian was a portly, balding former basketball and boxing champion who could use the ball like a magician. His sleight of hand would regularly result in teammates being put into gaping holes to score. Sometimes, when the opposition held back, waiting for McTigue to make his move, the crafty forward would burst into the clear himself with a surprising turn of speed. Brian terrorised Australia in internationals for years. I played against him when I represented Other Nationalities against England and we locked horns again in the 1958 Test series in Australia, the 1959 Ashes series in England and the 1960 World Cup. Every encounter was an education. A miner most of his life, he was yet another football great who died young.

Just as I had done from my earliest rugby days, I would make a point of positioning myself to catch failed attempts at goal and line kicks that didn't find touch. My lineout skills enabled me to soar high to pluck the ball out of the air when the other side kicked off to us, and off I'd go for a gallop. I had developed deft ball skills, sure, and putting teammates into a gap gave me wonderful satisfaction, but I still loved to run with the ball.

Kirk was born in 1952, when I was well settled into the club. The night before he was born I was trying to get a good sleep in preparation for a big local derby against our arch-rivals Wigan. So important was this match that the Leigh boss Jimmy Hilton had promised us 15 pounds extra a man if we won. Some time around 4am Joan began having labour pains and I rushed her to the local infirmary where a grand old Irish matron took over. "Now Mr Mossoop," she soothed, "Joan is in good hands here. Get on back to bed and finish your sleep. You've got a big game today." I did as I was told.

That afternoon when I was about to run onto the field there was still no news from the infirmary so I arranged for our club secretary to stand on a certain spot near the players' tunnel and as soon as word came that Joan had given birth he was to stand up and rock his arms in a cradling motion. It was a fierce game on a rolled mud track played before a huge crowd. At halftime it was 2-all and there was still no word from the infirmary. All through the half I'd been catching the secretary's attention and each time he'd shake his head. In the dressing sheds Jimmy Hilton helped to refocus my mind on the football when he increased our bonus from 15 pounds to 50. In those days you could live for a year on that.

Out we went for the second half and with 18 minutes to go our five eighth Jack Baxter scored a try to give us a three point lead. Wigan kicked off to us and they never touched the ball again in the match. With all that money at stake, there was no way we were going to throw the ball around and run the risk of them gaining possession, scoring a try and doing us out of the small fortune we'd been promised. We all took it in turns to take the ball from dummy half, tuck it under our wing and get tackled. This continued for the remaining 18 minutes of the match, to the anger and frustration of the Wigan players and the crowd. Near the end of the game I lifted my head out of the mud and searched for our club secretary in the crowd. At that, he leapt from his seat and started rocking his cradled arms back and forth furiously. I was a father. I had mud in my eye at the time, but I swear he also wiggled his index finger to indicate the new baby was a boy.

That night Joan and I showed off little Kirk to all our friends. They handed the little bundle around, cooing, "Oh aye, look at Mossoop's baby!" When our next door neighbours first saw the baby they looked at me expectantly. I assumed they wanted to know whether it was a boy or a girl. But no, Leigh was a rugby league town. The pressing question on our neighbour's lips was, "Who won the match?"

In spite of the endless dreadful weather I ran every day, continued to work out on weights and did my best to avoid the stodgy, fattening food that the people up there ate to keep the cold at bay. I remained lean and as physically fit as I had been back home. When I arrived I was amused by the flabby physiques of the Pom forwards. To me they looked soft and out of condition. How wrong I was. The climate over there tends to put blubber on your physique as a natural protection against the cold. And most people's diet, with plenty of beer and potatoes, also stacks on the weight and keeps it there. But underneath all this insulation were strong, hard-working men — miners, most of them — with plenty of stamina, and many of these human beer barrels could run like deer. Australian teams for years paid the price for underestimating roly-poly blokes like McTigue, Ab Terry, Brian Edgar, Derek Turner and Alan Prescott.

We had a forward in this vein at Leigh called Charlie Pawsey. Charlie could be a nasty customer on the field who'd have a whack at anyone. An international, he'd been one of the instigators of the infamous Great Britain-NSW brawl at the SCG in 1954 which resulted in referee Aub Oxford abandoning the game. Pawsey was a dock worker and a real roughie. Inevitably caked with dirt from his working day, and with unwashed and uncombed hair, he would wear the same clothes for months on end — working boots and pants, a soiled collarless shirt, an old tie fastened around his bare neck, a grime-encrusted vest and coat, and a cloth cap. Good old Charlie was always the first bloke into the communal bath after a game — and the first bloke out. Imagine my shock when, in 1988 at the Centenary league Test between Australia and Great Britain at the Sydney Football

Stadium, I ran into a dapper old gent in a beautifully tailored bermuda jacket, pressed grey slacks, striped club tie and neatly parted hair. It was Charlie, out here with a group of ex-internationals to mark the occasion. "Charlie, Charlie Pawsey!" I was incredulous. "You look like a bloody tailor's dummy!" "Well, Rex," he explained, "we living legends have to look the part!"

Another great character was Arthur Clues. Arthur was a Sydney cop who played three Tests for Australia against the Poms in 1946, then signed a contract with the English club side Leeds. He starred for Leeds for many years, and formed a lethal second row partnership with Harry Bath in Other Nationalities games. He lined up 14 times with the Aussies, Frenchmen and Kiwis who were playing in England, and from whom these strong international teams were selected. I made a number of appearances myself for Other Nationalities during my English stint.

Clues was a rogue. A big, funny, profane man with literally thousands of friends. Swear? I've never known anyone with such a colourful grasp of the English language. So well-known, well-liked and influential was Arthur that he was known as "The Mayor of Leeds". When he retired from league in the 1950s he opened a sports store in Leeds and his wife started a private school. Whenever an Australian team toured, Arthur would take them under his wing. Arthur is still causing trouble over there today, but his hips have given up on him and, sadly, he can now only walk with the aid of sticks.

If he likes you, nothing is too much trouble for Arthur. During the 1978 Kangaroo tour I was in the Old Dart commentating for Channel TEN and renewed my friendship with him. One night after an Aussie Test victory Arthur and I went to the team hotel, the Dragonara in Leeds, to celebrate. There were so many well-wishers you couldn't move in the bar. "Do you want a drink, Rex?" asked Arthur. "I'd love one," I replied, "but I'm not fighting my way through that lot." "Follow me, lad," said the big, bluff Aussie, and he barged his way through the tightly-packed throng. He was like a human ice-breaker, with me in his wake. In that broad Australian accent that he never lost even after 40 years away from home, he shouted to the man behind the bar, "Two brandy, lime and sodas, mate." The flustered barman replied irritably, "Wait your turn, sir, I've got all these other people to serve before you." Arthur smiled, then reached his huge hairy paw across the bar, grabbed the barman and pulled him off his feet and over the counter until the poor bloke's face was only inches from his own. Arthur bellowed, "I said two f . . . . . . brandy, lime and sodas — *now!*" "Of course, Mr Clues," said the barman. That was Arthur all over.

One night in 1953, brother Kirk telephoned to tell me Mum was dying. Her heart was gone, he said, and she had only days, possibly hours, to live. I offered to catch the first flight home to Australia to be with her at the end, but Kirk said she would not survive that long. I have never felt such helplessness. I told Kirk to put Mum on the phone. We both cried as we said goodbye. Her voice sounded faint, far, far away. A short time later she was gone. Mum was just 56.

The wonderful warmth and generosity of the Leigh fans made tough times easier to bear. They accepted the expatriate Australians — such as Tubby, Geoff Bourke and me — right from the start, and we repaid their support by contributing to some wonderful wins over the years. For most of the season we'd play two games a week. They ran two competitions simultaneously over there: the Lancashire Cup, which was the premiership; and the Challenge Cup knockout comp, which culminates in a big cup final at Wembley. We gave a good account of ourselves in the Challenge Cup, and in 1952 won the Lancashire Cup in a superb final against St Helens before 30,000 fans.

League supporters in the north of England would die for their team. Many of the people up there in that depressed part of the world have precious little apart from football to get excited about. They treated the players like kings. Back then, clothing and food was still being rationed and you needed a coupon to purchase things to wear and eat. These wonderful folk would come up to us in the street and try to give us their coupons to show their appreciation of a good win. "Here," they'd say, "take these two coupons and get yourself half a piece of steak." Or, "You played well on the weekend, Mossop lad, have a pound of butter on me." I loved these loyal supporters, the way they'd cheer and sing at matches and shout you a pint in their cosy, friendly pubs. They made you feel part of a community.

Footballers enjoyed celebrity status in Leigh and it was a contest among many of the local lasses to see who could bed the most players from the first XIII. Sexual conquests were celebrated by the embroidering of the player's name on the successful seductress's scarf. Some of these young ladies' scarves were very long, but I'm proud to say the name Mossop did not appear on any of them.

The football was hard, and there was plenty of it. I played 136 games in just three and a half seasons with Leigh. It was a gruelling program, but what a footballing education. Being an Aussie made me a marked man in most of the matches I played, and my hard-man reputation for loving a stoush and never taking a backward step fuelled the fire. I took and gave plenty. I got on no better with English league refs than I had with the rugby whistleblowers back home.

I was sent from the field just once, however. And my dismissal cost my side a shot at Wembley cup final glory. It was 1952 and we were playing a Challenge Cup match against Leeds, the winner to play Featherstone Rovers in a semi-final. In the opposing pack was a Welshman named Bryn Day. Day was an ordinary player but a first-rate menace. Balding and with a bony, angular 16-stone frame, he'd been bashing me, trampling me and dropping his knees into me all day. But we were winning the game, so for once in my life I was determined to turn the other cheek. Wembley and a big pay cheque of 500 pounds each — half a year's pay for most of us — was ours for the taking if we beat Leeds. We knew we would beat Featherstone in the semi, but to do so we needed to be at full strength. Getting sent off and suspended would be a disaster. So what happens? With only minutes to go against Oldham Bryn Day belts our tiny five eighth who hit the deck like a poleaxed steer. I saw red and suddenly Day and I were rolling all over the ground, locked in a vicious wrestling match. After about 50 seconds of this, the referee raced over blowing his whistle. Day slumped to the grass, pretending to be unconscious and con the referee. This enraged me even more. I dragged him to his feet and knocked him down again. "Get off, the pair of you!" screamed the ref. "Oh, Christ!" I thought, "I've really done it this time."

The Welshman and I faced the judiciary together. He had first say. "Oh, this Mossop," he started, in his sing-song accent, "he's come over here and he thinks he's a bloody five thousand pounds man but I'm telling the lot of you now that I don't care how bloody much he's being paid, next time we meet on the field if I get the opportunity I'm going to bash him again!" I angrily weighed in, my voice rising, "Look, gentlemen, you've heard from this unintelligent clod and all I have to say is that if he wants to go on with this thing I'll take him out in the street and finish it now!" Such were the great heights of debate reached that night. The chairman of the judiciary was not impressed. "Seeing as you both have adopted this attitude and appear to have learned nothing from your dismissal, I have no option but to suspend the pair of you for two weeks." Goodbye Wembley. I've done some stupid, thoughtless things in my time, and getting into a slanging match with Bryn Day was one of them.

After the verdict was delivered, Tubby Allan was furious with me. "You're a mate, but I'm bitterly disappointed in you Rex," said the captain who'd just seen his chance at winning the cup final go down the drain. "You mad bastard! All you had to do was keep your mouth shut in there and they would have let you off with a caution and you could have played in the semi-final." I watched from the stands as Featherstone downed us the following Saturday to qualify for the Challenge Cup decider.

Early in the 1954 season Trevor Allan sustained an ankle ligament injury that ended his English career. So popular was he that for months he was deluged with home remedies from well-meaning fans. Trevor was desperate enough to try some of these weird and wonderful potions but the injury did not respond and he and Judith left England for Australia. Joan and I were sad to see them go.

With just one year of my four-year contract remaining I was hell-bent on making every post a winner in the 1954-55 season. Before the competition started Joan and I took the chance to have an idyllic holiday in Switzerland. I returned to Leigh relaxed and in a fighting frame of mind, determined to end my English career in a blaze of glory then link up with an Australian club for the 1955 Sydney premiership. Just before our first match, Leigh honoured me by making me captain. The first part of the season was all I wanted it to be. My club was winning games and I was selected to represent Other Nationalities against England, France and Wales. Then disaster struck.

We were playing Halifax, a team with a big, strong pack of forwards who knew how to hurt. Leading the way for them was Jack Wilkinson, a huge man who loved to mix it for both his club and his country. The ground that day was rock-hard after a frost. Someone passed me the ball and I charged at Wilkinson. The big bloke picked me up, lifted me nearly two metres above the ground then speared me into the turf, crashing his 17 stone on top of me to finish the job. On the way down I tucked my head in to prevent my neck from being broken and ensure that my back and shoulder took the brunt of the impact. As Wilkinson landed on me I heard a creak and felt something go in my spine. Hoping for the best but fearing the worst, I staggered to my feet and continued to play in agony. There were no replacements in those days and I didn't want to go off and leave my teammates short-handed in this vital match. Added to this, I was proud of my record of not having missed a single game through injury in my three and a half seasons with Leigh.

In the days that followed I knew I had done serious damage to my back. It still hurt like hell, and I would get shooting pains up and down my legs. I had lost all elasticity, I could not even bend far enough to touch my knees, let alone my toes. The club sent me to a specialist who diagnosed a degenerate disc in my lower spine that had been damaged in Wilkinson's spear tackle. He informed me that I had played my last game of football and wanted to encase me in a plaster cast from my shoulder to my hip. "Forget that!" I told him, then underwent extensive physiotherapy for the next four weeks that made not one bit of difference. Next it was off to an orthopaedic specialist in Manchester. He took one look at my x-rays, confirmed the first specialist's opinion that my football days had ended and added that I'd need a major operation or I would be racked with pain for the rest of my life. The Leigh club, not accepting that opinion, then sent me to an eminent Leeds back expert who wanted to operate immediately. Again, I told them I would not have an operation. I was terrified of spinal surgery, and had decided that if an operation really was necessary, then I wanted it done in Australia. It was time to go home.

Leigh management had a meeting to discuss my future and released me from my contract with their best wishes. They then made the splendid gesture of paying for our passage home and paid me a full season's wage even though my contract still had a half season to run. They said it was their way of thanking me for three and a half good years. I'd tried my heart out for my English club from that first day when I necked Brian Bevan. I'd played 136 games, scoring 31 tries and ending up club captain. Until my back problem, I'd not missed a single game through injury, and I'd been a solid clubman off the field. The Leigh club and I parted company on the happiest of terms. When I returned to Leigh as vice-captain of the 1959 Kangaroos, I was given a marvellous reception by my old town. I returned, too, in '73, '78, '82 and '86 as a commentator, each time renewing friendships forged in my playing days.

Last time I was there, Leigh, like just about everywhere else in the north of England, was having a rough trot. The economy was shot to pieces and unemployment stood at 25 percent. But in spite of their woes the people of Leigh were as friendly as ever, still keen to buy you a pint and talk about their great sides of the early '50s.

Joan, Kirk and I set sail for home onboard the *Orsova*. It was late 1954. I was depressed by the specialists' verdict but didn't accept what they said for a second. As soon as I arrived home I would be seeking further opinions. I knew I would play again. However, in the meantime, there was nothing to do but lie back and enjoy the voyage. We thought how exciting it was to be returning home, to catch up with our families and friends, to get back into the lifestyle we loved, to build our new home and make plans for the future.

The voyage was enlivened by the presence of the 1954-55 English cricket team, bound for Australia for an Ashes series. They were a terrific bunch. I remember striking up friendships with a number of them, Colin Cowdrey, a charming gentleman, Godfrey Evans, Johnny Wardle and Trevor Bailey in particular. "Barnacle" Bailey was a very funny guy. I took him water-skiing on the Hawkesbury River that Australian summer. On board, too, was that great Yorkshire character, Freddie Trueman, one of sport's most outrageous men. Today he is a much-in-demand after-dinner speaker, but even then he had a fund of hilarious stories guaranteed to break you up. It was impossible not to notice how unpopular the team's skipper, Len Hutton, was with many of his players. They told me they found him aloof and resented the fact that he would never mix with them.

Many a young girl lost her heart to an English cricketer on that boat trip, and the players made the most of the situation, as red-blooded sportsmen will. Thank heavens the travelling British press corps had the integrity to confine their reporting to cricket. The jackals of Fleet Street today, had they been on that particular voyage, would have had enough ammunition about the sexual exploits of the English cricketers to make their readers back home choke on their breakfast kippers.

Although Joan and I have a host of happy memories of that voyage, it was a wonderful experience to steam through the Heads and into an Australian summer. Not for the last time in my life I reflected on how fortunate we are to live in this wonderful land. Dad and my brother were there at the dock to meet us but it was sad to see him on his own, without his wife of 32 years.

Joan, Kirk and I moved in with my father while we picked up the strands of our Australian lives. Before long, what with all the attention lavished on us by our families, not to mention the slobbering affection of my new boxer dog Grock, we felt as if we had never been away. We were glad we'd bought our block of land at Balgowlah, near Reef Beach and not far from Dad's house. I got a job selling cars with Stack and Company and we saved like mad to build a home of our own.

My back had not improved. Swimming was the only exercise I could handle. Running was out of the question. I sought the advice of a sports medicine specialist. He, too, considered it unlikely that I would play again, but he conceded I had a chance if I underwent a lengthy and gruelling program of exercises with weights to strengthen the muscles around my spine. That's all I wanted to hear from the sports medicine expert: that my condition was curable. So long as I knew that, I was prepared to put myself through anything to get back on the rugby league field. Willpower is not a problem with me. It has nothing to do with bravery or heroism. If someone says, "It's going to hurt like hell, but if you keep on lifting these weights long enough and often enough you're going to get better," I'll lift the weights. And if I'm told to do 100 repetitions of a weight exercise, I'll bust a gut to squeeze out 200. If I'm told 200, I'll go for 400.

I put the intense pain out of my mind and worked at those exercises like a man possessed. After six months of this nightmare regime I could run again. I kept up the weights and ran hundreds of kilometres, often with Grock bounding along beside me. I boxed, wrestled and played shuttlecock endlessly at Phil McEwan's gym at Fairy Bower, all first-rate routines for strengthening my back and regaining flexibility. By the time the 1955 football season rolled around I was in peak shape. On medical advice, though, I decided to sit out the year, get my back absolutely right, maintain my fitness, then pick up in 1956 where I left off, playing first grade rugby league. I would be 28 years of age.

As soon as we got back to Australia I found myself back in the Manly whirl and ran into many of my old rugby mates. The friendships were resumed as though I'd never been away, and I decided to approach officials of the Manly rugby club and offer my services as reserve grade coach for the 1955 season. I figured it would help keep me fit as well as allow me to put something back into my old team. Though my offer was received enthusiastically by most of the members, I was made aware that some people in the club considered me a traitor when my nomination as reserve grade coach was put before the annual meeting. Some blokes spoke bitterly about my desertion of the amateur code to pick up the fast money in league. Nevertheless, after a close vote, I was appointed.

I gave coaching everything I had, trying to instil a winning attitude in my players, but I learned then that I was too much the perfectionist, too serious about my sport, to coach these guys. Some of the blokes in the team gave 100 percent effort, but most were there only for enjoyment. To me, winning was everything, to them a game was just an excuse for a get-together at the club after the match. I would boil with anger, to the extent of threatening to belt my men for their lackadaisical attitude to training and playing. Later I would train my son Kirk's junior rugby team until he reached 14, but this was my first and last year as a coach of adults.

Meanwhile I was right into touch football, spreading throughout the parks of Manly the gospel of this terrific game that Joe Egan had taught me on the fields of England. With plenty of touch footy, my coaching activities and an unrelenting personal fitness program, I was as fit as I had ever been and my back was coming good fast. One day Manly-Warringah Rugby League Club officials approached me. They'd heard I was in good shape and asked did I want to wear the maroon and white in '56. I did.

PLENTY TO PROVE

My new teammates at Manly learned early that if they shadowed their new ball-playing forward through the rucks, there was a damn good chance I'd pop them a pass and send them into the clear. Before a game they'd come up and say, "Look for me, Moose, I'll follow you through." In the match I'd hear the cry, "Moose!", "With you, Moss!" or "Yes!", position the caller and send him away. In the early '60s, we had a rugged young lock from the bush named Jack Sinclair. He went on to play for Australia. Jack had a few rough edges. His way of letting me know he was sweating on my pass was to charge up alongside me and bellow a much-used Anglo-Saxon oath at the top of his lungs. Jack would stand way deep, watch as I took the ball and drew the defenders, then race flat-chat for the gap I'd created, screaming "F........!" I've never been sure whether it was my deft passes or the startling effect Jack's war-cry had on the opposition that was responsible for the many long breaks he made for us.

I turned up for the 1956 pre-season trial matches leaping out of my skin. My back was 100 percent, I was fit and rested after my year off, and I stripped at my ideal playing weight of about 14 and a half stone. Although I was 28 years old I knew my best playing days were all ahead of me.

My years learning the forward's trade in the school of English rugby league put me way ahead of the game in Australia. The typical Australian forward in those days was a big, fit bloke who'd tuck the ball under his arm and charge head-down-arse-up at the opposition all day. He was hard and tough and could handle himself when a stoush broke out. If he found himself in the clear he might even be able to get his pass away. If you were a forward you were a "pig", a toiler. Creative flair was confined to the backs.

I could barge, tackle and biff with the best of them, but old Joe Egan had added a few extra strings to my bow. He'd taught me that some very effective attack can be mounted close to the ruck. In England I'd learned to vary my game. I would lower my head and charge moose-like into the opposing forwards, then the very next play I'd run wide, carrying the ball in my hands, draw a man and put a teammate through a gap. I might stand wide of the dummy half, receive the ball and then throw a pass that would cut out two or three teammates and send the backs on their way. If I saw that defences were light-on on the left I could switch our attack that way, then when the opposition scrambled to cover, back we'd go to the right. My time at Leigh had taught me to read a game and act accordingly.

Of course, all this was standard procedure for English forwards. That's why the Poms had been smacking our bums for decades. English forwards had known since rugby league began what ours didn't tumble to until the 1960s, that a forward who can mix strength with subtlety, intimidation with creative flair, can create confusion in opposition defences and lay a foundation for victory.

Those people who remember me from my playing days tend to think of me mainly as a roughnut who was always being cautioned or sent off. The way I'm always going on about biffo probably hasn't helped dispel that myth. The truth was, though, that I *could* play a bit. In my eight years with Manly I represented my country in 10 Tests and three World Cup games, was vice-captain of the 1959 Kangaroos, played for NSW and City on numerous occasions, participated in two epic grand finals, won plenty of club awards and most years figured prominently in the media's best and fairest competitions in an era when such giants of rugby league as Clive Churchill, Jack Rayner, Keith Holman, Harry Wells, Norm Provan, Brian Carlson, Reg Gasnier, Brian Clay, John Raper, Keith Barnes, Ken Irvine, Noel Kelly, Brian Hambly and company were at their peak. In 1958 I held out a hot field to tie with Keith Holman as winner of the prestigious *Sun-Herald* best and fairest poll. Between 1956 and 1963 I played 137 matches for Manly-Warringah, every one of them in first grade.

When I fronted at Brookvale Oval back in February, 1956, my Manly teammates left me in no doubt that I had a lot to prove. I'd played league for three and a half years in England, but all that was a world away. As far as the other blokes were concerned I was still a rugby union Rah-Rah who had it all to do.

Known as the Seagulls in those days, Manly was a moderately successful club who had only been in the Sydney comp nine years. They'd been admitted with Parramatta in 1947. There was a bit of talent at Brookvale in the middle-'50s, but not enough to worry the big guns of the competition, South Sydney and St George. Our coach was the ex-international Pat Devery. Big, bald Roy Bull, a grand forward and an inspiring leader who'd been away in '52 and '56 with the Kangaroos, was skipper. Other prominent players in 1956 were the nippy Peter "Chimpy" Burke at five eighth, former great Test hooker Kevin Schubert who'd had many a keen duel with my mentor Joe Egan, rugged lock George Hunter, wing speedsters Ray Ritchie and John Tenison, and a sturdy little ex-Canterbury and Queensland fullback named Ron Willey. Like Roy Bull, Willey had been a 1952 Kangaroo.

What could I offer this mob? From my very first game in the maroon and white I set out to prove that I could add the skill, experience, fire and will to win that could turn a good side into a premiership contender. My first trial was against St George. The match was a portent of matches to come against the ferocious Dragons. They split my head wide open. Our next trial was against Easts and my old friend Trevor Allan turned out for the Roosters. Shortly after he departed for Norths where he played out the remaining few injury-plagued years of his career.

My back stood up to plenty of rough treatment in those pre-

season games and when the names were read out for the opening premiership match of the season, against St George, "R.
Mossop" was down for the second row.

Saints then were just beginning their amazing run of premiership victories — 11 in a row from 1956 to 1966. The foundation
of the great years to come was in place in the form of such stalwarts as Norm Provan, Ken Kearney, Billy Wilson and Bob
Bugden. Soon they would be joined by Reg Gasnier, Johnny
Raper, Brian Clay, Ed Lumsden, Johnny King, Kevin Ryan,
Monty Porter, Graeme Langlands, Billy Smith, Elton Rasmussen and, for three seasons, my bitter enemy Harry Bath, and
together they would form the best club team ever, a team that
proved a thorn in my side for as long as I played the game.

That first game against Saints at Kogarah Oval said plenty
about the way rugby league was played back in the '50s. St
George won: situation normal. There were 44 scrums in the
match, real contests where the ball was placed squarely in the
tunnel between the front rows. Unlike today when scrums are
almost always won by the side whose halfback feeds the ball —
the packs come together, the half throws the ball blatantly under
the feet of his own second rowers, and a split second later the
ball is out among the backs — scrums in my day could not be
won without a fast-striking hooker, wily, scrummaging props
and a huge, co-ordinated heave from the back rowers. Also, in
those days of unlimited-tackle football it was not unusual for a
side to have to defend for 15 minutes or more without a break,
and I can remember us tackling desperately for long stretches in
that game. And there was plenty of rough stuff. From the kickoff, St George adopted the softening-up tactics that they later
turned into an art form. Often the Dragons would purposely lose
the scrums in the first 15 minutes of a game to allow their savage
defence to pulverise the opposing attackers. When the other
team was stuffed, St George would spin the ball out to their
speedster backs who would do the rest. Rugby league '50s-style
was summed up by their big centre Merv Lees who had belted
Roy Bull in the game, opening up a nasty cut over his eye. Lees

told reporters, "Of course I hit Roy, but he kicked me first." Rough justice, dispensed quickly, with no hard feelings afterwards.

Referees in those days allowed rival players to sort each other out. If a punch-up got out of hand, a Darcy Lawler or a Col Pearce might step in and award a penalty or, in extreme cases, send the combatants off, but usually a blind eye was turned to a bit of harmless biff. I had a bit of trouble one day with a strapping Eastern Suburbs prop by the name of Jack Gibson. This bloke opened me up with a punch in an early scrum. Referee Lawler saw the incident but took no action, nor did I expect him to. All three of us knew I'd even the score in my own good time. A few scrums later, after I'd been stitched up, it was my turn. I belted Jack back just as hard as he had hit me. Old Darcy chipped us, "Righto, you two, you've had your fun, now cut out the rough stuff."

Jack Gibson has always been a bit of a mystery to me. Today we are friends, but I have never been able to equate the mean, no-holds-barred bastard I used to pack down against in the old days with the master coach of the '70s and '80s who despises on-field violence and would drop any of his players who whacked an opponent. Jack in his playing days had a beautiful build for a forward. He was about my height, 6ft 3in, but a bit more thickset. He did not have much skill, but made up for that with his forceful, bustling style of play. He was a ruthless, uncompromising competitor who wasn't opposed to throwing a punch — or worse — if the situation called for direct action.

Today rugby league is in a six-tackle rut: two or three forward hit-ups to settle play, maybe try to pop up a pass on the third, move the ball wide for two tackles, then kick. This is so stereotyped, so boring, but still better than the panic play that set in when the game was conducted, thankfully briefly, under the four-tackle rule: three helter-skelter tackles and then a bomb, ad nauseum. Way back before they started monkeying with the rules, in the days of unlimited tackle football, you had time to give creative play free rein. There was no pressure to come up with something within a set number of tackles. You could play it tight or free-flowing and spontaneous, depending on the state of the game. You could work steadily to force an advantage with constructive forward play or continual switching of the point of attack, or whip the ball out along the backs: halfback to five eighth to the inside centre to the outside centre. He gets tackled, forwards who have trailed the action acrossfield wrap around to take the ball from the dummy half, full-steam ahead until tackled. Meanwhile the backline has stretched wide and deep across to the opposite side of the field. Out flies the ball along the line again to the winger who streaks over in the corner. To all those who say unlimited tackle football was dull, I recommend you check the tryscoring lists of the period. Wingers would regularly score 25 or 30 tries a year, many more than a good winger scores today.

The other top sides back in 1956 were Balmain, who went down in the grand final to St George, and South Sydney who were backing up after their phenomenal string of victories to win the comp in '55 after being near last on the ladder 10 rounds into the premiership. At their peak for the Rabbitohs in my debut season were the all-time greats Churchill, Rayner, "Chicka" Cowie and Ian Moir. Clive Churchill broke his arm in a mid-season game against us and Souths missed him as they dropped out of premiership contention.

Manly was never a threat that year, managing just seven wins and three draws out of 18 games. We did take comfort in running St George close in our two encounters. We lost 9-6 in the first round and held them to an 11-11 draw in the second. It was clear that we were an emerging force in the premiership. I had a fair season first-up, alternating between prop and second row. It's a fact that when a ball player is running hot he makes himself and his teammates appear worldbeaters, but let his timing stray or his runners not be where they should be, and everybody looks like a park player. That first year, I learned a lot about my teammates and they learned a lot about me.

One thing there was no doubt about. Teammates, opponents,

fans and the media knew I was no shrinking violet when it came to dishing out punishment. I thrived on the dog-eat-dog aggression of league. It was a matter of honour with me that I simply would not take rubbish from anyone. I was no great shakes as a fighter, but I would whack anyone who I believed deserved it — and I was happy to go on with it as long as it took to prove my point. To show weakness in those days was to be eaten alive. Each side had a number of hardheads in their pack and every week it was the same: stand over them or they would stand over you.

For years the more-fancied sides had been intimidating Manly teams with strong-arm tactics. And just as it fell to Malcolm Reilly and John O'Neill to put backbone into the Manly pack in the '70s, in the '50s the job fell to me. I thrived on the challenge. The old Australian opening batsman Sid Barnes had a column in *The Sunday Telegraph* called "Like It Or Lump It". After a spate of biting and king-hitting incidents in '56, Barnes wrote: "There is only one answer — and cure — for biting and other dirty tricks practised in the security of a ruck. And that is for the injured player's teammates to scientifically work over the culprit. There is a St George player who could do with a 'treatment'. I saw this particular individual deliberately and viciously knee a Manly player — a little bloke — in the face as he completed his tackle. Five minutes later Rex Mossop and Kev Schubert, both meaty types, closed on the St George man. From then on there was no more knee action from our friend."

Over the years my win at all costs attitude rubbed off on my teammates, although some had to be coaxed more than others to develop killer instinct. Once in the early '60s we were playing an end-of-season match against a Queensland country side at Ingham. It was a nothing game played in heatwave conditions on a dustbowl, but I was captain that day and I would accept nothing less than a big win. Soon after the game started, the opposition kicked the ball into our in-goal. Our winger Nick Yakich, one of the fastest men ever to play league, ambled back to retrieve it as if he was on a Sunday afternoon stroll. From out of nowhere came a Queenslander and almost touched down under Nick's nose for a try. It was a hot day, but it became much hotter for Nick. I rushed over to him and shouted, "Get off!" He looked incredulous. "What?" "Get off the field right now or I'll knock you out!" Remember that this was in the days of no replacements. "What for?" he stammered. "For not trying!" I barked. He left.

There was another occasion on the 1959 Kangaroo tour when I was captaining the Roos against an English club side. Elton Rasmussen, a big strapping Queenslander, was in our side. Elton, sadly dead now, was one of our bravest, most willing forwards, but he was also a gentle man who did not approve of brawling on the field. Anyway, a fight broke out among the rival forwards and players rushed in from all over the field to get involved. All except Elton. I stormed over to the big fellow and roared, "If I ever see you dog a fight on the field again, I'll kick you right up the arse!"

Manly, in a new uniform that featured an outsized seagull across the chest, and with a new coach in former player Ken Arthurson, really hit their straps in 1957. We stormed all the way to the grand final. "Arko" was as good a coach as he is chairman of the Australian Rugby League. A wonderful player whose career was cut short by a depressed fracture of the skull, he couldn't bear to be away from the game, and the club, he loved. After his coaching days ended, Ken became a selector, treasurer and later secretary of the Sea Eagles. It was his astute administration and inspired buying that paved the way for the club's first two premierships in 1972 and '73. The rest is history, how he succeeded Kevin Humphreys as el supremo of the Australian League in '83, joined the board of the New South Wales Rugby League the same year and later, in 1986, became director general of the international Rugby League Board.

Arthurson, who coached us in '57, '58, '59 and '60, was a supreme motivator of men. He wasn't a ranter or a raver. He just had a knack of letting every bloke in the team know what was expected of him. He'd come up before a game and pull you aside and whisper, "Now, you're the only bloke in the team capable of doing this. It's all up to you. If you succeed in your job, we all succeed." There wasn't a man in the maroon and white who wouldn't have run through a brick wall for Ken Arthurson.

We gave our fans something to cheer about in '57, winning 12 and drawing one of our 21 games. Ray Ritchie, a real flyer, made the Australian World Cup side. He soared like a meteor that year, but could not sustain his form and faded from the scene. Roy Bull had another strong year. The former Kangaroo won the club's award for the most consistent player, and I was runner-up. The current Manly club secretary Doug Daley was a first grade regular in 1957. Doug was a game lightweight second rower. He was given good support by George Hunter, Barney McEvoy and newcomer Dennis Meaney. Ron Willey, Bill Lloyd, Chimpy Burke and heavyweight winger George Hugo were stars of a backline that, while solid, probably lacked the pace to match it with the greyhounds of league when the chips were really down. Our forwards were definitely our strength.

The year 1957, my second with Manly, was a World Cup year, and I had hopes of making the squad. League writers Tom Goodman and George Crawford were writing that my constructive ballwork, high workrate and enthusiasm and surprising pace for a big bloke had caught the representative selectors' eyes. I hoped the veteran scribes were right. Wrote Goodman in an early-season edition of *The Sun-Herald*: "The effective English-style work of Manly forward Rex Mossop, standing wide of the rucks, was a spectacular feature of yesterday's match against Wests. The tall second rower's positioning often confused the defence and he made several strong bursts . . . he dictated the trend of play with quick and tricky passes that continually switched the direction of Manly's attack."

Such good reviews are all very well, but opposition coaches read the paper, too. Before I knew it I was a marked man. From about then on, there would always be a "hitman" in the other team detailed to blot me out of the play. Probably the most effective assassin was St George's Brian "Pop" Clay. A short, balding, blocky man who was one of the most destructive tacklers rugby league has ever seen, Clay gleefully demolished me every chance he got. If I went well against Saints, I knew I'd earned my money.

In spite of the extra attention I was receiving each time I ran onto the field, things went to plan early when I was selected for City Firsts against Country. I was included when the big Wests second rower Kel O'Shea withdrew through injury. I had some illustrious teammates in my first rep match, including Clay, Keith Barnes who kicked 10 goals in the game, Ian Moir who scored four tries, Dick Poole and Harry Bath. Bath and I called a truce long enough to pack down together against the bush boys, as we did whenever we played together in the Other Nationalities team in England, but our hostility was too deep-seated not to flare again once we returned to our club sides.

It was a pleasure to partner my great St George rival Norm Provan in the City second row. We gave each other hell every time we played and it was a pleasant change to be on the same side as the 6ft 5in, 17-stone "Sticks". Just as Pop Clay always had a contract out on me, Manly coach Arthurson always singled me out to take care of Norm whenever our club teams clashed. Wrote Tom Goodman of City's record 53-2 victory thrashing of Country: "Tall second row forward Rex Mossop completely justified his inclusion in place of injured Kel O'Shea. He was the best forward of the match — even better than Provan."

I made the NSW side that beat Queensland 49-11 and 29-12, but when the World Cup team was announced, the second row spot I hoped would be mine went to the Queensland forward Tommy Tyquin. I was disappointed, but more certain than ever that I'd realise my dream of becoming a dual international before too long. I knew the Poms were touring in '58 and I made a green and gold jersey that year my goal.

Meanwhile, there was a premiership to win. Our resolute forward play and Ron Willey's accurate goalkicking had us well on course for a semi final berth. Although we lost to St George in both our competition games we had handsome wins over Norths, Easts, Canterbury and Parramatta, a game in which I scored two tries.

I sustained my form well all year, but there was one match, against Newtown, when I played well below my best, thanks to a snowy-headed, 17-year-old rookie forward. I'd checked the Newtown team list before the game, and found nobody in the side whose name filled me with any foreboding. In fact, I hadn't even heard of most of the Bluebags. Anyway, early in the match I took the ball and ran wide of the ruck. Suddenly I was hit hard just below the knees with the sweetest tackle you've ever seen and crashed ignominiously into the Henson Park dust. I looked down to see who'd done the damage and it was this athletic-looking young lock forward. "Who the bloody hell is this bastard?" I thought. The youngster buried me all day. I'd get the ball and *bang*, I'd be eating dirt. Before long I'd had enough and blew my cool. Every time he'd tackle me I'd punch him repeatedly. It made no difference. He kept hurling himself at my legs and I kept hitting the deck. At fulltime when we were walking from the field, I searched out the young bloke. Like the big-time rep player I was, I put my arm magnanimously around his shoulder, just like Wild Bill Cerutti had put his arm around mine so many years before, and said, "Well played, son. You did quite well out there today. What's your name, boy?" Shrugging my arm away, he snapped, "My name's John Raper, and you'll be hearing plenty more of me!"

We believed we were a big chance of upsetting premiership favourites St George in the big games at the business end of the season, but it didn't quite work out that way. The Dragons battered us 21-7 in the first semi, with Bath outstanding. He showed me that day that I wasn't the only one with British ball skills as his marvellously-timed passes sent Provan and Clay careering towards our line. We were forced to defend for long periods and when it was our turn to attack we had no steam. In the second half of this game we were required to hold out St George for 17 minutes without a break. I laugh today when commentators tell us how hard it is to defend for two sets of six tackles. We probably would have made more than 100 tackles without getting even a sniff of the ball that day.

The following week Roy Bull played a blinder and inspired us to a 15-11 win over Souths and a grand final showdown with St George. Bull was magnificent that day. He even scored a try, but had a little help from his friends. Roy was held up a metre or two short of Souths' goal-line and was struggling in the tackle, hoping to break free and plunge over. Dennis Meaney, our hooker George Lenon and I saw what was happening and raced in together, picked up the heavyweight prop and we all surged over the line in a tangle of arms and legs. Referee Darcy Lawler signalled a try.

Saints were too good for us in the big one. Marshalled by skipper and hooker Ken Kearney, they out-thought, out-fought and out-played us and came home winners 31-9. I contributed to the thrashing by throwing a loose pass that was intercepted and resulted in a St George three-pointer. I recall Saints looked a bit thin on the blindside so I ran wide and dummied to a forward who had come inside me, hoping to create space along the touchline for our powerhouse winger George Hugo. After dummying inside I flung the ball out to where I thought George would be, but my pass found St George's flying international Tommy Ryan, who took off toward our line with only an out-of-position Ron Willey to beat. I punched the ground and swore in rage and frustration at my blunder before jumping up and chasing Ryan all the way to the line. He had 30 metres on me when I gave chase and when he touched down he was 40 metres ahead. There was no chance of my catching the speedster but I had to make the effort. He might have tripped or been struck by lightning before he reached our tryline. Those men in red and white dashed not only Manly's dreams, but every other team's dreams for more than a decade with their trademark combination of brute force and magical attacking skills.

That year was Manly's most successful to date in its 11-year history. For the first time we'd made it to a grand final, and on the way attracted a record number of fans to our games. With the promise of a big club and representative season the following year, I couldn't wait for the 1958 season to start and threw myself into my off-season fitness program with a vengeance.

Life was good on the home front, too. Joan and I had a second son, Greg, that year and by combining my football earnings with my salary as a car salesman we could at last afford to build a house on our block of land. Joan supervised the building with a stern and demanding eye. As I looked forward to an Ashes year, life seemed full of promise.

⑨

DUAL INTERNATIONAL

Victory against St George was a rare jewel in the late '50s, and when we knocked off Killer Kearney's men first up in 1958, the portents were wonderful. It was our first win against them since 1955, and it came in the first premiership match. St George captain-coach Ken Kearney made our job easier when he was sent off for kicking George Hugo, but that day we had Saints' measure and would have won anyway. Our forwards gave the Dragon six a bitter taste of their own medicine by battering them mercilessly from kickoff until fulltime. Frank Burge awarded Ronny Willey three points in the *Sun-Herald* Best and Fairest Competition, I scored two, and a new boy to first grade, Peter Diversi, picked up a point as third best in the match.

Diversi was a hardhead from the bush and we shared both the second row and the enforcing duties at Manly. We were about the same height and weight and formed a good back row combination. I remember Peter single-handedly destroying Western Suburbs at Brookvale one afternoon. First he shoulder-charged Kel O'Shea, dislocating Kel's shoulder. Then he upended the legendary Wests hard man Peter Dimond, breaking his collarbone. Two Magpies off; no replacements; an easy Manly win. Football was a joke to Peter. He'd go around wrecking blokes, all the while laughing his head off. He'd sit in the shower after a game, scraping the dirt out of his cuts with a scrubbing brush. When the wound was red-raw he'd douse it with methylated spirits, cackling when I'd turn white at the sight of his masochistic medical routine.

As things turned out, Australia could have used a bloke like

Diversi in that season's Test series against Great Britain. It rates right alongside the 1990 series in England as one of the mightiest Ashes contests of all time. I made all the early rep teams, captaining City Seconds and then playing in the third and fourth interstate matches against Queensland. Jack Gibson took my second row spot in the Sydney side that was beaten by Great Britain. This match was our first good look at the tourists. The Poms let us know exactly what kind of series this was going to be when they ripped into our forwards from the outset. They seemed to single out big Jack and the rookie lock Johnny Raper for special treatment. First Gibbo was king-hit by a youngster called Karalius and then ganged up on by rival second rower Brian Edgar and the wildman winger Mike Sullivan. In the melee that followed, our heavyweight centre Harry Wells rushed in and shoved Sullivan away from Gibson, but this was no deterrent to the winger. For the rest of the game he went berserk, lashing out viciously with his fists and boots at every opportunity. First blood to Great Britain, 20-15, and it was clear changes would have to be made if we were to have a chance of taking the Ashes.

The Poms of '58 were a superb mixture of experienced, skilful players and raw youngsters of tremendous promise. Leading the side was the veteran Alan Prescott, a massive, balding prop from St Helens. His forward henchmen included the skilled ball-player Brian McTigue, and big, speedy sidestepping runners in Ab Terry, John Whiteley, Brian Edgar and young Dick Huddart. Mick Martyn, a flashy young try-scoring second rower I remembered from my Leigh days, was also tipped to make the Test side. The hooker was wily little Tommy Harris. Vince Karalius we didn't know much about but had heard he was a young lock on the verge of Test selection. The classy Eric Ashton was one centre, Alan Davies the other. Quick-finishing Ike Southward was on the right wing and Sullivan, a stirrer and a troublemaker who, unlike a lot of bad-tempered wingers, could handle himself very well indeed, was on the left. At fullback was Eric Fraser. Directing the backline was the quicksilver pairing of five eighth

David Bolton and the supremely talented and confident 19-year-old halfback Alex Murphy.

The NSW side picked to play the Poms a week before the First Test was a strong one. We had powerful backs — Brian Carlson, Harry Wells, Peter Dimond, Greg Hawick — and a strong, in-form forward lineup — Clay, O'Shea, Billy Marsh, Kearney, Bruce Olive and yours truly. Norm Provan and Keith Holman, two Test certainties, missed the game with injury. The match was open warfare, fought out in front of a crowd of 52,963 at the SCG. When the dust settled, four players had been sent from the field: Karalius, Hawick, Dimond . . . and Mossop.

Col Pearce had his hands full as the two sides tore away at each other. Karalius was marched for kicking Dimond, Dimond for kneeing Sullivan, Hawick for lashing out with his boot at a group of Englishmen who had him on the ground and were belting him. I was charged with punching Sullivan. As I told the judiciary that night, the little bastard had it coming.

I can cop a lot on the football field, but one tactic I will not stand for is testicle-squeezing. This English side had some accomplished nut-crackers. It's an old ruse: two blokes hold you in a tackle, one grabs your balls and squeezes hard, you lose your temper and lash out, they get the penalty. Simple. One English back with a reputation for ruggedness had been doing it all day. He tried it on me a couple of times. After the second time I snapped. Standing there with his fingerprints all over my privates, I determined there and then that I would make this mug regret his actions. When at last I caught up with him I made it count. Positioning the bloke sweetly, I timed the tackle to perfection, driving my shoulder hard into his chest. The testicle-squeezer collapsed winded. Standing over him, I gave him a serve, telling him he would be well-advised to keep his grubby hands to himself in future.

I caught up with Sullivan, too. He'd been giving it to me all day, running in from his wing to belt me, then racing back to the safety of the flanks before I could get to him. He was having a grand time, taunting me, then with a laugh scampering out of harm's way, or so he thought. Ten minutes into the second half, Sullivan got the ball and veered infield. "Come on, you Pommie bastard," I roared as he ran right into my arms. I picked him up and dumped him to the ground, then fell on top of him, smashing my forearm across his throat. As he lay there dazed I punched him in the head. Englishmen flew at me from all directions. Col Pearce, with a riot on his hands, blasted on his whistle and yelled, "Mossop, get off!"

I knew I was a near-certainty to make the First Test side the following Saturday so I was hoping and praying that I wouldn't be suspended by the judiciary. Karalius copped three matches. and Hawick and Dimond 10-day suspensions that would keep them out of Test contention, so things were looking bad. When I finally fronted judiciary chairman "Snowy" Justice, himself a rugged veteran of Test clashes against the Poms, my only defence was that Sullivan had had it coming and besides, I said, "I thought Englishmen were fair game." Justice's eyes twinkled and he outed me for just one match. As luck would have it, Manly were playing next day, Sunday. I'd miss that game, then be eligible to fulfill my dream when I ran onto the Sydney Cricket Ground in the green and gold of Australia the following Saturday.

On Sunday night the Australian team was announced and I was in it. So nine years after first representing my country in rugby union I'd achieved the ultimate in rugby league. I had joined a small, select band of dual internationals. If ever I felt like a party it was that night — Dad and Joan were so proud — but apart from a few quiet drinks with my family it was a sombre celebration as I tried to focus on the job I would be expected to do six days later.

We had four training runs together that week, trying to cobble together a combination that would trouble the Poms. The team was a strong one. Newtown's Gordon Clifford was fullback; Ian Moir and Ross Kite were on the wings; centres were Harry "Dealer" Wells and the mercurial Brian Carlson; halves were Tony Brown and Keith "Yappy" Holman; Kel

O'Shea was lock, I partnered Norm Provan in the second row; our props were Brian Davies, the captain, and Billy Marsh; "Killer" Kearney was hooker.

Match day dawned, and after hours spent lurking around the house like a moose with a sore head, Dad and I bundled my football gear into the boot of my old FJ Holden and left Balgowlah at 1pm for the SCG. Joan was travelling to the ground with friends. With kickoff at 3pm, two hours would normally be ample time to get to the SCG, but this Test had captured the imagination of the Sydney sporting public as no other Test had for years and traffic was at a standstill for kilometres around the Moore Park area as cars jockeyed for parking spots. For a long time I was sure we'd be too late and that I was destined to be the only player ever to miss his Test debut because he was stuck in traffic. Already keyed up, I was starting to get frantic.

I was in a frenzy as we drove into the SCG carpark at 2.30. By then, there was no spot to park, but luckily an attendant recognised me and let Dad leave the car in a driveway. Dad and I leapt out, slammed the doors shut and went to the boot to get my gear out. The boot was locked. No keys. Where the hell are they? Search pockets, abuse Dad, swear, stomp. Christ! There they are, still dangling in the ignition with all four car doors locked.

By this time a crowd of 30 or 40 people had gathered to witness the spectacle of Australia's newest Test hero trying to break into his own car. There was no shortage of helpful suggestions, believe me! Finally, there was nothing else to do. With just 20 minutes remaining before kickoff, I picked up a brick and smashed the window. Cheers rang out from the crowd which now numbered about 60. My face burning with embarrassment and fury, I grabbed the keys, unlocked the boot, took my gear and bounded through the Members' Stand and into the dressing room.

There I found my teammates in a state of high nervous tension. Some were retching and others were going to and fro to the toilet. A few were sitting stock-still as if in a trance. I laugh when

I hear of players needing to watch American gridiron films and listen to the theme from *Rocky* to psyche themselves up for a big match. To me, this is utter bullshit. I know that I never needed any fake hype. Whether playing for my club, my State or Australia, my motivation came from deep inside, a combination of ego, adrenalin and a driving will to win at all costs.

The Australian XIII burst out of the dressing room into the bright winter sunshine then limbered up on the sideline. Loud boos from the crowd told us the Englishmen had commenced their blood-chilling slow walk onto the arena. Both teams lined up to shake hands. I noticed my former Leigh teammate Mick Martyn among the Englishmen. Approaching him with a wide grin, I shook hands, told him what a thrill it was for me to be playing against him in such a big match and then enquired after the health of a few of our mutual friends in Leigh. Martyn, whose nerves were stretched tight as a drum, seemed to relax at this show of friendship from a rival.

Our kickoff was accompanied by the roar of nearly 70,000 spectators, all baying for the blood of Englishmen. We gave them what they wanted. The ball went high, straight to Mick Martyn with Provan and me in hot pursuit. As the ball spiralled down towards Martyn I started screaming at him and waving my arms like a banshee. "Catch that ball and you're dead, you bloody Pommie bastard! When I get my hands on you I'll break you in two!" The poor bloke froze. The ball went into his arms and rolled right out again. Norm and I, with our combined weight of 32 stone, crunched him anyway. A horror start for Martyn and for England. For the rest of the game I stood opposite Mick in the ruck and let him know what a coward I thought he was. His confidence shattered, he couldn't get into the game and was not picked for another Test on tour. I wasn't particularly proud at playing such a dirty trick on an old friend, but I'd do almost anything to win a Test.

After some violent exchanges in the early scrums the Australian forwards, led magnificently by Queenslander Brian Davies, established their superiority and Yappy Holman took the opportunity to play the best game of his long career. He set the tempo for the rest of us with driving tackles and snappy, darting runs that punctured the Poms' defence time after time. Holman gave young Alex Murphy a lesson in halfback play, but, unfortunately for us, Murphy was to prove a quick learner. Little Holman terrorised the British that day. He knocked Dave Bolton out of the game for a while with a crash tackle and stiff-armed their centre Davies, who needed medical attention. Gordon Clifford could have been sent off for a late high tackle on Bolton. Mike Sullivan was going out of his mind, lashing out at anybody in a green and gold jumper. Prescott almost knocked Billy Marsh's head off with a roundhouse right but Marsh returned the compliment.

We bested England at football as well as fighting. Australia scored five tries to Great Britain's two, and some of them were beauties. After just five minutes British fullback Fraser fumbled in his dead ball area, and Kel O'Shea fell on it to score. Three minutes later, Provan burst upfield to within six or seven metres of the English line. I'd supported big Sticks all the way. When he was halted I charged to dummy half, picked up the ball and plunged over the line for a try in my first Test. I scored quite a few tries in my career, but none gave me as much satisfaction as this one. The roar of the crowd as I touched down was deafening. I was over the moon with delight, but showed no emotion other than accepting the handshakes of my teammates. Manly rugby union team were playing at Manly Oval that afternoon and I learned that when I scored my try the news was announced over the public address system. For a little while the rivalry between the codes was forgotten as the Rah-Rah fans cheered for an old Manly boy.

Back at the SCG, Carlson, Kite and Provan went on to score three-pointers in the match and Clifford banged over five goals. For Great Britain, Southward and Bolton scored tries and Southward kicked one goal. Australia 25, Great Britain 8. The Aussies went out to celebrate and the Poms took off for a week on the Gold Coast to regroup and lick their wounds before the

Second Test, to be played at the Brisbane Exhibition Ground three weeks later.

Their time in the sun seemed to work wonders for the English players and when they slow-marched onto the field for that Second Test they looked fit, strong and determined. They had a new second row for the game. Dick Huddart was making his Test debut, replacing the hapless Mick Martyn, and Whiteley had moved forward from lock, making room for Vince Karalius who had completed his suspension. The switches were instrumental in our downfall.

The Test, which Britain won 25-18, was one of the great ones, and will be remembered as "Prescott's Test". The big skipper broke his arm in the third minute of the game, but played out the full 80 minutes, tackling with his shoulder and one good arm, scooping out one-handed passes to supports and rallying his troops with his enormous courage. All match Prescott's teammates and the British management pleaded with him to come from the field, but this was the era of no replacements and he wouldn't hear of it. Early in proceedings the Poms lost five eighth Dave Bolton with a broken collarbone then centre Challinor and fullback Fraser were also injured and remained little more than passengers for the rest of the afternoon. With his arm dangling at his side, Prescott led his depleted forces superbly in one of league's most courageous efforts.

My thoughts on the matter are that Prescott had no choice but to play on. He was in enormous pain and his arm was useless, but he could still run, tackle and pass after a fashion, and direct his men. I don't think any of the Australians knew that the English skipper's arm was broken, although we could see he was favouring it. Speaking for myself, I kept tackling Prescott as hard as I could, but I did not especially target his injured arm. Sledging a bloke like Mick Martyn and putting your body on the line for your country in a Test match is one thing, but I always tried to draw the line at blatant brutality. In the notorious grand final of the following year, when I was singled out for special treatment by some of the blokes I packed down with in the Australian teams of 1958, some St George players crossed over that line.

With Prescott doing it tough in that Second Test of 1958, Dave Bolton off the field and Eric Fraser and centre Jim Challinor injured as well, Vince Karalius took it upon his broad shoulders to get Great Britain back into the series. He took us apart that day. Vince was not a huge man, but he was immensely strong, 15 stone of muscle and fury. He played the whole game with his face distorted in hatred of the Aussies and his taunting and sledging was as creative as his ballwork. Alternating between lock and five eighth he took the game right to us, ripping our defence to shreds with his wild bull charges. His tackles, often high and always hard, took their toll as the match progressed.

As the enforcer of our side, there was no way that I was going to let Karalius continue with his one-man demolition job on the pride of Australian rugby league. I lined him up as he stood in a tackle, looking to unload, and belted him as hard as I have ever belted anyone. He didn't flinch or even alter his expression, just stood there and took note. I knew I'd hurt him but he wasn't about to show he'd been rocked. Late in the game I had another go at Karalius. I swung at him, he ducked, then punched me in the face. Down I went, my eye laid wide open. This was not the last time Vince Karalius increased my doctors' bills.

The Englishmen played inspired football. Karalius was the decisive factor in the victory, but it was in this match, too, that Alex Murphy came of age. He set up three tries and scored one himself in a 25-8 English win. Australia at no stage threw in the towel, hitting back hard in the late stages of an absolute thriller. But this will always remain a classic Great Britain Test win.

Darcy Lawler, who had refereed the first two Tests, was replaced by the little moustachioed Queenslander Jack Casey for the Third and deciding Test at the SCG. A capacity crowd of nearly 70,000 crammed into the old ground, hoping to cheer the home side to an Ashes-winning victory. Our selectors had kept faith with the Second Test side, dropping only Tony Brown and

Ross Kite and replacing them with Greg Hawick and Ian Moir. Great Britain went into the game without Dave Bolton and Jim Challinor. Skipper Alan Prescott watched the game from the sideline, his arm encased in plaster.

The opening minutes were ferocious. Anything went as these two great teams battled for superiority. We forced our way to the British 25-yard line and, taking the ball first pass off the ruck, I probed for an opening. Seeing a support, I offloaded and as I did I was hit by a runaway train called Karalius. The "Wild Bull" has stiff-armed me and knocked me cold. When I regained consciousness my lips and gums were in shreds, I was bleeding heavily and I was badly concussed. At halftime, League doctor Len Greenberg put 11 stitches in my mouth and gums so I could return to the fray. I can remember virtually nothing about the match, but as I lay in bed eating my meals through a straw for the next two weeks I had plenty of time to read the newspaper reports.

Ike Southward scored early, then Ab Terry, a huge prop, tore through like a back to cross for a try and make it 12-2 after 22 minutes. Keith Holman, with a magnificent individualist's try, and Norm Provan touched down to get us back into the match by halftime, 14-12. Straight after, Alex Murphy bamboozled Wells and ran right past fullback Clifford to take the score to 22-12. Then hell broke loose.

Kel O'Shea shot the ball out to Ian Moir on our 25 and the winger kicked over his opposing winger Southward's head and took off downfield after it with the English line wide open. Southward, also in pursuit, then illegally obstructed Moir. The Australian players and the crowd screamed for referee Casey to penalise Southward. "Play on!" yelled Casey. Meanwhile British fullback Fraser had raced to recover the ball back on his own goal-line. Attempting to pick it up he fumbled it. The crowd now screamed for the referee to whistle a knock-on, but Casey again let the Poms play on. Fraser shovelled the ball out to centre Davies who booted it deep into Australian territory. Mike Sullivan, who had followed through, scooped up the ball and scrambled his way across the Australian line for a try. England 25-Australia 12. The Ashes were all but on their way back to England.

The crowd erupted in rage at Casey's blunders, pelting him with fruit and bottles. Debris littered the field as missiles rained onto the playing area. Play was held up as the rubbish was cleared away. Some of the Englishmen, quite satisfied by the turn of events in the game, calmly munched away at oranges or apples that had landed in their vicinity. Karalius was less sanguine, motioning to a group of throwers in the stands to come out onto the field and throw things at him, if they dared. No one took up his offer.

The demonstration and the unexpected try, which was scored against the run of play, knocked the stuffing out of the Australians and Great Britain piled on another four tries — two more to Sullivan, and one each to Davies and Whiteley — to wallop us 40-17.

After the match I sat in the dressing room in a daze, my mouth bleeding and my teeth loose, trying to remember where the hell I was. There were bitter recriminations. One back was made the scapegoat for our heavy loss in the Ashes-decider. One of the Australian selectors charged into the room and turned on this bloke whose defence, it must be said, had been bloody awful. The selector raged: "You gutless f. . . . . . bastard. You didn't tackle. That's your last f. . . . . . game for Australia." And it was.

Next day the newspapers continued the tonguelashing. Wrote Tom Goodman in *The Sun-Herald*: "England ran Australia ragged in the tough and sensational deciding Third Test at the SCG yesterday . . . Keith Holman celebrated his record 14th Test against England with a brilliant individual try and he did a terrific lot of tackling. But even he did not always get his man . . . The forwards many times let fast-running Englishmen through the rucks, right through to fullback Gordon Clifford, who gave one of the most wretched displays of tackling ever seen in a Test match."

THE MOOSE THAT ROARED

George Crawford in *The Sunday Telegraph* was no kinder. "Norm Provan and Kel O'Shea seemingly are over the hill and far down the other side. Ken Kearney can still win the ball from scrums, but aside from that he is now a passenger in the team. Gordon Clifford gave the most pathetic fullback display I have seen in a Test match. Five eighth Greg Hawick has slowed so much he is far short of Test standard."

In many ways this series was the end of an era for Australia and the beginning of one for Great Britain. Although they had played well in attack and tackled their hearts out, such Test stalwarts as Greg Hawick, Ian Moir, Brian Davies, Ken Kearney, Kel O'Shea, and the great little warrior Keith Holman had all been up a long time and many were showing wear and tear. With next year, 1959, a Kangaroo year, it was time for the selectors to find new blood. The Poms, on the other hand, had unearthed a new generation of stars in this series. Karalius, Murphy, McTigue, Huddart and Edgar would be giving Australians headaches for years to come.

The season wound down. Manly finished third on the ladder and made the semis, but we were knocked out of contention by Balmain who in turn were blown away by the eventual premiers St George. It was a thrill when I shared first place in *The Sun-Herald* Best and Fairest Competition with my teammate and friend Keith Holman. Yappy and I beat out a hot field of Churchill, Provan, Raper, Bugden, Clay and Keith Barnes to poll 20 points each. We split the 225 pounds prize money.

Yet in spite of all the applause that came my way when the accolades for '58 were handed out, something nagged away at me. I was nearing 30, definitely in the veteran class, but I had to make that Kangaroo team to tour Britain and France at the end of '59. There would be fierce competition for spots in the squad but I just had to be on the plane. After the events in the Test series just completed I had a score to settle with the Poms, and with one Pom in particular who had made me look bad. A bloke named Karalius.

10

OPEN WARFARE

The year 1959 was a watershed year for rugby league. The standard of the domestic competition was at an all-time high with St George, as ever, setting the pace; Queensland had gathered a group of talented youngsters who were expected to make NSW fight hard to continue their domination of the interstate matches; New Zealand was visiting for a full Test series; and at the end of the year the 10th Kangaroos were departing for a four-month, 37-game tour of England, France and Italy. So how does an old bloke of 31 prepare for such a gruelling season? He trains his butt off.

Right through the summer months I pushed myself to the limit, and when I turned up at Brookvale for pre-season training I was by far the fittest player in the club. Coach Kenny Arthurson rewarded all my good work by switching me into the front row. I'd played there a fair bit in the past, but regarded myself as a specialist second rower. The move upfront meant I would have to play tighter than I was used to, no more scouting wide of the rucks and running with the backs. I wasn't put out by the change. I had lost a little pace, after all, but none of my skills, and I knew my ability to play both positions would count in my favour at Kangaroo selection time.

If ever we were going to take the title from Saints, we knew that this was the year. The perhapsers of 1956 had matured into one of the best teams in the premiership, with Diversi, Bull, Burke, Willey and myself acknowledged as among the best in our positions. Promising youngsters such as Bob Batty and Billy Delamare were also making their mark.

Looking back, we were unlucky to be playing in the great St George era. If it wasn't for the mighty Saints, Manly would not have had to wait until 1972 to win their first premiership. 1959 was the season when Johnny Raper and Reg Gasnier burst into the big-time. St George had been good enough to win the past three grand finals without them, but "Chook" Raper and "Puff the Magic Dragon" Gasnier put Saints even further ahead of the rest.

Gasnier had lightning acceleration and fine-tuned anticipation. He could swerve, step and tackle. He was fast over a distance, and when he burst into the clear, shoulders back and head high, he was a dream to behold, unless he was playing against you, when he became a nightmare. Raper was simply the best all-round player I have ever seen. He was a freak who could break the line himself, send supports through with his exquisitely-timed passes, and there has never been a tackler like him — either in the front line or as a cover defender. He was also courageous, durable and clever. The key to Raper's greatness was his mastery of the basics of rugby league. He could perform every skill, with the possible exception of goalkicking.

We knew the St George style backwards, but countering it was another matter. For the first 10 or 15 minutes of the game they'd let you have the ball so they could smash you. Their fearsome defenders — Clay, Provan, Bath, Porter, Kearney, Raper and Bill "Bluey" Wilson — brutally snuffed out the most organised attack. These blokes usually played it hard and clean, but if things turned nasty, they didn't mind dishing out the dirt. When the opposition was pulverised, Saints' constructive ballplayers — Bath, Raper, Bob Bugden and Clay, would open up the game, sending the dashing flyers of the backs — Gasnier, John Riley and Eddie Lumsden — on their way to the tryline. In their heyday St George regularly racked up cricket scores of 40, 50, 60 points a game.

Manly started the season with three good wins and in spite of being sent off and cautioned for over-violent play in a match against Easts I was one of the first men selected in the early rep games. On the plane with me when the NSW side flew to Brisbane for the first interstate match were Gasnier, Raper, Clay, Carlson, Provan, Brian Hambly, and young Ian Walsh, a pig farmer from Eugowra who had starred in that year's City-Country game. We were a good side, but not good enough. Queensland shocked us by winning 17-15 in the first clash. In that game I had my first encounter with a ruthless, no-frills hooker with a wild shock of white hair standing out from his otherwise dark thatch and dynamite in both fists. His name was Noel Kelly. "Ned" and I would meet again many times — on and off the field.

NSW squared matters in the return match, 24-14, although we finished the game a man short after Brian Hambly saved Gasnier from a hiding at the hands of Queensland prop Dud Beattie by knocking Dud out with a rabbit-killer. It was in that game that the Queenslanders Bob Banks and Don Meehan had their skulls split open after crashing heads with bald Pop Clay.

The Blues lined up next against the touring New Zealand side and were pipped 23-22 in a thriller at the SCG. Gasnier, Raper, Bill Wilson, Wells and Moir played themselves into the First Test team, but I had a below-par match and missed selection. Everyone knew the Australian side would form the nucleus of the Kangaroos and I was disappointed to be left out after my good work against Great Britain the year before. The team was Barnes, Lumsden, Moir, Gasnier, Wells, Brown, Muir, Raper, Provan, Paterson, Wilson, Kelly, Beattie. I was behind the eight-ball and knew I would have to redeem myself in club football, while my rivals for Kangaroo selection hogged the limelight in the big games. I was continually overlooked by the representative selectors for the rest of the Kiwi Test series, but in this period I picked up a string of best player awards as Manly surged to the semi finals.

Alan Clarkson reported on the Manly-Wests game for *The Sydney Morning Herald*: "The match, played in semi-darkness for the last 15 minutes, was one of the most bitterly-contested of the season. It developed into a gruelling forward battle with both packs giving — and taking — plenty of punishment. In this play, Wests prop Nev Charlton and Manly second rowers Peter Diversi and Rex Mossop were outstanding." And Tom Goodman wrote of our narrow loss to Saints in the second round: "Rex Mossop played one of his best club games. He rose to the occasion when Diversi became disabled and did a trememdous amount of work. His handling and his passing were grand, and Mossop had an eye to positioning his supports."

Norm Provan was everybody's pick as Kangaroo captain until the big bloke announced mid-season that work and family commitments would keep him at home. With Ken Kearney and Dick Poole also retired from rep football, speculation then raged over who would win the prestigious post. The press and fans picked their shortlist. Harry Bath, Kel O'Shea, Nev Charlton, Keith Barnes and myself were all on it. I didn't really concern myself with this debate. All I wanted to do was make the touring team. If I went as captain that would be icing on the cake. I leaned strongly towards Keith Barnes being picked as skipper. He was a fine man and a fine player, and was chosen as captain for the last two Tests of the series victory over the Kiwis. *The Sun's* E.E. Christensen made his prediction: "Mossop appears to be the pick for Kangaroo captaincy, but the ultimate choice rests with the Board of Control." W.F. Corbett of *The Sun* also chose me as his captain, with Queenslander Bob Banks as my deputy.

We accounted for Newtown easily in the first semi final, swamping the Bluebags 17-0 on a heavy SCG. The following week St George beat Wests in the second semi and went straight into the grand final. We lined up against Wests to decide who would be Saints' opponent in the premiership decider.

Midway through the first half of the Wests game I was king hit from behind by Magpie prop Mark Patch. When I was revived a minute or two later, I saw the League doctor, my very good friend Len Greenberg, leaning over me with a worried expression. He was holding an ice pack to my swollen face. I climbed to my feet and asked my teammates who had decked me. I chased Patch all game, but he managed to keep out of my way. I never did get my revenge. The bloke left Wests at the end of the season to finish his career in the bush, and that was his good fortune. In a dour game played in light rain, we held Wests out to win 14-13 and secure a place in the grand final the following Saturday.

By the end of the match my face had ballooned grotesquely. An x-ray on Monday confirmed my worst fears. My cheekbone was broken. Cursing my bad luck — at stake was a grand final and a Kangaroo tour — I made an appointment to see Doc Greenberg and asked him to do me a very special favour. "Don't let on I'm hurt to anyone," I pleaded. He replied, "My advice is that you'd be crazy to play a grand final in your condition, but you're a grown man, you know the dangers you're facing, and if you're prepared to go ahead and play I'm not going to stop you. I won't say a word to a soul." When the League asked Len whether I was fit to take my place in the Manly lineup he said only that my x-rays showed no fracture. He wasn't lying. The first set of x-rays came out opaque so couldn't reveal a thing. The second set, however, showed three fractures and a depression. But that was our secret. All week the papers ran stories of how my cheekbone was only bruised and that I was in no doubt to play.

I decided to let Ken Arthurson know the real story about my cheekbone. Ken stuck by me, adopting the same attitude as Len Greenberg, that I was big enough and ugly enough to look after myself. And, besides, I was needed in the grand final team. Then we bunged on an elaborate charade for St George's benefit. We brought a photographer down to training and he took pictures of me tackling, being tackled and even sparring with a professional boxer. The papers lapped up the shots, even a posed one which had me being socked fair on the suspect cheekbone by the pug. Over at Kogarah Oval, argument raged over whether I was fit or foxing. My mate Johnny Raper told me years later that the Saints forwards adopted an attitude of, "Well, if Moose's cheekbone is not broken now, it bloody well will be when we're finished with him!"

THE MOOSE THAT ROARED

Before a crowd of 50,000 at the SCG, St George kicked off high and deep. Standing back close to my own goal line I was perfectly positioned to catch the ball and tear upfield into the swarming St George forwards. *Belt!* Saints' captain Killer Kearney, who in his speech after the match said, "And I'm sure everyone here today will have enjoyed a game played in such fine sporting fashion", smashed me bang on the cheekbone. Down I went in agony. Minutes later it was Harry Bath's turn to test out my injury. He came at me with fists flying. He hit his target and I hit the deck. When I picked myself up my face was aching and beginning to swell all over again, and to make matters worse Bath's tackle had torn and dislocated my thumb. It was cut and bleeding and sticking out at a weird angle. Referee Darcy Lawler called for ambulance assistance and out ran Doc Greenberg. Snapping my thumb back into place, he chuckled, "You knew what you were letting yourself in for. These bastards know you're carrying an injury and will be at you all game."

Len was spot-on. I was singled out for treatment by the St George forwards all game, except for Johnny Raper who never tackled above the kneecaps. Monty Porter took a swipe at me, then Bluey Wilson, then Bath again, then Kearney, then Bath once more. In the opening seconds of the second half, Bath flattened me for about the 10th time. This sparked a fracas involving about eight players. Harry and I stood toe to toe trading punches until we were separated by referee Lawler who warned us that if we didn't wake up to ourselves we'd be off. Bath and I, however, had reached the point of no return.

Peter Diversi and Roy Bull, playing his last game for Manly, fought back bravely, but Saints' head barrage on me continued. Few men escaped injury: Diversi broke his hand and Raper, Clay, Bugden and Wilson all sustained bad injuries. Norm Provan's younger brother Peter, a fine forward in his own right, broke both his nose and his collarbone in the savage match. I was literally out on my feet, but kept charging into the rucks and putting my teammates through. Never let the bastards know you're hurt.

OPEN WARFARE

Unlike many teams, St George could fight and play football at the same time — and as the match progressed they slipped further and further ahead of us. With 10 minutes to go it was 20-0 and we were shot seagulls. I was hurting badly by then. Harry Bath had done his work well. As the game went into the dying stages I'd taken all I was going to. The pain in my cheek was excruciating, my thumb was aching, my team was getting flogged. I'd copped the trifecta. Suddenly I saw Harry on the ground at my feet. I did something then I'd never done before and never did again. I stomped hard on his head. For good measure I ground my studs in, opening a gash on his face. I left him lying on the grass, in urgent need of attention.

Two minutes later, play was continuing when Diversi screamed "Duck!" I dropped to my knees as Harry Bath, crimson-faced with fury, sailed over my shoulder. He hit the turf in an awkward heap. "Stuff it," I thought in that split second, "Saints have beaten us. There's nothing to lose. I might as well settle the score." I leapt on Harry and hit him again and again. He recovered and got stuck into me. Scuffles flared like brushfires all over the field. Harry and I separated ourselves from the melee and waded into each other once more. The blue lasted almost a minute, but seemed like an hour. Our feud, which started back in the north of England eight years before and which we'd enthusiastically fuelled every time we'd locked horns since, reached its climax that day.

Harry was a better fighter than me, but I knew as many dirty tricks as he did and I was giving as good as I got when Darcy Lawler raced over, blew his whistle and barked, "Righto, you two gentlemen — piss off!" In a weird throwback to my sendoff in the 1950 rugby union grand final when my partner in crime Bomber Miles winked at me as we left the field, old Harry gave me a cheeky smile as we jogged off the arena for our early showers.

We fronted the judiciary together that night. Judiciary chairman Snowy Justice asked Harry if he was guilty of fighting and Harry replied, "Of course I'm bloody guilty — and if I had the chance I'd do the same bloody thing again!" I chipped, "And I bloody-well would, too!" Bath and I broke up as Justice suspended us for one match each. That night Harry Bath and I decided that we liked each other after all. We're good mates to this day.

A week before the grand final I had been picked in the last Kangaroo tour selection trial, a Sydney-Country match at the SCG to be played the day after the premiership decider. That was the game I missed through suspension, but I was not unduly worried. I had it on good authority that I was already on the plane. A day or so before the grand final, Len Greenberg had called me into his office. Sitting me down, he told me that I had not only been selected for the Kangaroo tour, but there was a strong push to make me captain because of my long experience of English conditions and good form throughout the year. All I had to do, he said, was keep my nose clean in the grand final and the captaincy would be mine. I had no reason to doubt Len's words. As League doctor he was well-connected with the game's hierarchy.

It's history that I did not keep my nose clean and the general consensus of opinion in the days before the Kangaroos were picked was that by being sent off I had blown any chance I had of leading the team away. Wrote George Crawford in *The Daily Telegraph*: "I have no doubt Mossop would have been Kangaroo captain if he had not met this trouble (my being sent off in the grand final). Board of Control members must now be worried about Mossop's position. His appointment in these circumstances would become strong propaganda against the Kangaroos if they got into trouble early in the tour."

11

KANGAROO QUEST

The following Saturday night the Kangaroo team was read out and I was in the side, although not as captain. That honour went to Keith Barnes. I was named vice-captain. I believe the selectors and the Board of Control made the right decision by appointing Keith skipper. Not only was he the form fullback, and sure of a Test spot, but he was a wonderful ambassador for the code.

The announcement of the '59 Kangaroos was met with derision. Almost to a man the critics panned us and said that the Poms would eat us for breakfast. "Too inexperienced" and "Not tough enough" were the most common criticisms, although in my case it was "too old" and "too fiery". Frank Browne, writing in *The Daily Mirror*, echoed what many were thinking when he wrote, "As far as the forwards are concerned, they are a run-of-the-mill bunch with Rasmussen and Hambly my picks to be the successes of the tour, and Raper and Mossop the failures." Chook and I took great pleasure in proving Browne wrong.

It *was* an inexperienced side, with 18 of the 26 players aged 24 or younger. What the doomsayers could not have known, however, was that many of those youngsters would evolve on this tour into some of the finest players ever to grace the game. Blokes like Gasnier, Raper, Irvine, Lumsden, Parish, Muir, Hambly, Walsh and Kelly returned four months later as household names. Nevertheless, there was a huge responsibility on Billy Wilson, Harry Wells and myself, the old hardheads in the side, to keep the campaign on the rails. Clive Churchill was coach, and Ern Keefer and Colonel Jack Argent the managers.

THE MOOSE THAT ROARED

I was flattered when the chairman of selectors called me aside before we flew out and told me he expected me, with my English experience, to help the younger men come to terms with the foreign conditions. First thing I did was tell Reg Gasnier to protect his head when running with the ball through that forest of coat-hangers that passes for defence in England. All tour long I did my best to get on the same wave length as the younger blokes, many of whom were born a decade after me.

We flew out on September 5 in a BOAC Brittania. The club rivalry of the past season evaporated immediately as blokes who'd been doing their level best to kill each other just weeks ago shared beers and laughs. I hit it off at once with the St George contingent, especially Johnny Raper, Brian Clay and Bluey Wilson.

We settled in at the Victoria Hotel, Stockton Heath, near Warrington, for the first part of the long campaign. Later we moved to the Troutbeck Hotel at Ilkley, Yorkshire. Personalities began to emerge. The most commanding presence of all was our manager Jack Argent, a former army colonel and a disciplinarian of the old school. Ramrod-straight and abrupt of manner, Jack made it clear from the start that his word was law. Clashes were inevitable.

Among the younger players were quite a few free spirits who rebelled against Jack's edicts. Nobody would be late — either coming back to the hotel after dinner at night, or for training every morning at 7am. Repeated offenders would be sent home. Players would wear boots at training. Those who did not would be sent home. There would be no beards grown. Offenders would be sent home. To mark a British military holiday we would all dress up in blazers and hats and march through the streets of Warrington. Anybody who didn't turn up would be on the next plane home.

Jack was a good man and a first rate manager, but, for Christ's sake, you can't just lay down the law to young blokes like we had on that tour and expect them to take orders blindly. They were rugby league players, not commandos. As a senior member of the tour I acted as an intermediary between Jack and the players. Once I pleaded with him long into the night that he change his mind and not send my Manly teammate Peter Burke home for refusing to wear boots at training. In the end Jack relented, but to this day I'm sure Peter doesn't know how close he came to the ultimate Kangaroo disgrace.

By tour's end Jack and I were good friends, but we had our moments. In the dressing room after the Second Test, which we lost, he got stuck right into the players. I cut his harangue short when I loudly demanded, "And how many f . . . . . . Tests have you played for Australia, Jack?" Jack froze, and I could see that many of the players thought I'd way overstepped the mark, but it had to be said. Jack was being bloody unfair and my heat-of-the-moment words rammed that home to him.

Another time, during the French leg of the tour when everybody was homesick, I tried to lighten things up by starting a beard-growing competition. I grew a suave black one that had the French press calling me "Barbu" — Blackbeard. When Jack saw what we were up to, he demanded that we shave them off at once. "Australian representatives will be clean-shaven!" he ordered. I refused point blank, telling him to jump in the lake, or words to that effect. A beard did not hamper either my training or playing and it was staying on. Jack backed off and I kept the beard, in spite of the efforts of those two lovable rogues Bluey Wilson and Noel Kelly who came at me with razors when I nodded off in the team bus.

There wasn't a man on that tour who did not finish with a grudging respect for Jack Argent. He won us over forever when he stood up at the dinner after the Third Test, a game marred by biased refereeing, and in front of the English league hierarchy called referee Eric Clay a cheat to his face. Jack is a dyed-in-the-wool league man, still active out at Parramatta club, and the game could do with a lot more like him.

Keith Barnes and I got on very well, and are still firm mates. He was a good and popular captain and one of the gutsiest players I've ever seen. His physique then could only be described as frail, but he was a dependable custodian, never flinching as he took high kicks or brought down Englishmen such as the flying steamroller Billy Boston, a man much bigger and faster than himself. We had a running joke that we repeat to each other today when our paths cross. Keith would say, "Moose, can you do such-and-such for me?" and I'd always reply, "Of course, skipper, I'm the loyalest vice-captain a captain ever had."

As vice captain, or "captain of vice" as I became known, I had my work cut out for me. Apart from trying to get across my knowledge of English conditions and playing styles to the other blokes, I also took on the role of father confessor. Many was the time I had to pep up men who had become distraught with homesickness. I had to settle off-field squabbles between the players and on more than a few occasions separate brawlers. It's inevitable that on such a long trip, healthy young blokes' thoughts will turn to women. I had to step between two of the smallest men on the tour who were belting each other over an English lass they'd both fallen in love with. "For God's sake, here you are in a country where there are millions of eligible women, and you two boofheads are fighting over the same one." That settled them down, but they seemed a bit doubtful about my logic.

There were a couple of men in the team who couldn't read and they'd usually ask me to read them their mail from home when it arrived. The hardest thing I had to do on that Kangaroo tour, far harder than facing up to the toughest Pom, was read a letter to one of these blokes in which his wife said she was leaving him. It was dreadful, for him and for me. He took it badly and I spent a long, long time comforting him.

There was a bad incident at the Ilkley Moor Golf Club. Members of the club decided to have the Australian team as their guests for a golf day. The players were allowed to use the members' lockers in the club house. A couple of idiots stole their hosts' clubs, balls, caps and even cashmere sweaters. They returned that night to our hotel and started laughing and bragging about their daring heist. I blew my stack. "How bright are you bastards!" I roared. "The people at the club know your names and are bound to call the police. And, apart from anything else, by being thieves you've let your country down. Now take the bloody gear back before anyone notices it's gone!" At a stopover on the way home, one of our light-fingered Roos knocked off a camera from a duty-free shop. I demanded that he return it, which prompted a few of the other blokes to return items that they'd pilfered, too. The captain of vice earned his bloody money on that trip, I'll give you the tip!

Generally, though, we were a happy bunch and team spirit was high as we prepared for the First Test. The Test side was taking shape as various combinations were tried out in club games, but there was no ill-feeling from the guys who looked like missing out. They cossetted the top XIII so they would be at their peak for the battle ahead. The final match before the First Test at Swinton was against the top English club side of the time, St Helen's. The match was a special one for me because Saints fielded nine internationals and enjoyed the biggest following in the English league. St Helens was also the home club of Vince Karalius.

It would be nice to be able to report that I paid Vince back that day for all the pain he'd inflicted on me in the home Test series the year before. But football doesn't always work out the way you want it. The fact is that Karalius got the better of me again, in the biffo stakes at least. He sent me to Disneyland at least once in that match. I didn't worry too much, because Vince was a Test certainty and I'd have at least three more occasions to even the ledger with him. Sadly, he suffered a bad injury in a club match just days before the Test and that was the end of his season. We would not meet again until the World Cup, to be played in England the following year.

Karalius won the fight, but we won the football. Australia flogged the champion club side 15-2. The match was the perfect preparation for the Test. That was the game when I realised that Johnny Raper was something very special. In the 25 minutes he was on the field he gave one of the all-time great displays of sustained attack and defence. He cut Saints to pieces around the rucks and many times tackled three or four St Helens players in succession. Once he was picked up and dumped but got away a perfect ball to put a teammate into a gap a split second before he was barrelled upside down into the turf. Midway through the first half I saw him sitting on the ground gingerly rubbing his leg. "Get up you lazy bastard!" I bellowed and cracked him across the back of the head. "Nobody lies down today!" He looked up at me surprised, then climbed to his feet and played on, stopping another succession of rampaging Saints in their tracks. Suddenly he collapsed to the ground in obvious pain. "What's the matter?" I asked. "I broke my bloody leg back there," he moaned. As he was carried off he assured us he'd be back as soon as he could. The injury kept him out of action until the Third Test.

For the past month I'd been plagued by boils on my leg. I caught the infection after cutting myself in an early tour game. I'd been to doctors who gave me temporary relief, but on the Wednesday before the First Test I woke up with an enormous boil on the top of my left thigh. The lump and surrounding infection were the size of a tennis ball and it was clear that only urgent attention would allow me to take my place in the Test team. Off I went to a doctor, a Canadian who, as it turned out, was much better suited to butchery than medicine. This idiot took one look and told me the boil would have to be drained. Producing a huge needle, he fobbed off my suggestion that a local anaesthetic might be in order. Instead he commanded a couple of male nurses to hold me down. He then slammed the syringe into the infection. The pain was excruciating and I sat bolt upright shouting like a maniac as the boil burst. My leg remained as sore as blazes but I would not have missed that Test for anything.

Coach Clive Churchill deserves much of the credit for our showing in that Test — and for our success throughout the entire tour. In the lead-up weeks he'd been working on set moves to make the most of young Reg Gasnier's blinding acceleration. Reg had been kept under wraps to that point, but he was all set to unleash his mighty talent on the unsuspecting English.

On a typically foggy, sunless day, the old enemies joined battle once more. Great Britain fielded quite a few of their '58 Test heroes — Fraser, Ashton, Davies, Sullivan, Bolton, Murphy, Huddart, McTigue, Harris and Terry — and were the bookies' favourites. Our team bore little resemblance to the outfit thrashed 40-17 in the deciding Test the year before. Barnes was fullback, Lumsden and Johnny Riley on the wings, Harry Wells and Reg Gasnier, who blossomed on this tour into one of the most potent pairings ever, were our centres, Pop Clay and Barry Muir were the halves. The forwards were Hambly, Mossop, Parcell, Beattie, Walsh and Wilson. Clay, sturdy and destructive, directed the attack from five eighth and it was he who did the spadework for Gasnier's slashing debut against the Poms.

After just 10 minutes our forwards had England backpedalling on the dry, unusually hard Swinton surface. On halfway, Harry Wells, the perfect robust foil for the rapier skills of his centre partner, put Gasnier into a gap. Reg left the British fullback Fraser struggling in his wake as he streamed down the touchline to score. After 33 minutes I sent Wells over for a try with a reverse pass that caught the defence on the wrong foot. Just after halftime I took the ball from the dummy half on the open side of the ruck. Then, instead of doing what the Poms expected me to do — run ahead myself or pass the ball out along the line — I switched it straight back to the blind side where Barry Muir waited. "Garbo" took a couple of steps then gave it to Gasnier on the burst. Gas cleaved between Ashton and Boston to score his second try. As we jogged back to halfway for the restart of play, the tough little Pommy hooker Tommy Harris passed by and quipped to me, "Where the bluddy 'ell did ye get that racehorse from?"

Great Britain came back as we knew they would, with McTigue and Derek "Rocky" Turner leading the way. Several times we hurled attackers into touch just centimetres short of our line. Then Gasnier put a cork on their comeback. Accepting a line drop-out by Dave Bolton, Reg shot into a yawning gap and touched down for his hat-trick. Australia 20, Great Britain 4. In the closing minutes, Boston dribbled the ball over our line and fell on it for a try, then Rocky Turner, a big, fast, mean lock forward, took the ball on the burst 15 yards out from our line and powered through my weary tackle to score. I was furious with myself about that. At fulltime the score was 22-14. The First Test was ours, and the tour a guaranteed success.

Gasnier bewitched, bothered and bewildered the Brits that day and, with Harry Wells, asserted a centre three-quarter dominance that plagued England for this series and the next. Another wonderful memory I have of that Test is of Brian Clay — bless him, Pop's gone now, too, along with Elton Rasmussen, Ken Irvine, Brian Carlson and Clive Churchill from that wonderful side. Brian demolished his opposite number, Dave Bolton, in that match. Dave is now an Australian resident after a long and distinguished career in England and later with Balmain and Penrith. I'm sure he still winces when he remembers the buffeting he took courtesy of Poppa's demon tackling. Brian Hambly, too, tackled with controlled destructive fury. Even the partisan Swinton crowd, freezing in the grandstands, warmed to us that day and by the end of the game were wildly cheering our enterprising display.

In a departure from the norm, the '59 Kangaroos played the First Test against France after the First Test against Great Britain. The way the schedule was worked out, we would then return to England to complete the British leg of the tour, then fly back to France for the rest of our matches there before travelling south to Italy for some exhibition games against local sides.

One of the few subjects I had done well in at school was French, and my halting efforts came in handy in Paris when I did my best to argue the point with the most dishonest referee I have ever played under. Georges Jameau, later kindly described by embarrassed French league chief Antoine Blain as "a staunch

French patriot", penalised us 24-5. Although we scored four tries to one, with three super long range three-pointers to Eddie Lumsden, the deluge of penalties against us allowed French full-back Pierre Lacaze to kick six goals. Lacaze also potted two field goals. Because, or in spite of, the efforts of this French cheat Jameau, we sneaked home 20-19.

Our battle plan had been to tackle in twos and threes, one man to hold up the runner and the others to pick him up and bury him. The French hate that sort of manhandling, and sure enough they got rattled early, dropping the ball, shirking tackles and running around accusing each other of real or imaginary wrongs. The Parisian crowd expressed their disapproval of their countrymen's performance by whistling at them. One French player reacted by dropping his trousers — he was wearing no jockstrap or briefs — and exposing his derriere to the north stand, the south stand, the east and the west. I couldn't help it. I gave the bloke a cheer. One of his teammates was not so complimentary. He ran up behind the flasher and kicked him right up the backside. That's French football for you.

After the match, Jack Argent fired off an official complaint, accusing Jameau of blatant bias. He noted that the French forwards had been allowed to kick us without penalty; that French second rower Aubert had been allowed to kick and punch in the open as he liked and that he had kicked me while I was lying on the ground; and that their halfback Farges had stomped on Barry Muir's back as Garbo was stretched on the turf.

After the match we went out on the town. The high life of Paris is the perfect antidote for blokes missing the warmth and comforts of home. Again my schoolboy French came in handy for ordering food and drink and asking the way to the nightclubs of the Latin Quarter. Late that night, after long and alcoholic celebrations, four of us — me, Tony Brown, my old mate Arthur Clues from Leeds, and, for some reason I've long since forgotten, Tom Mitchell, an English official who was manager of the '58 Lions touring team — decided to soldier on. At about 3am we came upon the Place Pigalle. Even at that ungodly hour, the square was abuzz with music, dancing in the streets and thousands of people out for a good time. Mitchell, who could not hold his grog, started acting like an idiot. As he came upon a parked car, this fool would bend the aerial. Seeing a big American car, he made a beeline for the bonnet and bent the aerial back. The car's owner, a hugely-muscled black US soldier, built like Mike Tyson but taller, saw Mitchell and knocked him to the footpath. Mitchell picked himself up and fled into a wine bar, with the American in hot pursuit. By this stage we were so annoyed by Mitchell's behaviour that we were at first happy to let him cop what was coming to him. Then Arthur said, "Oh, shit, he's too drunk to defend himself, we'd better help him out."

Clues, Brown and I waded into the bar where a brawl was already proceeding. As usual in such set-tos, drinks are spilled, clothes are torn, but nobody really gets hurt. I was belting some bloke who was belting me, Brown, living up to his nickname of "Slipper", was dealing with another customer, and Clues was swinging John Wayne haymakers at anything that moved. The blast of a gendarme's whistle sent everybody scrambling out into the street. We escaped, dragging the drunken and semiconscious Mitchell with us. We stopped in a cafe and sobered him up, but the man was a menace. As soon as he could walk again he ran out into the road and climbed to the top of an ornate fountain in the middle of the square. There, with the water cascading all around him, he started abusing police and passersby. For a while he avoided arrest by trampling on the fingers of the cops as they tried to pull him down from his perch, but finally they got him down and bundled him off. We left him to his fate, which turned out to be 48 hours in the local bastille.

Back in England, we faced Bradford Northern, Wigan, Halifax and Featherstone Rovers before fronting up at Leeds for the Second Test, the match we hoped would win us the Ashes trophy. We won two of these club games and lost two. In those days, matches against club sides were always rugged encounters. The local lads would be pumped up for a big effort against the visiting "convicts" and they'd be backed by a large and partisan crowd. Fireworks were inevitable. Usually there'd be a flareup in the first or second scrum and when that happened we knew what to do. We'd single out our opposite number and whale away, whether he'd been an instigator of the trouble or not.

There were plenty of enforcers in our team. Bluey Wilson was one, a cold, cruel man on the field but one of nature's gentlemen off it. Bluey was a wonderful practical joker and one of his specialties was biting your tie in two while it was still attached to your neck. He'd come up to you, put the end of your tie in his mouth then splutter, "OK, Moose, what are you going to do about it?" I'd reply, "Well, Bill, there's not a damn lot I *can* do about it." He'd say, "You're absolutely right" and bite the bloody end off.

This was the tour when I first came to know Noel "Ned" Kelly well. Noel off the field was a decent, funny and warm-hearted bloke who liked a beer and would do anything for a friend. On it, he was a holy terror. A mighty forward, whether playing hooker or prop, Noel rates among the most feared en-forcers rugby league has seen. In a long career I never saw any-body get the better of him in a one-on-one confrontation. He specialised in sticking up for his smaller teammates. Ned rarely started trouble, but he always finished it.

In a club game on that tour, one of the Pom forwards was get-ting stuck into Barry Muir. Barry had probably asked for it, but that was no concern of Ned. Noel walked over to the English-man, calmly and with a quizzical smile on his face that gave no hint of what was going to happen next. Then with a lightning left that could have travelled no further than a few inches, he knocked the forward unconscious. Ned was lethal and one of the few men I have known who could knock a bloke out with a single punch. I saw him do it at least half a dozen times.

Another time, years later, I was calling an Australia-New Zea-land Test match from Brisbane. I was still reading the teams out to viewers when the ball was kicked off to Johnny Gleeson, the Aussie five eighth. The giant Maori forward Robin Orchard then laid Gleeson out with a stiff arm from behind. Up strolled Ned, that little smile on his lips, and with one of his left-hand specials knocked Orchard cold. Ned was marched immediately and then when Orchard was revived, some minutes later, he was sent off too. The game was just 10 seconds old.

It's funny the number of rugby league tough guys who are charming, amusing gentlemen away from the paddock. Wilson, John Sattler, John O'Neill, Mal Reilly come to mind. Ned Kelly had us all in stitches so many times on that tour and every time our paths met in years to come we got on well. When I was looking for a quick-witted, knowledgable league expert with a sense of humour to join my Controversy Corner panel at Channel 7 years later, I didn't have to look further than Noel Kelly.

The pitch at Headingley for the Second Test was as muddy and slow as the Swinton surface had been firm and speedy. The heavy conditions suited the bulkier, slower Englishmen better than it did us, and they beat us 11-10. It was a real Test match, hard-fought all the way. Britain scored a try after only 55 seconds when their skipper Jeff Stevenson caught us napping after we'd been penalised and ran the ball instead of going for goal. A quick pass to second rower Dave Robinson who scored and we were behind the eight ball.

Lady Luck was cruel that day. We were leading 10-6 with 30 minutes left to play when Brian Carlson's goal shot hit the upright and bounced back into the field of play. A successful kick would have given us a six-point lead, enough to make the Poms score twice to beat us. Then Muir and Wells combined to send Gasnier away. Reg passed back to Carlson who sent Muir over for a try, but referee Ron Gelder ruled Carlson's pass forward. After the match, Gelder made the astonishing admission to me that he had erred in disallowing the Carlson pass.

The try that gave Great Britain their one point lead at the end was also questionable. Eric Ashton kicked through and Gasnier caught the ball behind his line and was tackled. It should have led to a line dropout, but Gelder ordered a scrum. The ball came out England's way, Stevenson ran wide then passed back inside to Whiteley who scored. Neil Fox converted. The series would go to a decider after all.

In the run-up to the Third Test we defeated Swinton, lost to Wakefield Trinity, beat Huddersfield and struggled to down Hunslet in a vicious brawling encounter. At one stage spectators ran onto the field to help the cause of the local heroes when an all-in stoush broke out.

We'd played 24 matches since touching down back in September and we were dog-tired, physically and mentally, by the time we ran onto the field at Central Park, Wigan, to play for the Ashes trophy. The week before the Test had been cold and wet. The glorious autumn weather we'd enjoyed through October and early November was replaced by driving rain and bitter winds. Our disposition was not helped either when we learned that the notorious Eric "Sergeant-Major" Clay would be refereeing the game. Clay was a bad-tempered, tin-pot dictator and another man not averse to giving the home side a little help if it needed it.

It's history that we were beaten by Great Britain in the deciding Test. I have no excuses. The Poms, particularly their forwards, outplayed us. They suckered us into a barging test of strength up the middle when we would have been much better off throwing the ball wide and turning loose Gasnier, Wells, Lumsden and Carlson.

The first half was tryless. The neglected backlines froze as the forwards slugged it out. It was much warmer in the rucks where Billy Wilson and Jack Wilkinson, the bloke who had fallen on me and wrecked my spine four years earlier, waged a two-man war. At halftime, England led 6-2, three penalties to Neil Fox and one to Keith Barnes. Right after the break Fox kicked another penalty, then five minutes later kicked ahead and regathered to cross for a try which he converted. Great Britain 13-2.

The game then burst wide open as we at last realised we'd have to rattle up a few tries if we were going to win. Gasnier came into his own, making bust after bust. In one glorious run he sliced through, drew the fullback Gerry Round and found

Johnny Raper in support. Raper, back in the Test side after recovering from his broken leg, flashed over for the try. Gasnier then gave the Englishmen a preview of what he was going to do to them for years to come when he scored the try of the series. Receiving the ball on his own 25, he threw his head back and glided majestically through the defence. He swerved past fullback Round, and delicately lofted the ball to Brian Carlson who touched down. At 15-12 we were back in the game, but an Australian victory wasn't to be. Minutes from the end we dropped the ball, Whiteley picked it up and passed to Southward who scored a soft try. The game ended at 18-12. As the British celebrated after the game they could not have known that it would be the last time in more than three decades (at time of writing) that they would defeat Australia in a home series.

At the post-match function we mingled with our opponents and congratulated them, but our manager Jack Argent spoke for us all when he stood up and addressed the gathering. "Gentlemen, it is easy to understand why an Australian side has never won the Ashes in England when you have such biased referees," he announced to the stunned room.

After that, there was nothing more for us to do than pack our bags and head off to France. There, we beat the Frenchmen in the two remaining Tests, 17-2 and 16-8, and won seven out of our eight club games, but along the way encountered the usual laughable refereeing, wild scenes and fantastic events that make every Kangaroo tour of France an occasion to remember. I recall a local fire brigade pumping thousands of gallons of water off the field before a match so play could proceed. I remember Kenny Irvine being hit on the head by a chair-wielding spectator at Perpignan, and Ken being tackled by a Frenchman who jumped off the reserve bench as the winger sped by. Then there was the day when Carcassonne scored two tries against us when their players ran outside the field of play, dodging by the coaches, reserves and medicos to run around and touch down behind the posts. On another occasion Gary Parcell and a French opponent settled a dispute by rubbing mud in each other's face.

Bizarre happenings were not confined to the field. One Kangaroo teammate, much the worse for wear, stuck out his arm one day while walking down a French street and stiff-armed an unsuspecting Frenchwoman cycling by. Then one day, Barry Muir got worked up over something and wanted to fight Brian Clay. The incident took place on the third floor of the team hotel. "Barry," said Poppa, "I'll give you 10 punches start . . . then I'll throw you out the window." Three months away from home is a long time, and it is inevitable that tempers will flare.

Tempers certainly flared back home in Australia when one newspaper really dropped me in the muck. After the Third Test in England I sought special permission to take a week away from football to accompany an official visitor, Jack Brown, to Paris. Because Jack was an ex-president of Easts Leagues Club and a stalwart of country football, and because I'd played more games to date than any other Kangaroo and needed a break, permission was granted. Jack was a generous fellow and usually picked up the tab as we caroused through the nightclubs of the City of Light. He was a master of rhyming slang and the colloquialisms of the racetrack. If somebody had body odour he'd say they were "Anna May Wong under the Warwick Farms" — a bit strong under the arms. Imagine the problems he presented to the French who were trying to make some sense of "tip the bucket", "bag o' fruit" and "tit for tat".

Anyway, when I rejoined my teammates in the south of France a blistering telegram from Joan awaited me. She had just read a clipping from a Sydney newspaper which read: "Pity the poor Kangaroos, away from home, in snow and sleet, while their vice captain holidays in Paris." Joan took one look at this and jumped to the conclusion that I was playing up. Of course, nothing could have been further from the truth. I deserved my break and the tour management knew it. This was not the last time that a big-mouth from the press caused ructions in my family.

After running up 104 points to 37 in our two Italian exhibition games in Padua and Treviso, we were glad to catch that Qantas Super Constellation home to Australia. Joan was there to meet me at Sydney airport with the boys, and there were marvellous scenes as the weary, battered Kangaroos were reunited with their loved ones. After one last official lunch at League headquarters the men of the 10th Kangaroos shook hands and went our own ways. It was good to be back home in the January heat after all that ice and snow.

I was disappointed that we'd come home without the Ashes, but we'd come bloody close. Many of those untried youngsters who went away in 1959 with the scornful laughter of the critics ringing in their ears returned to England as superstars in 1963. With Raper, Gasnier, Kelly, Walsh, Irvine and Hambly calling the shots, the 11th Kangaroos plucked the Ashes trophy right out of the Lions' den.

As for me, by playing in all five Tests on tour, appearing in 26 of the 37 matches, second only to winger Eddie Lumsden (it's tough out there on the wing!), captaining Australia to a big win over Hull, and carrying out my vice captain's tasks way beyond the call of duty, I believed I'd rammed home a point to the scribes who said I was too old and hot-headed to be of any value on the Kangaroo campaign.

12

STAYING POWER

I turned 32 just before the 1960 season got underway. Although definitely in the veteran class by then I was fit and enthusiastic and had every intention of kicking on forever. As Manly's 1960 premiership campaign began, I'd been playing league week in, week out for the past 12 months, but my twin goals of winning a competition with Manly and playing for Australia again — against France at home and in the World Cup in England — drove me on. Many pressmen and opposing players were predicting that the old Moose would fade quietly out of the game following the Kangaroo tour. We'd see about that.

The older I got, the harder I trained. I know for a fact that there were few players of my era who worked harder or longer than me at staying fit. It was no chore. I couldn't get enough of the training routine, and that's why I was able to play first grade until I was in my middle 30s. A great inspiration to me in my playing days was the legendary conditioner George Daldry. He was, and is, a tough man, hardened in the dreadful conditions of Changi prison camp in World War II. I worked out with George quite a bit and he was a tyrant, a real taskmaster, but he would never ask you to do anything he wouldn't do himself. He had a variety of ways to make you sweat. George would put you through a gruelling training program consisting of long distance running, sprints, calisthenics and weights, but he'd save one final exercise — usually a tough one — until last. "OK, let's go!" he'd say. "Just 60 more seconds . . . don't stop until I tell you." On you'd plough, your muscles burning like mad. "Gees," you'd think, "this is the longest 60 seconds I've ever experienced." But you wouldn't be game to call it quits until George gave you the word. At last George would shout, "Right, that's enough", and you'd look at the clock and see he'd kept you going for an extra five minutes or more.

Ken Arthurson again had the coaching reins at Brookvale and under his astute hand we won six of our first seven matches. Sadly, a spate of injuries saw us fall in a heap in the second round, when we won only three games out of nine. Athough we missed the semis I was mighty pleased with my own performances that year. In one purple patch I won three *Sun-Herald* best and fairest awards in a row and before falling victim to injury I was leading the prestigious poll by four points.

In those days, the league world waited with baited breath each year for the highly-respected league writer George Crawford to name his five top players of the season. His selections would feature in the grand final edition of the *Sunday Telegraph*. So that Sunday morning when I opened my paper to read how Saints had flogged Easts 31-6 in the premiership decider, I was delighted when old George named Raper, Gasnier, Provan, Jack Gibson and Rex Mossop as the best in the Sydney competition. Wrote Crawford in his citation: "Rex Mossop was by far the most constructive front rower in Australia. Mossop's skill in initiating plays from rucks with clever switches made him a valuable asset to Manly, NSW and Australia. He showed this skill to great effect in the NSW-Queensland game in Brisbane. It enabled the pack to give its best display in many years. Mossop missed several matches late in the season because of an ankle injury he suffered in the Australia-France Third Test. Manly faded in his absence and missed its usual spot in the premiership semi finals. This revealed clearly his great value as a team man."

The French arrived mid-season, and for a while it looked as though I'd miss my chance to play once more against the erratic but often-brilliant Froggies. An ordinary game for Sydney against Country saw me overlooked for the first three games of the four-match interstate series, the City versus France clash and the First Test against the Frenchmen. After some good club form, however, I was reinstated to the NSW side which walloped

Queensland in Brisbane. Raper, Provan, Hambly and I took the Maroons apart and we all made the Second Test side.

Two weeks before, France had snatched an 8-8 draw when fullback Pierre Lacaze goalled seconds before fulltime. Changes had to be made and fortunately for me I was brought into the team at the expense of Gary Parcell. At Brisbane Exhibition Ground in the Second Test, Australia massacred the visitors 56-6 with Bob Bugden and Kenny Irvine each crossing for a hat-trick of tries. I gave the final pass for each of Bugden's three-pointers.

After such a hiding everybody — fans, press, and the Australian players — considered an Aussie win in the remaining Test a formality. It's hard to believe, but those bloody French, so pathetic just a fortnight before, came out and beat us 7-5 at the SCG to square the series. Our cause wasn't helped by some shocking injuries, but, no excuses, the men from France rose to the occasion magnificently and proved once again that there is no such thing as a certainty in rugby league.

After just 20 minutes of the Test Johnny Raper sold me a dump and as I went down my ankle was crunched in a tangle of players. I collapsed over the sideline in agony. Doc Greenberg couldn't diagnose exactly what the problem was. All I could tell him was that it hurt like hell. In those times of no replacements I had to play on, so Len whacked in several shots of novocaine to kill the pain. He also slit my boot up both sides with a razor blade, because the swollen ankle was strangling the blood circulation in my foot. I hobbled around for the rest of the game, tackling when blokes ran within arm's reach and playing dummy half whenever I could. Running with the ball and pushing in scrums was out of the question.

X-rays the following day were bad news. A piece of bone about the size of a one cent coin had broken away from my tibia and lodged in my ankle joint. Greenberg advised surgery, but warned me that going under the knife would keep me out for the rest of the season and end my hopes of being selected in the World Cup team to England, due to be chosen in September.

Doctor Len had one alternative to surgery. He told me that if I could stand the pain of running on the ankle for long periods, the friction would gradually grind away the bone that had lodged itself in the ankle joint. He left me in no doubt that the pain would be crippling, but I had no choice.

So began the most excruciating time of my life. Right throughout July and August I'd shamble every day around North Harbour Park, near my home, logging mile after painful mile. At the end of August x-rays showed a vast reduction in the size of the rogue fragment and by the middle of September it had disintegrated completely and I was able to declare myself fit to play in the World Cup squad selection trial, a match between Metropolitan and Country. The selectors showed faith when they named me captain of the city team, and even more faith when, two weeks later, they included me in the Australian side to travel to England to contest the World Cup with the other league-playing nations.

I knew that at my age this would be my last hurrah as an international so I worked hard to make the top XIII. It was wonderful having Noel Kelly as my roommate. We shared many adventures, some of which are fit to print. Arthur Clues joined the squad as coach and many good times were had with him as well. There was a nice touch, too, at the end of our match against France at Wigan. A contingent of fans from Leigh turned up at the ground and every time I ran with the ball or tackled somebody they gave me a cheer. When the game was over I showered and changed and walked out of the dressing sheds to find a group of about 200 of these old friends waiting to wish me well. It was good to be remembered.

We squeaked in 13-12 against France and my appalling record of injuries against the French continued. During the game one of the opposing props charged at me and his head slammed into my groin. The blow ruptured my stomach lining. There was nothing I could do about the injury except protect it by playing in a girdle-like contraption wadded with sponge rubber for the rest of the campaign. Not a day passed when Ned

Kelly didn't make some crack about his elderly roommate having to wear a truss.

We then beat New Zealand at Leeds and immediately knuckled down for our next game, against England, at Odsal Stadium, Bradford. The old enemy had also beaten France and the Kiwis so our clash would decide the winner of the World Cup.

Although I am as patriotically Australian as the next Aussie, the cakewalks we've enjoyed against Great Britain over the past 20 or so years have given me little real satisfaction. Back in the '50s and '60s, the Poms could play, and although we hated them we respected them, too. An Australia versus Great Britain Test match was the ultimate clash, the best our game had to offer. Beating the Englishmen really meant something then. Today, grand finals and State of Origin matches rate above Tests but, believe me, that wasn't the case when Brian McTigue, Rocky Turner, Alex Murphy, Eric Ashton, Billy Boston and Vince Karalius wore the English jersey.

French referee Edouard Martung lost control from the kickoff, allowing much offside play and plenty of biffo. Gasnier ran riot in the first few minutes, but none of his slicing runs brought tries. The Poms, on the other hand, crossed for two early three-pointers, to the wingers Boston and Sullivan. At halftime it was 10-0 and that's how the score remained for most of the bitterly-contested second half. Brian Carlson scored for us with nine minutes to go to make it 10-3, but his try came too late and we could not bridge the gap.

A dour, gruelling struggle, this match rates as among the hardest I've ever played. It wasn't so much a game as a war. Brawling broke out regularly. Every tackle was accompanied by a punch. The succession of rugged incidents shocked the crowd and had the Australian and British sporting press demanding an inquiry. Everybody was upset except the players. We enjoyed ourselves mightily. The forwards tore into each other, with Parcell, Kelly, Hambly and yours truly squaring off against McTigue, Turner, Wilkinson and Karalius. Volatile little half-backs Muir and Murphy were at each other's throats all day.

Vince Karalius and I had been sniping away throughout the match, swapping blows on two or three occasions. I gave him my best shots every time, but as before I just couldn't hurt him, I couldn't even make him alter the expression on his face which, as usual, was one of stony hatred. Then, with only minutes to go I suddenly realised that this would be the last time we would ever meet on the football field. I don't know why, but it made me a little sad. I loved playing against this implacable foe. I decided it was settling time. Positioning myself directly opposite him across a ruck, I called out to Karalius, "Vince! Time's running out. Let's get into it." An enigmatic smile flickered across that hard face, then, like two old gunfighters facing each other in the final showdown, we waded into each other. Suddenly my arms were pinned from behind by two English forwards and we all collapsed in a melee of flying fists and feet as the biggest all-in of the game broke out. Arthur Clues leapt over the fence to lend his men a hand. The ref blew fulltime and the combatants separated, looked sheepishly at each other, and shook hands.

Karalius and I did meet again. In the '70s the New South Wales Rugby League invited Vince to Australia to be the special guest on Rothmans Medal night. I caught up with him there and made plans to get together before he flew home. Joan and I shouted Vince and his wife to dinner at the Coachman Restaurant in Bourke Street, East Sydney. My old adversary looked every inch the millionaire he had become. Trim, fit-looking and smartly-dressed, he was greying a little at the temples. The man known as the "Wild Bull" was softly-spoken and a complete gentleman. He wanted to know about my TV career and showed interest in Joan's painting. He didn't mention football at all. I talked about the bad old days just once, at the beginning of the meal. Hoping to get the reminiscences flowing, I reminded Vince of his string of knockout victories over me. He didn't take the bait, just smiled that enigmatic smile.

I battled on with Manly for another three seasons, lean seasons for the club, as it turned out. My enthusiasm for the game I loved never flagged, but as I hit my middle 30s I was slowing down, and my reflexes were not what they used to be.

Midway through the 1963 season we were playing Wests at Pratten Park and they were giving us a hiding. Nothing was going right for me. I couldn't bust the line, my passes were not finding runners and I was dropping off tackles. Noel Kelly had linked up with the Magpies by then and with Kel O'Shea and Peter Dimond as his henchmen, Ned had turned Wests into a powerful outfit that came close to ending St George's record run of premierships in two memorable grand finals. The worse I played that day against Wests the crankier I got. O'Shea was an old mate of mine, but I decided to take my frustrations out on him, whacking him at every opportunity. Kel was more interested in winning the game than fighting, but my actions stirred up a few of his teammates who started sledging me.

Late in the game I dropped a simple pass. This prompted a tirade of abuse from one Magpie. I lost my temper completely and charged at this bloke, bellowing obscenities and swinging like a windmill. The Wests pack closed on me. Someone grabbed me while two others started hitting me. Then Noel Kelly, unflustered in any crisis, strolled up and soothed his teammates down. "Come on fellas, leave him alone." Ned's word was law and they backed off. My old friend then turned to me and said, "Listen, if you don't settle down, you silly old bugger, you're going to get yourself killed." Ned's advice sank in. I knew then that my long career was nearing its end. I played my last grade game for Manly against Easts two months later, the final competition match of the 1963 season. We won 18-5 at Brookvale Oval.

Some years before I had made a pact with Ken Arthurson. He knew I'd have to be dragged kicking and screaming into retirement, so we agreed he would be the best judge of when I should give the game away. I would have continued playing into my 40s and 50s if I could have, but Ken was keen for me to get out while I was still a respected first grader. My old friend advised me to retire after that game against Easts. I had every intention of doing so, too, until the countdown to the 1964 season when I decided I'd wear the maroon and white for one final year. I'd played well over 500 games in both codes of rugby, including nine union Tests 10 league Tests and three World Cup matches, and 137 first grade games for Manly, but I wasn't satisfied, I wanted more. So I worked hard on my fitness and was feeling good when I saddled up for a trial game against Souths at the start of the 1964 season. It didn't work out. I was hopeless. Poor timing, dropped passes and missed tackles proved to me that at 36 I was too old to compete any more. I retired that day.

I found it hard to cut my ties with the game that I had played for so long. I attended every match, straining and flinching every time a former teammate would make a break or drop an opponent in a tackle. And that first year out of the game I couldn't quite break the habit of turning up at training every Tuesday and Thursday night. In time, I quit hanging around the Manly camp, but I never stopped training. Fitness became a habit that has lasted all my life.

I threw myself into my career as a car salesman with Stacks, where I'd been employed since 1955, but no matter how good the pay, no matter how many sales records I broke, selling Holdens, Chevrolets and Pontiacs could not fill the gap that retiring from football had left in my life. There was a terrific bunch of blokes working for Stacks then, including Trevor Allan, champion cyclist Lionel Cox, boxers Tony Madigan and Keith Dudley, rugby star Denis Cleary, and St George skipper Ian Walsh. We had a fierce competition to see who could sell the most vehicles each week, then on Fridays we would all meet at the Angus Steak Cave for some epic lunches. I have a hazy memory of driving home from one of these lunches in those pre-RBT days and stopping my car on a traffic cop's foot while trying to turn right into Martin Place.

There were many good times with the boys at Stack and Company, but I was burning for a new challenge. I had all this energy and nothing to channel it into. Selling cars just wasn't extending me. I became irritable around the home, wondering what I was going to do with the rest of my life.

Some time in March, 1964, my boxing mate Keith Dudley told me he had read where Channel 7 were looking for a sports director. I'd done a little TV commentary during Great Britain's victorious tour of Australia in 1962, and accepted a few awards on radio, but I'd never considered a career in the media. I looked at Keith doubtfully when he suggested I should apply for the Channel 7 post. He said, "Mate, it's right up your alley, you're a dual international and your knowledge of other sports is pretty good. And what you don't know, bullshit about."

I turned up, had my interview, then promptly forgot all about it. A couple of months later Channel 7 contacted me and said they wanted to see me again. The personnel manager told me I had been chosen out of 63 other applicants for the very important position of sports director — then he offered me 40 pounds a week! I told him that was a ridiculous amount, and left. Soon after, I had a call from Harry Chester, a shrewd and successful executive who taught the young Kerry Packer plenty about the media when later he joined Sir Frank Packer's organisation. Entering Chester's plush office at the Epping headquarters of the station, I said, "Look, I really don't know why you've asked me in here. I'm a family man and I can't afford to work for peanuts." Chester replied, "Well, things have changed since that first offer. We have some exciting things planned in sport this year and we need someone to start running the show now. We're prepared to pay you more." "How much more?" I said. "Around 110 pounds." "Sorry, Harry. I'd like the job but that's much less than I'm earning selling cars." "OK," he said, "One hundred and fifty, tops." We shook hands.

That night I broke the news to Joan and Dad. Joan was wary. "You're throwing away a solid job with Stacks," she said. "What are we going to do for money if you fail in TV?" I turned to my father. "What do you think I should do, Dad? Should I try my luck in TV?" "Son," the old man said, "I reckon you should give it a go."

13

LIGHTS, CAMERA CONTROVERSY CORNER

Viewers who switched on the Channel 7 evening news for my debut appearance back in May, 1964, would have seen a snappily-dressed, smartly-groomed 36-year-old former footballer confidently relaying the day's sports information from behind what appeared to be a businesslike desk in a spacious, hi-tech newsroom complex. That was the impression, the reality was something else again.

TV studios then were hot, stuffy little makeshift pigeonholes — a table plonked in a spare space of the studio floor with a few backdrops hastily thrown up and a tangle of lethal wires connected to cameras, lights and power sources twisting all over the floor. Behind the scenes there would be directors, technicians, lighting staff, sound and camera men, all jostling to function in the cramped space. As for the suave and composed sportscaster, this night he was in a lather of confusion.

Whoever was floor manager of this fiasco had neglected to clue me in about any of the signals all on-air personalities have to know: signals that tell you which camera to look at, when you have to start talking, when your segment is coming to a close. Out of the corner of my eye, I could see all these people frantically signalling to me, but I had no idea what any of their sign language meant. So, like any moose would, I ignored them and thundered straight through my five-minute report. And as for my sartorial elegance, chances are that my carefully pressed shirt, smart tie and blazer would have been complemented, under the desk and out of camera range, by a pair of old shorts and sandals. In the world of television at least, what you get is not always what you see.

John Bailey was the newsreader at Channel 7 in those days and afterwards he pulled me aside and told me I'd done fine and then explained to me what all the signals meant. I owe John a lot. If he'd told me the truth and said I'd been bloody awful, I probably would have chucked in my TV career there and then, but, as John laughed at the time, "TV is the place to work if you don't mind being thrown in at the deep end." I knew I'd been pretty rough that night, but management had obviously seen a spark of talent somewhere and were as supportive as John Bailey.

I was given great heart by the Seven executive who had hired me, Harry Chester. Harry said to me at the outset, "I'll give you one tip and then I'll leave you alone to run your own race. Don't ever try to be anyone else when you're in front of a camera. Be yourself. You've got a strong personality, so don't try to water it down. If you try to copy other commentators you can say goodbye to your credibility. You've been employed because you're Rex Mossop. If we wanted you to be like anyone else, we would have employed them!"

John Bailey's words about the deep end had even greater significance for me shortly after when I was instructed by Seven's then general manager Jim Oswin to organise a telethon to raise money for Australian athletes competing in the 1964 Tokyo Olympics. Dad had always drummed in to me that when your employer tells you to do something, you do it, so I jauntily said, "Sure, Jim, no problem," then wondered silently what the hell a telethon was.

In the weeks that followed, I found out. A telethon — a marathon TV variety show where appeals are made to viewers to phone in donations to aid a worthy cause — is a logistical nightmare. Again John Bailey, who would co-host the show, gave me mountains of help. I had only a short time to set the whole thing up, and the workload was terrifying. I had to book all the talent who would be appearing on the program, then slot the entire hodgepodge of singers, musicians, magicians, comedians, jugglers, sports stars, actors and other celebrities into a slick entertainment package that would keep viewers glued to their sets for nearly 20 hours. I had to hire all the telephone answerers and the switchboard staff, masterminding their shifts so we'd have a full complement of alert operators throughout the evening, through the night and into the next day. Then there had to be people to keep track of the contributions being phoned in, and other workers to collect the money and make sure it reached the athletes. And all these people had to be fed, so I had to organise catering as well.

Then, on the night of the telethon, my first major TV presenting job, I came down with laryngitis and had to croak my way through the entire production. Apart from this pain in the neck, the telethon was well-received and served its purpose by raising a large sum for the Olympians. Viewers saw a new side to Mossop during the 27 hours straight I was on-air. As well as introducing the acts and keeping the public informed how much money was rolling in, I was kept busy taking on viewers' dares to sing in exchange for a donation, clowning, dancing, swordfighting and playing indoor cricket. I'm afraid I couldn't resist when one member of the public rang in and said he would give the appeal a large cheque if I sang selections from *My Fair Lady*. Accompanied by Seven's musical director Franz Conde, I pulled it off, sore throat and all.

A couple of novelty events I set up were especially popular. There was a weight-lifting competition, cyclists riding bikes on rollers attempting to break speed records, and Olympic boxer Tony Madigan sparring in the studio. The success of these novelty contests started a few bells ringing and I wondered how a live to air football passing competition or a televised armwrestling championship might go down if ever I got the chance to stage them.

Another live TV event I organised was coverage of the 1964

World Surfing Championships at Manly beach, where a little northern beaches surfie named Midget Farrelly beat the world's best to take the title. Televising surfing presents many problems. For a start, you never know whether there will be any waves, and this day there were hardly any at all, just a two-foot chop. To try to make the telecast more interesting for viewers, we put a camera in a helicopter — the first time this had been tried in Australia — and the chopper hovered over the competitors' heads, giving viewers a seagull's eye view of the action. This technique turned a drab event into a visually interesting contest. I learned then that televising sport is a lucky dip, and you have to be flexible enough to accommodate any conditions.

Soon after this, ATN decided to televise speedway racing live from Sydney Showground. It was my job to set the whole telecast up. Speedway was a sport I knew nothing about, contested at night under lights on a dirt track with sound levels pretty near deafening — quite a challenge for a novice. But I learned fast, and with a lot of help from Seven's Mike Raymond, pulled it off, and continued to survive as sports director.

Early in 1965, Jim Oswin came to me and said that the outside telecasts were doing well and could I think of any other sports that we could cover in this way. Straight off, I said, "Rugby league." "Oh no," said Jim, a nice man, but very old-school-tie conservative, "nobody wants to watch professional football. Why don't you contact the rugby union schools convenor and see if we can televise the GPS matches?"

It took me a while to talk Jim out of broadcasting private school rugby but finally I wore him down. "Oh, alright, Rex," he said at last, "contact the Rugby League and see how much money they'd charge us to televise the second half of a match each week." Today TV rights for rugby league are negotiated in an atmosphere similar to that of a presidential summit, with the league and network chiefs, supported by a battery of bankers, lawyers and accountants arguing over millions of dollars. Back then I captured the rights for Channel 7 by making an appointment with the then League president Bill Buckley and offering him 500 quid a match. He accepted my offer, but old Bill had his doubts. He was afraid that people would not go to the games if they could watch football from the comfort of their loungeroom. I countered that TV exposure would introduce the game to a host of new fans who would flock to the grounds. The huge crowds *and* high television ratings that rugby league enjoys today is proof that I was correct.

The final details were ironed out, and weeks later live league was being beamed across the state. The outside broadcast van would wheel up to Leichhardt Oval or Kogarah Jubilee or wherever, one or two cameramen would fix their heavy equipment in position, I'd squeeze myself into my tiny commentary perch in some hastily constructed scaffolding, Bill Kerr or, later, Barry Ross would feed me the statistics, and off we'd go. Compared with the slick presentation and state-of-the-art camera work today, what we offered viewers back in the '60s and early '70s was primitive fare, real Dark Ages stuff. Once at the SCG they rigged up a large wooden backdrop for me to stand in front of and conduct interviews. I'd just said, "Welcome to the important Cronulla-Western Suburbs clash ..." when this great bloody backdrop came crashing down on my head. The cameras caught it all as I roared, "I can't work under these f . . . . . . conditions."

The accident and my furious reaction did not make it to air, but mysteriously they found their way onto every blooper show in the world. In spite of, or perhaps because of, incidents such as these, the public tuned in each weekend and my career as a football caller was underway.

That first year in television was not easy. Many times, confounded and frustrated by the technical demands of my job, I nearly gave it all away and returned to selling cars. But then I would think that if only I could master this strange new medium I could set Joan, the boys and myself up for life. So I worked 14-hour days, I filled pad after pad with notes about the intricacies of TV, I listened to the production experts and learned from pros like John Bailey, and I would practice my on-air delivery and mannerisms driving from Balgowlah to the Epping studios and home again each day.

For a while I attended speech classes given by an elderly actor in an office at the lower end of George Street, Sydney. First up he asked me to say something, anything, so I reeled off about a minute of football commentary. "Well, Mr Mossop," he said, "the voice is fine, but we've just got to make it a little more, er, *mellifluous*. Now, repeat after me, 'How now, brown cow . . .' No, Mr Mossop, not so nasal! Now, again . . . 'The rain in Spain falls mainly on the plain'" . . . all that Henry Higgins crap. I recited my elocution exercises, but not very enthusiastically, and soon the old fellow saw the light and gave me the same advice that Harry Chester had given me at the beginning. "Mr Mossop," he intoned with a Shakespearian flourish, "my advice to you is to act naturally." This is exactly what I was hoping he'd say.

In time I developed an excellent working knowledge of the technical side of TV, and my on-camera style, too, fell into place. There was no point in being forced or fake, trying to be slick and smooth. No, I decided, Harry Chester, the old voice coach and my own instincts were spot-on: the best way to make my mark in TV was to be myself, down to earth, opinionated and forthright. If I had an itch I'd scratch it, if I felt uncomfortable in my seat I'd squirm. I never bothered with idiot boards or cue cards because I had a natural talent for ad-libbing, always saying whatever came into my skull. And I never worried too much about dropping the odd "bloody" or some other healthy and harmless Australianism. I was a boots 'n' all football player and I became a boots 'n' all TV personality.

I have never suffered from stage fright. Getting up in front of people and performing was second nature to my Dad, and it is second nature to me. I had nerves before going out to play a big football game, I'd have terrible butterflies and be continually urinating for hours before kickoff, but I can honestly say that I have never been nervous on TV. I am perfectly relaxed in front of a camera or microphone. The bloke you see on your TV screens is exactly the bloke I am in real life.

In my time, TV critics have branded me abrasive, aggressive and pig-headed. I'm proud to stand guilty of all of these. TV is no place for shrinking violets. I long ago realised that I was not blessed with a bland, pleasant personality. I am big and loud and forceful, I *can* be a bastard, and I have been this way all my life.

I never set out to be controversial, and, God knows, I would have had a quieter, happier life if I had compromised more often, but I am a simplistic, black and white person. When I form an opinion — whether it's about why rugby league is not the game it used to be, what makes a man a man, or why Australia is in moral decline — I'll fight for it. And I'm happy to tell those who disagree with me that they are wrong. I'm not afraid of a blue. I learned early on to be comfortable with being both loved and hated in equal measure for my TV work. When I make a statement about something I never care what people think. It's my view and I'm not concerned whether viewers like what I'm saying or not. They can please themselves, I don't have to account to anybody. As long as people say, "Gee, that bloke really believes what he's saying," I'm happy.

One of my very first projects at ATN back in 1964 was to host a Sunday morning general sports program. Once more we were breaking new ground. A program of this type had never been done before on Australian TV but I had enormous faith that such a show would succeed. That first half-hour program which kicked off at the graveyard hour of 11am was called *Sports Action*. High ratings saw it lengthened to an hour and then, under its new name of *Sports World*, it was extended to two and a half hours and then three hours, stretching from 9am until noon. I hosted and produced the program for 24 years. Apart from the news, it remains the longest running show in Australian television history.

We started off on a shoestring budget, just me at the desk with a couple of sports photos or trophies as props. I'd run though a variety of sporting news, and sometimes they'd screen a film clip to illustrate what I was saying. As rough and ready as the show was when it started out, people tuned in in droves. Like roast dinners and backyard family cricket matches, the program became a Sunday institution in hundreds of thousands of homes. So many people come up to me today and tell me their favourite *Sports Action* or *Sports World* memory, often reminding me of incidents I'd long ago forgotten. As the ratings picked up, Channel 7 decided to spend a little more money on us, extending our time, giving me a few co-presenters and allowing me to run more film.

I reckon I had the mix just right. In our extended version, we'd kick off a winter Sunday program with an hour of general sport: overseas news, a rugby segment, five or 10 minutes of soccer with Johnny Warren, a terrific racing roundup with Ian Craig, Max Presnell and Frank Kennedy, some athletics or motor racing perhaps . . . And then it was into the rugby league.

The show gave me a terrific opportunity to promote my great sporting love. I was always so concerned with doing the right thing by league. Yes, I'd been sent off a few times and had a wildman reputation when I played, but I'd always worn a coat and tie when interviewed on TV or when accepting awards, could speak well, and was ever-conscious of projecting a good image for the game and its players in public. I carried this stance into the show. I always tried to portray league matters intelligently and constructively and was always exhorting viewers to get out to the ground to see the match live as soon as the show ended.

I had an iron rule that all guests and presenters on my programs be decently attired — from the waist up at least! I always wore a jacket and tie but, because I usually conducted the show from behind a desk, I could remain cool below decks in shorts and sandals. Roy Ferguson, the St George centre, turned up one day in shorts and T-shirt, so I made him put on a jacket and tie and asked the cameraman to film only Roy's head and shoulders. He did so, but at the end of the interview he pulled back to reveal Ferguson's shorts and thongs. Thousands of people in their lounge rooms copped an eyeful of Roy's hairy legs under the table. What an awful sight to inflict on viewers early on a Sunday morning!

Sports World was telecast from Channel 7's Studio A. In the show's heyday in the '70s, there was a desk which seated three people for general sport presentations and interviews, and a racing desk where Presnell, Craig and co did their segment. Behind these desks there was a rear screen projection set-up on which relevant footage was shown as the presenters talked. As host of the show, I had a desk to myself on the right hand wall of the studio. There was a space where we positioned the giant target for the Commonwealth Bank Passing Competition and other areas where we'd conduct arm-wrestling and cycling competitions. Cameras would be wheeled from set to set as the show progressed.

One segment everyone remembers is the passing competition. Each week we'd invite two prominent league players into the studio. Dressed in their club jersey, shorts, socks and sandshoes, they'd stand on a chalk line on the studio floor and pass footballs at a huge plywood target, marked out like a dartboard but with a cartoon elephant painted on the top, about six metres away. The object was to pass the ball through the bullseye on the target, upon which, a loud bellowing sound would blast out from behind the prop.

There was a strict procedure to follow every week. I'd introduce the segment and then ask, "Well, who's first cab off the rank?" at which one of the players would step forward and do his thing. Retrieving the balls was my Controversy Corner panellist Ferris Ashton, a former Easts star who would pick the used footballs up one-handed and toss them back to the other contestant who would then have his go at making the elephant roar. It was an elimination contest and at the end of the football season we'd invite all the winners into the studio for a finals series. The eventual winner received a handsome cheque from the Commonwealth Bank.

In 1972, Manly won their first grand final and Sea Eagle captain Freddie Jones, a notorious knockabout, was scheduled to compete in the final of the passing competition the day after the historic win. We knew this was fraught with danger. As expected, Fred turned up at the studio straight from the victory celebrations and he was as drunk as a parrot. You could smell his boozy breath from 30 feet away. Getting the preliminary interview with the staggering skipper over and done with as fast as we decently could, we positioned Freddie on the chalk mark and pointed him in the general direction of the target. He was so under the weather he could barely stand up, let alone see what he was supposed to be aiming at. Then, to our everlasting astonishment, Fred passed every ball right through the bullseye. The elephant trumpeted itself hoarse as Freddie cleaned up the prize money.

The Passing Competition was cheap, basic entertainment, but it was a lot of fun. One day the international forward Ron "Thirsty" Lynch was a contestant. A superb passer of the ball, we expected him to wipe the floor with the opposition. We don't know if Thirsty had been living up to his nickname before the program or not, but his first pass missed the target completely, sailing high over the elephant's head and into the gloom at the rear of the set. The entire studio broke up as we laughed and hooted at Thirsty's abortive attempt. Ron's pass brought the entire show to a hilarious halt.

Another great novelty was the arm-wrestling competition. Two footy players would grip each other's wrist across a table. We'd play the theme from *Rocky*, read the rules, which called for elbows to be square on the bench and no daylight between the contestant's bum and his chair, and they'd strain away until one man pinned the other's arm to the table. The bloke who won hands down was the former rugby union international Steve Knight, who played league with Wests and Manly. He was a beautifully-built fellow with a huge and powerful physique. Like many strong men, he was a gentle giant, but nobody could best him at arm wrestling. I'd run into him often down at Manly beach where he was a beach inspector. Being such a shy and self-effacing guy, he never considered himself an attractive man, but you should have seen the girls lust after him.

Looking back on my *Sports World* days, the best part for me was Controversy Corner. Just thinking about it makes me smile. Seated around an old square table mounted on a platform in the studio would be the respected *Sydney Morning Herald* league writer Alan Clarkson, my old football sparring mate Noel "Ned" Kelly who was as quick with a quip as he was with a right hand and should have had his own show, former top referee Col Pearce, good old Ferris Ashton, known to us all as "Ferdie", and a guest panellist, usually a league star. John "Rupert" Mudge, an old football mate, and sports publisher Jack Pollard also did stints on the panel.

Our mission? To discuss "pertinent league matters". Ned and Ferdie were funny, funny men who knew their football, and their antics would be balanced by the calm authority of the knowledgable Clarkson and Pearce. I'd be at the head of the table stirring things up, putting the panellists down when they got out of hand — and always having the final say. Sometimes, when I felt in the mood, I'd take the chance to pontificate about any subject that took my interest, whether it had to do with football or not.

With Noel Kelly and I on the panel, one recurring topic of discussion was biffo. Ned and I were quick to hand out a bit of rough justice when we played, but Col Pearce, who'd been a thorn in both our sides in his refereeing days, would have none of it. He reminded us that nobody ever won an argument with a referee — but on Controversy Corner I was the man with the whistle and I kept Col in his place.

Before the cameras rolled we'd put our heads together for 10 minutes, quickly run through the current crop of controversies, then set a very rough agenda for the segment. It was all very much ad-lib, we'd talk over the top of each other and arguments would break out like brushfires. No subject was taboo, and each panellist could say what he liked. But I had one hard, fast rule:

that we never forget that we were there to entertain the viewers. The Controversy Corner panel was guilty of many things, but we were never dull. I loved to get under Ferdie's skin. He'd bite at anything. Once he proudly told the viewers that his son was playing that day in a grand final in the country. "That's all very well, Ferdie," I grumbled, "but if he was any good he'd be playing in Sydney!"

Controversy Corner, like the passing competition, had a basic format. Each panellist would dissect a game from last week's round, then the show would be thrown open for a general free-for-all, we'd tip that afternoon's winners, and finally the guest panellist would be presented with a swagful of prizes. There was no money in the budget to pay guests an appearance fee in those days so we loaded them up with the sponsors' products. "No guest goes away empty-handed," I'd say, then weigh the poor bloke down with a Fabiani shirt, a Meapro ham, Pantene "for the wig", Bernard moccasins, Brut aftershave, Dencorub, Patra orange juice and a voucher that would get them a session in a Viking sauna. When giving away this last prize, I'd always turn to Ferris and say, "You're looking good today, Ferdie" and he'd respond, "I *feel* good, Rex. And here's why. I've just had my Viking sauna." Then he'd launch into a spiel on the benefits of steam rooms. More than one person wondered at the time, however, that if the beefy Ferdie spent so much time in saunas, how come he never lost any weight!

Unlike today, when the players are instructed to dutifully thank the sponsor whenever they receive an award on air, way back then they'd make do with a simple, "Thanks, Rex" and be off. And, unlike many of today's programs, we always encouraged our guests to say what they thought. The panel pulled no punches and it was expected of guests that they earn their booty by making honest, straight from the shoulder comments. These days players give interviewers the same old stock responses to every question: "We stuck to our guns and we came up trumps" or "Hats off to the opposition but we were the better team on the day" or "We beat ourselves with some silly mistakes". You've heard it all. The interview ends and nobody is any the wiser.

I have so many memories of the old Controversy Corner days . . . of towering Norm Provan leaning back on his chair, over-balancing, and then, like a big oak tree after it's been felled, toppling slowly backwards off the platform. The cameras caught the big man crashing to the studio floor. It seemed to take an age for Sticks to hit the deck and as he went down we all chorused "Timberrrr!"

Then there was the time I had to do a live commercial for a sponsor who manufactured portable toilets. We'd cut to a commercial break as I took up my position beside the toilet. Thinking I had plenty of time before we were back on air, I looked at the damn thing there on the studio floor and announced to the panellists, "Gee, just looking at it gives me the shits!" Of course, the cameras were rolling live and all of Sydney knew what I thought of the bloody portable toilet.

And I'm still reminded of the day I declared Controversy Corner a non-metric zone. The metric system had just been introduced, but like the dinosaur I am I wanted no part of it. "It was the 25-yard line when I played and it will remain the 25-yard line. There will be no 22-metre lines on my show!" I declared. Occasionally management winced at some of the things they heard us say and I can remember after I'd made my notorious comment about the toilet I received a gentle reminder from management that Sunday was not the day for bad language.

A little showmanship went a long way. I remember being given a sporting book to promote on the program once. It was a huge, thick thing that was riddled with errors. Instead of eulogising it as I was supposed to do, I held the book up and told the viewers, "Now this book has been written by a supposed sporting expert and it's full of mistakes and is not worth a cracker." I then hurled the volume as hard as I could and it hit the studio wall with a resounding *crack*. Another time I made a bet that I would kiss a bulldog if Canterbury won a particular

The long walk. Sent off playing for NSW against the 1958 English rugby league tourists.

News Ltd

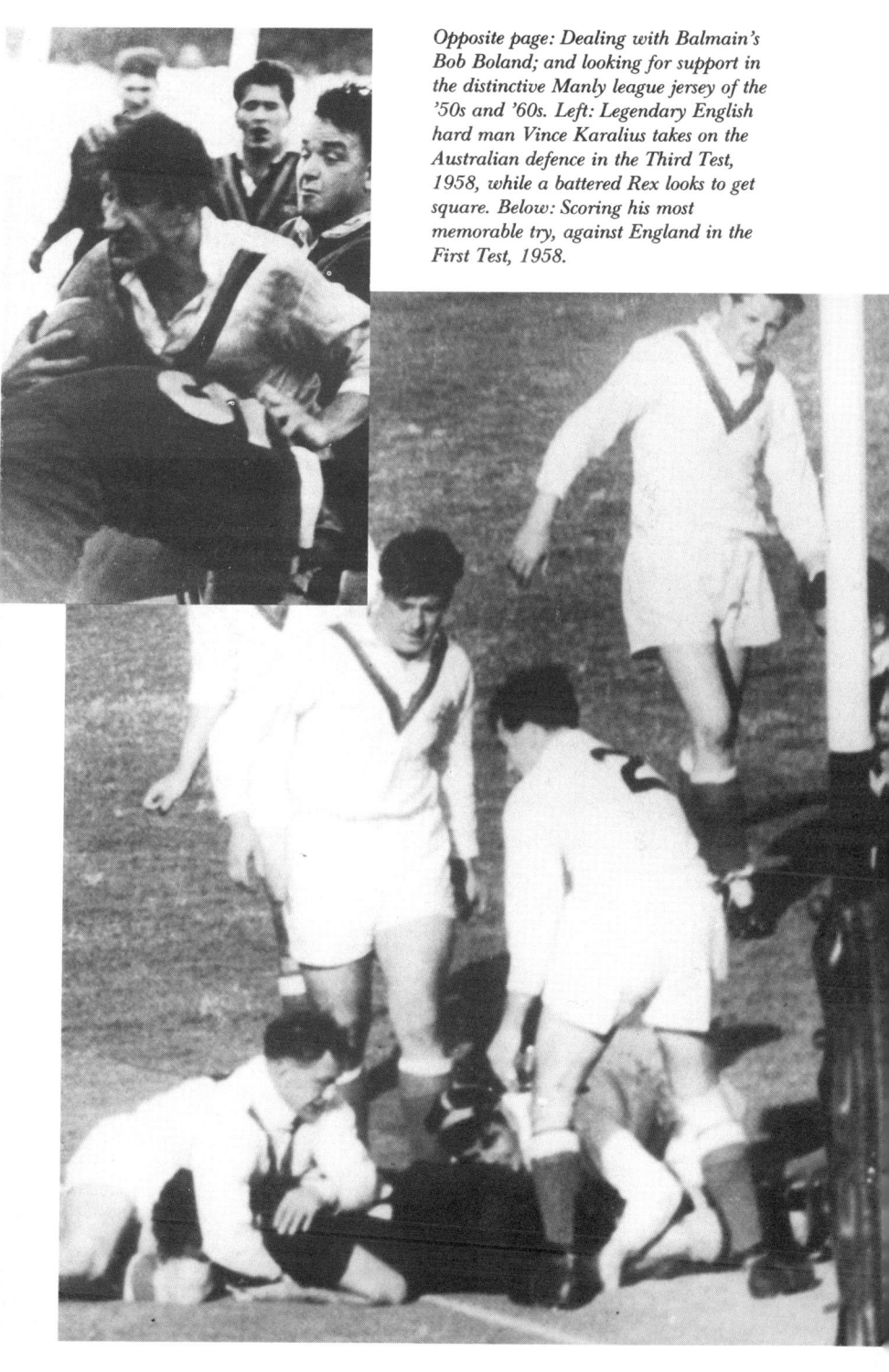

Opposite page: Dealing with Balmain's Bob Boland; and looking for support in the distinctive Manly league jersey of the '50s and '60s. Left: Legendary English hard man Vince Karalius takes on the Australian defence in the Third Test, 1958, while a battered Rex looks to get square. Below: Scoring his most memorable try, against England in the First Test, 1958.

SMH

SMH

Opposite page: Crunching Wests' Mark Patch; and being wrong-footed by the classy English centre Eric Ashton during the 1958 Test series. Above: A flareup with rival St George forward and 1959 Kangaroo teammate Billy Wilson. Saints swept Manly and every other team aside in their run of 11 straight premierships between 1956 and 1966.

Opposite page: The charging Moose; and copping a broken cheekbone against Wests in the '59 final. This page: The Mossop-Bath feud erupts in the 1959 grand final. Above: Bath belts Diversi, who had come to Rex's aid. Mossop cautioned by referee Darcy Lawler. Below: Bath and Mossop (far right) get their marching orders after their marathon punch-up.

Top: The '59-'60 Kangaroos. Noel Kelly is second row, first on left; Harry Wells is next to him; manager Jack Argent is fourth from the left; Ken Irvine and Reg Gasnier are seventh and eighth from the left in the second line; Rex is fifth from left in the third line; in the back row, John Raper is first on the left, Clive Churchill and Brian Clay fourth and fifth along the line. Above: The Second Test team, 1958. Provan, O'Shea and Mossop are third, fourth and fifth in the second row. Right: Vice captain Mossop with Kangaroo skipper Keith Barnes.

Next page: Six of the best: Clockwise from top left — Norm Provan, Jack Gibson, Reg Gasnier, Johnny Raper, Brian Bevan, Clive Churchill.

Top: French league boss Antoine Blaine tries to quell trouble in a '59 tour match. Above: Setting up Raper and Gasnier for NSW. Right: On tour in '59 with Clive Churchill, Tony Brown and John Raper.

Above : Turning a cauliflower ear to Controversy Corner panellists Alan Clarkson, Jack Pollard and Ferris Ashton. Left: The Sports World compere in trademark garb.

Channel 7

Right: Sports World's passing competition was a viewer's favourite for years. Here another contestant tries to make the elephant bellow.

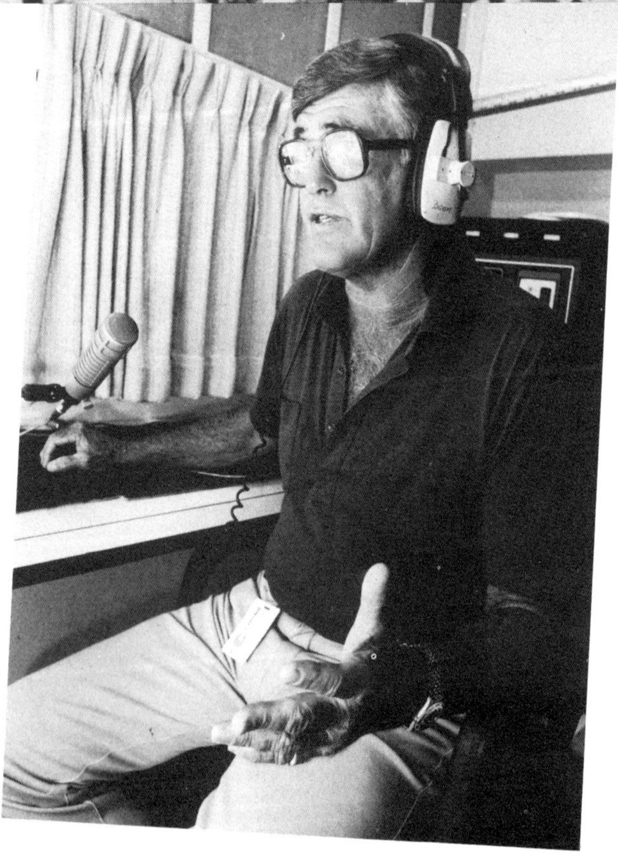

Above: Starring in a beer commercial. The marlin was tagged and set free. Right: In the Channel 7 commentary box.

Phillip Lock/ SMH

Opposite page: With Sixty Minutes' Jeff McMullen; and keeping fit with Wayne Pearce.

Opposite page: Talking sport with fellow veteran commentator Mike Gibson.

Above: The doting granddad with grandchildren Jessica and Rebecca. Right: Romping with Sam and Sheba. Below: Relaxing by the pool at home.

Happy and mellow, Joan and Rex today.

A face in the crowd.

game. They did win and I was true to my word and gave this ugly old bulldog a big smack on the chops for the cameras. To my shock and embarrassment, not to mention the viewers', the amorous mutt reciprocated by doing his darndest to make love to my left arm.

Sydney journalist Mike Colman reminisced in an article a few years ago about the old Controversy Corner days. He was an avid watcher of the show. I believe he summed *Sports World* up for a lot of people when he wrote: "It was a comforting feeling to know Rex would be there every Sunday with his right wing views a little to the west of Ollie North, his editorials ranging from Iran to Henson Park, his unsubstantiated claims of having mastered every sport from lacrosse to the Eton Wall game. And, above all, it was nice to know that however close the Yanks were to dropping the bomb on the Russians, however bad the famine got in Biafra or the flood in Bangladesh, however far the dollar dropped and the size of Weston's Waggon Wheels shrunk, one thing remained constant — the panel would always tip Penrith at Penrith.

"In the early days there was Rex first, daylight second. Sunday *was* Rex Mossop. The show might have been called *Sports World* or some such thing, but to us it was just 'Rex'. Not 'Rex's Show', not 'The Rex Show' — just 'Rex'."

14

IN THE COMMENTARY BOX

What makes a good rugby league commentator? After 27 years in the job, I feel qualified to judge. The first thing is that you must know what you're talking about. Sounds obvious, but, believe me, there are plenty of callers who don't. Television commentators need different qualities to radio broadcasters. On TV there is no need to say, ". . . and Meninga passes to Lewis who gives it to Ettingshausen", viewers can see that for themselves. But if you can read the game of rugby league, if you have a feel for the sport, you can help people understand tactics, give them an overview of proceedings on the field and really increase their enjoyment of the match. A good commentator can tell viewers in advance that there's a move on if the ball is switched to the blindside, that if the fullback is up in the defensive line a chip and chase might bring results. A caller who knows his business can tell people when a side is beginning to wilt.

I hold a referee's ticket, and that's a good credential for a commentator to have. You're dead if you don't know the rules. You have to do your homework and get to recognise the players; not just their names, but their shape, their physical characteristics and idiosyncrasies, what their strengths and weaknesses as footballers are. You need a good eye and accuracy. You need credibility; it's not necessary for viewers to love you, but they have to believe what you are telling them. A caller worth his salt requires a good working knowledge of the tons of technical equipment that beams his voice into millions of homes. And if all this is not enough, you have to be an entertainer. It is a skill to recreate for viewers the atmosphere of a game, to make them believe, when they listen to your description, that they are actually in the crowd.

A match can be brought to life when a commentator raises and lowers his voice, when he gets excited and makes outspoken comments about incidents or players.

Being a high-profile commentator has given me the opportunity to campaign for the return of the man to man punch-up, which was such an exciting part of league in my time. I'll believe until the day I die that two men relieving their inevitable frustrations in a one-on-one stoush is far preferable to a bloke getting even by snidely driving his knees or elbows into his opponent when the referee is not looking. The powers-that-be are sanitising our game to death. Rugby league is a fierce body contact sport, for goodness sake. It's not ballet. TV and radio are terrific platforms for me to get stuck into the League bigwigs about my other pet hates: the replacement and interchange rules. These rules eliminate the courage and endurance factors from a game which once was based on these qualities. Nobody can ever accuse me of not making my feelings known.

Among the present crop of TV commentators, I've got time for Darrell Eastlake; his raucous style does not suit everyone and he cops a lot of criticism but his enthusiasm is infectious. Darrell only covers a few games a year and it's hard coming in cold. Quite a few times I've phoned him at his home in Newcastle to give him a pat on the back. Billy Anderson, too, has an encyclopaedic knowledge of football, but finds himself in the difficult situation at Channel TEN of having to compete against the other commentators to get his precise insights across. Billy's strong suit is analysis, yet he was hired at TEN to provide the "colour" - that is, "It's a fine, cool day here at North Sydney Oval, streamers are flying and here come the Bears in black and red . . ." — and he admits to being uncomfortable with this kind of commentary. Warren Boland on the ABC does a good job. Way-

ne Pearce is a nice, good-looking young fellow, an acknowledged expert and a terrific personality, but at present seems
more comfortable on radio than television. In a short time, he'll
be one of the best. Junior just needs a little more experience,
that's all. Same goes for Peter Sterling. On radio, John McCoy
and Jon Harker on my station 2GB are as good as they come,
while Ray Hadley, a trained race caller and auctioneer, does an
excellent job on 2UE.

The man all commentators owe a debt to is Frank Hyde.
Frank is a true gentleman who stands for everything that is good
about league. He was a man who could really bring a game to
life. An accomplished player in his day, Frank knew and loved
league and can lay claim to being the doyen of all callers with his
"It's long enough, it's high enough, it's straight between the
posts!" There, seated at his little 2SM desk on the sideline, he
would call the game, read the ads, do the interviews, present the
awards. Frank had tremendous dignity, which he only let drop
when delivering one of his trademark tonguelashings to some
poor ballboy who had the temerity to stand between him and
the action. And he could sing as well. The tragedy with Frank
was that he worked in an era where his station got away with
paying him peanuts. He deserved more.

England's answer to Frank Hyde was Eddie Waring, long
dead now. Eddie was a charming old guy who rated his ears off
in the north of England, but he didn't know a bloody thing
about football. His commentaries were a disgrace. "They don't
have lineouts in league, you know," he'd say in his broad northern accent. "In this game they don't have lineouts, oh no. Instead they have scrums, 10 yards in from the sideline they'll
have a scrum. You'll see this little laddie coming up on the left
hand side. He's the one who puts the ball in. No.7, yes, that's
him, Alex Murphy. He's put the ball in. I told you he would.
There's no lineouts in this game, you know . . ." and on and on
like this. He was a lovable conman who pulled the wool over the
BBC's eyes for many years. The fans knew better, though.
Whenever he'd come into a ground the whole crowd would

erupt in unison, "Eddie Waring is a bum! Eddie Waring is a bum!" That's what they thought of Eddie.

I've never made any secret of my affection for the Manly-Warringah side. For God's sake, I played with them for years and have lived in the area almost all my life. Why wouldn't I support them? I don't expect any of you to believe me, but throughout my commentating career I have always been tougher on Manly than on other teams. Perhaps because they are my team I try to avoid accusations of bias by being super-critical of them when I think they deserve it. When Manly score a sensational try, I'll pull right back and might grudgingly mutter that they've done well, but if poor Sea Eagle defence lets in a soft try, I'll give them hell.

I remember calling Manly's first grand final win back in 1972. I was almost out of my seat with excitement but of course I couldn't show it. And when Manly won their second premiership in that wild and woolly grand final of 1973, one of the greatest matches I have ever seen, I had to restrain myself from leaping out of the commentary box and belting big Cliffy Watson, the Cronulla forward who was inflicting so much damage on the Sea Eagle six. But, once again, I had to keep my commentary even-handed. However, the time when it was hardest for me to keep my loyalty in check was in a final between Manly and Balmain at the SCG in the 1960s. I'd bet $2000 on Manly to win and they were leading until the last 10 seconds when the big Tiger winger George Reubner crashed over to snatch the game for Balmain. I was devastated at losing my dough when my bet had looked safe for all money, but I gritted my teeth and enthusiastically congratulated the winners. No viewer would have guessed that the team I was praising so heartily had just cost me two grand.

In 1990 I copped a huge blast from Manly coach Graham Lowe when I got stuck into the Sea Eagle forwards for being too soft. He accused me of being insulting and negative. Lowie's a top bloke, but I treated his criticism with the contempt I felt it deserved. If I think something, no-one on this earth is going to stop me from saying it.

Sometimes the hardline views that I espoused on TV got me into trouble. I've been threatened by some very tall poppies indeed who took exception to my comments about them. Mostly the targets of my criticism write to me to complain or will have a go at me in the press. So far I have never been physically threatened, although some thin-skinned sportsmen have at times dealt physically with media critics. Just this year a rugby league Test player had to be restrained from belting a high-profile journalist who had criticised his performance in a State of Origin match. And back in the late '60s Bill Mordey, the knockabout Sydney sports journo who's now promoting Jeff Fenech's fights, had his car filled with garbage by a group of international footballers who were angry about something he'd printed. However, you can't worry about things like that. As I said earlier, a man without enemies is a pussy-footer. If you want the public to respect you, it's not enough to wear nice clothes, blow-dry your hair, put your face on TV, say something nice about everyone, and collect your six-figure salary.

There have been times when a coach has asked me to give one of his players a bake on air. If a bloke deserves it, I'll single him out. I never think twice about dishing out criticism. I copped plenty of knocks myself when I was playing, it's part of the game. If a player can't take constructive criticism, it's his problem, not mine.

I once fell out with Ron Coote, a great bloke and a superb footballer who has long been a good mate. I was calling a game at the Sydney Sportsground and my commentary went something like this: "So-and-so's broken through and the tryline's wide open, but here comes Ronnie Coote across in cover. He'll nail this bloke beautifully ..." Well, Ronnie didn't nail the bloke. The fellow pushed him off and went on to score. "What a terrible effort from one of the game's greatest tacklers," I roared, "a seven year old could have stopped that fellow in his tracks!" I really gave Ronnie a going-over. Some weeks later I ran into Ron and he said, "Gee, Rex, I thought you were my friend. Why did you criticise me like that?" I replied, "Ron, you're an international, one of the best cover defenders who ever lived. When you miss a tackle like that one, it's news. It was my duty to blast you." He knew there was nothing personal in my attack. Ron accepted my explanation on the chin and we resumed our friendship.

Not everybody is as nice as Ron Coote. One of the worst things about being in the public eye is that nutters and cranks consider you fair game. I've had death threats, obscene phone calls, had louts hurl insults from cars, and meals in restaurants interrupted by rude fools who want me to settle a bet about why the ref awarded a penalty in the 32nd minute of the 1947 grand final. There was even a shot fired at the Channel TEN gatekeeper's box. No doubt because of something I'd said!

If you establish a reputation as an aggressive, tough-talking bloke, there inevitably comes the time when you are forced to back up your words with action. I've never shirked a physical confrontation. What can anybody do to me that hasn't been done before? Break my nose, my leg, my hand, make me bleed? Been there, done that.

There was one incident at Leichhardt Oval. Easts were playing Wests in an Amco Cup match and this night I was a spectator at the ground. It was 1978 and Arthur Beetson was at the height of his powers and he was carving the Magpies to pieces. Suddenly I saw a clown in the crowd hurl a full can of beer right at Artie's head. Luckily it missed. A full can thrown hard from 40 metres' range could have terminated the great forward on the spot. I could not believe my eyes. Not only had this bastard tossed the can, but at least 50 other people had seen him do it and not one had done anything about it. Without a thought I plunged into the crowd and fronted the can thrower. "You idiot! And —" I looked around at the other spectators, "the rest of you are not much better!" I grabbed the culprit and told him off long, loud and colourfully, but it was not just him I was furious with, it was every single person there who had seen the incident and not had the guts to detain this bloke and hand him over to the police. While I was giving the can-thrower a verbal going-over he kept standing up in his seat and I kept pushing him back down again. He was quaking in fear. I ordered someone to call a policeman — "*Now!*" One spectator reluctantly attracted the attention of a cop who pushed his way through to the scene of the crime. "What's up, Rex?" he asked. I told him and he carted the fellow away, saying, "A can thrower, eh? We love to meet people like you!"

In all my commentating career the worst technical hitch I ever encountered was when I was presenting *Sports Action* and all the monitors went black. There I was giving a running commentary of some big event and all of a sudden I'm staring at blackness. I was forced to ad-lib for what seemed an eternity until they sorted the problem out. The biggest challenge I ever faced was when a technicians' strike meant I had to call the 1979 grand final from a monitor back in the Channel 7 studio at Epping. It was not easy trying to recreate the wonderful atmosphere of grand final day when you're sitting alone in a tiny studio 25 kilometres from the action.

There have been many exciting technical advances in sports televising during my time as a commentator. Colour, of course, which came in 1974, was the greatest boon to sports television. Rugby league is the ultimate TV spectacle in colour. The game is made for it. But there was also the video disc, invented in 1964 by the Japanese for the Tokyo Olympics, which replayed events as often as you wished. Then came the slow-motion replay, head-on cameras positioned in the in-goal area, the tracking shot where we put the big, heavy cameras of the early days on a little railway track set-up on the sideline and the operator would haul them along the chalkmark. As cameras grew lighter, cameramen were able to run up and down the sideline with them, soundman in tow with a microphone, to give a close-up view of a player being hurled into touch or a team pounding away at the opposition tryline. Before long, there were more and more cameras covering the game, from every conceivable distance and angle, until we reached the stage we're at today where our sports telecasting is the best in the world.

The commentator is the frontman everybody sees, but, really, it's the director who makes a telecast happen. He's the one who decides whether viewers see a medium shot showing, say, 15 or 18 of the players as the ball is kicked off, or a tighter shot encompassing seven or eight men in a passing raid, or a close-up that brings us tight enough to read the label on a player's boot as he dives across the tryline. A good director knows exactly what shot to use and when, and he calls the images and angles so deftly that the story of the game is told naturally in pictures without the viewer even being aware of the camera changes. As caller of the game, I'd watch both the action on the field as well as the monitor which showed the pictures viewers were seeing in their homes, so the commentary flow was in synch with what was happening on the screen.

Glitches are part and parcel of television broadcasting. Luckily in my time at Channel 7 and later at TEN I worked with excellent teams of professionals. The blokes behind the scenes — the producers, directors, floor managers, cameramen, sound and lighting people, electricians — are the unsung heroes of TV and without them you don't have a program. I was fortunate enough to have some terrific men and women backing me up. I always tried to be professional and do my presentations in a single take with as little fuss as possible and that made their job easier. I never had any problem getting on with the crew. Not all TV personalities can say that. If a star is conceited, a bit up himself, these backroom boys can make life bloody difficult.

Even so, I had a reputation for impatience and often I would have blow-ups when I felt someone in the team had blundered, but like all my outbursts they were short-lived and quickly forgotten. TV is a volatile medium and I was not Robinson Crusoe in angrily delivering character readings when deserved. I have only ever uttered the great Anglo-Saxon four-letter word on TV once. We were at the SCG at an important stage of a match and, from memory, a Telecom technician accidentally disconnected the line leading from the commentary position to the outside broadcast van, cutting transmission. I was left in limbo for some minutes while the crew worked feverishly to rectify the error. But they weren't working fast enough for me. I exploded, "For Christ's sake," I shouted at my director, "what the f . . . .'s going on?" My exasperation earned me yet another rap on the knuckles from a station management that, although they sometimes didn't know quite what to make of me, sure enjoyed the ratings I pulled in.

15

KING OF THE CLUB SHOW

B ack in 1968 Bill Collins ruled the Saturday night TV roost. The big, beaming, and extremely popular movie buff introduced his wonderful golden oldies with his inimitable mixture of gushing enthusiasm and uncanny ability to identify the third chorus girl from the left in an ancient Busby Berkeley musical as a young Lucille Ball. Viewers loved him — and still do — as much as the films he presented on *The Golden Years Of Hollywood*. Bill, like Brian Henderson and, I suppose, myself, is a great survivor in an industry that eats its own. The challenge facing channels Two, Nine and Seven was how to topple Mr Movies.

At ATN we decided we wouldn't compete head-on with Bill by screening films, but give viewers something completely different. We'd bring the atmosphere of the local Leagues or RSL club right into people's living rooms. General manager Ted Thomas sounded me out about hosting the *Club Show*, a new low-budget program which would go to air live from the studios every Saturday night and offer viewers variety, interviews, competitions, news and opinion and regular live coverage of the trotting and greyhound races to keep the punters satisfied. Franz Conde, a very talented and experienced chap, would be the producer. "We've decided to go ahead with it," Thomas said, "and the host's job is yours if you want it."

Presenting sport was what I was best at, and what I loved to do, but the idea of hosting *The Club Show*, simulating that very Australian club atmosphere in a TV studio, appealed to me. The show would be aimed at people who couldn't get out to their local club on a Saturday night and had already seen *Casablanca* 27 times. With Dad's words of advice that you should always do what the man who pays your wage wants you to do ringing in my ears, I accepted the station's offer on the spot.

Don't get the idea that I was a "yes man" at Seven. I got on well with a succession of bosses there, Jim Oswin, Ted Thomas, Bruce Gyngell who dreamed up the successful "Seven Revolution" campaign, but some of my rows with these fellows became legendary in media circles. I remember one rip-snorter I had with general manager Ted Thomas, the bloke who offered me *The Club Show*. It's funny, today I can't even remember what it was we were fighting about, but I was in his office and we were having a drink together when he began laying down the law to me. He said, "You'll do it this way!" and I said, "I bloody-well won't!" He came back with "Well, if you want to continue working here you will!" My back to the wall, I roared, "Then you can stick your job. I quit!" and stormed out. I rang Joan at home and said, "I'm finished at Seven. I'll be coming straight home." Ted Thomas let me stew beside a silent telephone for 36 hours. I was too proud to contact him and suggest we let bygones be bygones, and he'd be damned if he was going to let me off the hook until I suffered a bit. Finally he called and we got together and patched things up.

At 5.30 on Saturday night, *Club Show* night, I'd assemble all the acts who were booked for that evening's program, give them a rundown of the show and then they'd have the chance for a short rehearsal. At about 8pm a studio audience of about 300 would file in and seat themselves in the auditorium. Bang on 9.30pm, the Channel 7 orchestra would wheeze out the show's theme, the cameras would roll and we'd be on air live, no autocues or idiot boards. Flying by the seat of your pants like that can be a dangerous business.

There's no safety net with live TV. Blunders, boo-boos and mistakes cannot be edited away or covered up, they're beamed out to a hundred thousand television sets as they happen. The ability to ad-lib and think fast on your feet is essential, as is the talent for remaining calm when all around you is disaster.

I loved hosting *The Club Show*. There was always the chance that the guest singer would botch that final note of *The Impossible Dream*, the juggler would drop his flaming torch or the comedian would tell a joke so blue that the switchboard would be jammed by irate wowsers for days. We had many of the visiting American and British actors and singers appear on the show, and I interviewed some very high profile international sports stars. Most were terrific, but I could see that some were a bit taken aback by the rough and ready way we threw the program together.

The trickiest part of presenting *The Club Show* was preparing for the live crosses to the dog races each half hour or so. The dogs waited for nobody, so it was my job to get all the entertainment and interviews wound up and out of the way so we could make a smooth transmission to Wentworth Park. Often I'd have a minute or two to kill before the barrier gates would open so I would have to fill in the gap by ad-libbing, talking off the top of my head about any subject under the sun: politics, the economy, sport, why the latest long-haired singing sensation couldn't hold a candle to Frank Sinatra . . . anything. Management never had any input into this off-the-cuff editorialising, they let me rave on about whatever I chose. I became expert at reaching the conclusion of my little monologue just as the race caller yelled, "And they're racing!"

We always tried for something different on the show. Once we televised the rugby league sprint championships from Wentworth Park. Speedsters such as Mike Cleary and Ken Irvine were competing in a series of match races sandwiched between the greyhound events. My old friend, the race caller extraordinaire Frank Kennedy, who was to die soon after of leukaemia, did the commentary. I promoted the races on the show the week before and told everybody to tune in. The public took me seriously. A few days after we'd broadcast the football sprints, station chief Bruce Gyngell called me into his office. "What's going on?" I said as I sat down. "How can you explain these sensational ratings for last week's *Club Show?*" he asked. "Look," I said, "it's a good show. We always get top Saturday night ratings of nine or 10 points." "Forget that," Gyngell said, "last Saturday the show pulled in figures of 22 points, an astonishing rating." "It must have been the football sprints." I ventured. "Well," he said, "can you organise some more of them?" He'd just learned what I always knew: that rugby league rates its ears off.

The Club Show was tailor-made for an old ham like me. On four excruciating occasions in the show's five-year run, I inflicted my singing voice on viewers. Once I warbled *I Will* and then I bashed their ears with a song that goes "If I had the world on a string I could be a millionaire", or some such nonsense. By God I had a hide, but the audience seemed to enjoy my efforts, laughing, clapping and singing along before giving me a big cheer when at last I reached the final glass-shattering note. Like my father before me, I can carry a tune, and have no qualms about getting up in front of people and belting out a ballad, but I don't think Tony Bennett has too much to worry about!

On one memorable night I hosted the show in drag after losing a bet with Johnny Raper on the outcome of a cricket Test. The crowd packed into the studio enjoyed every minute of my discomfort. Now that was something Bill Collins never tried on *The Golden Years Of Hollywood*!

There was another occasion when I was the star turn of the show but, believe me, this time it was no laughing matter. A few weeks before I'd just arrived home after playing touch football when I got a jolt of pain in my back that sent me straight to my knees. I lay in the foetal position in agony until my brother Kirk found me and put me to bed. I had never known such agony. I was rushed to hospital where they diagnosed a kidney stone attack and kept me under morphine until I passed the offending particle. I recovered and went back to work. This night *The Club Show* was in full swing and I was mid-sentence interviewing a guest when the pain struck again. I was carted off the set. Comedian Brian Doyle filled in for me for the rest of the show. I have never experienced such pain before or since. The doctors told me it is about as bad as it gets. I'm a strong guy and I don't buckle easily, but that night I was crying in agony.

As bad luck would have it, I collapsed again on air a short time later. This time my problem was a legacy of the old 1954 Jack Wilkinson spear tackle that had damaged the disc in my spine and ended my English rugby league career. Over the years the disc had degenerated and suddenly I was again suffering nerve pains in my back and down my leg. On the show that evening while I was interviewing racing journo Max Presnell, I copped a particularly bad attack, too bad to continue with the show. Once more I had a date with the doctors. This time producer Franz Conde took over the microphone in my absence. Soon after I put aside my terror of spinal surgery and went under the knife to have the nerve in the degenerated disc severed. This rectified the problem once and for all. I was in the best of hands. The surgeon was a wonderful old specialist, Dr Skyrme Rees. A Welshman well into his 70s who wears a monocle and is several times larger than life, the doctor remains a friend today. To me, the man is a genius.

There was never a shortage of larger-than-life personalities on Australian TV in the '60s and '70s. Johnny O'Keefe used to be in the Channel Seven stable of stars. He was a regular guest on *The Club Show* and had a program of his own called *Sing, Sing, Sing*, a rock 'n' roll show. He was a very warm guy, and we had a good working relationship without being close friends. Often when he'd want a bit of privacy where he knew no-one would find him he'd ask if he could use my dressing room for a while. I was glad to oblige. I think he was a troubled bloke. He was always on the move and never seemed to relax — darting here and there in a very edgy, hyped-up way. I don't know for certain if he was into amphetamines in those days — it couldn't have been long before he died — but if he wasn't, Johnny O'Keefe had more adrenalin than anybody I've ever known.

Another troubled soul was the legendary English comedian

Tony Hancock, who came to Australia at that time to film a TV comedy series for Seven. His life was at a low ebb. The Channel 7 series was a last chance to resurrect a wonderful career that had gone badly off the rails because of a tangled love life, rampant egotism and the bottle. His lover was supposed to be meeting him in Sydney but had just cabled that she had changed her mind, leaving Tony very depressed and lonely. Everybody at the station was talking about the problems he was having on the set. He couldn't remember his lines, he was unreliable and temperamental. I was a great fan of his, however, and when I saw him being made-up in the dressing room I couldn't help introducing myself. "Hello, Tony. I'm Rex Mossop and I work here at the station." His face remained impassive as he greeted me in a very quiet voice and shook hands without warmth. He was the saddest man I have ever seen. I watched as he stood up from his make-up chair and disappeared into the studio. Next day he was dead, victim of a pills and booze overdose.

I had a happier experience with the American actor Eddie Albert, veteran of many movies and the hit TV series *Green Acres*. He had some wonderful stories, many involving the voluptuous figure of his co-star in the show, Eva Gabor, Zsa Zsa's sister. He was a keen sportsman in his younger days and was impressed that I had dug up a bit of background on his sporting career and was able to ask him about things other than acting when I interviewed him on *The Club Show*. The *Wagon Train* star John McIntyre was another charming guest and so was the soccer great Bobby Charlton.

In 1971 *The Club Show* was given a break and I was pitched into the Beast's role in the long-running daytime panel show, *Beauty And The Beast*. With my gruff, masculine image, management thought I'd be a natural foil for the Beauties, Pat Firman, Jill Forster, Melissa Jaffe, Pat Lovell, Freda Leslie and dear Ena Harwood. These were all very smart cookies, and reinforced my masculine prejudice that a brainy woman is a dangerous woman!

In spite of the fact that I was stepping into the shoes of such illustrious Beasts of the past as Eric Baume, Stuart Wagstaff, Noel Ferrier and John Laws, I considered the program a heap of rubbish. But, being the company man I was — I always said I'd host *Romper Room* if they offered it to me — I took on the show.

We'd tape five *Beauty And The Beasts*, a whole week's worth of programs, every Thursday afternoon. My job would be to sit at a desk surrounded by the women and read out letters from viewers seeking advice on personal problems (although I've always had a sneaking suspicion that most of the mail originated from no further away than the producer's office). I'd give my point of view about the viewer's problem, usually dismissing the letter as the ravings of a lunatic, then throw open the discussion to the Beauties who'd rattle on until it was time for a commercial break and a new letter.

The show and the ladies, even though they were all very nice, drove me to the brink. My job was to ride roughshod over my fellow panellists by being chauvinistic and obnoxious, which was not a problem. Their job was to fight back as best they could, and we all enjoyed the verbal sparring. But the letters would drive me berserk. One woman wrote asking what she should do about about a peeping Tom who would stand in the street and watch her undress through her bedroom window each night. "God spare me days!" I raged on air, "Ever tried pulling down the blind, you stupid woman!"

I stuck it out for three years, each week growing crankier and crankier as Thursday, *Beauty And The Beast* taping day, approached. At night I would arrive home to Joan like a bloody raging bull. *Beauty And The Beast* was dreadful garbage, but it was popular. More than 300,000 women a day all over Australia had nothing better to do than sit down and watch it. On a recent visit to Perth I switched on the TV and they were rerunning the old episodes of nearly 20 years ago on daytime TV. There I was, 40-ish with jet black hair, having a ding dong battle with Ena Harwood. Ena had been a raving beauty in her day. I often told her in jest on camera that if she was 15 years younger and I was 15 years older we could beautiful music together.

THE MOOSE THAT ROARED

In the early '70s the channel started a successor to *The Club Show*, *The New Club Show*. Again I was the host and again it was a lot of fun to do, but nothing lasts for ever and by the mid-'70s, the concept had served its purpose and Seven gave *The New Club Show* the flick. However I had no time to mourn its demise.

At that time I was doing *Sports World*, rugby league commentaries, the sports news each evening and any other special events that popped up. I was, to put it crudely, working my butt off, 12-hour days six days a week. Today if you look at the credits that roll by at the end of a program you see executive producers, producers, researchers, scriptwriters, a host of assistants — but back in the early days I had to make do with just a director and a secretary. We had to organise everything. At one stage there at Channel 7, if I'd been hit by a bus, about a third of the station's programs could not have gone to air.

No matter how busy I was at work, however, I maintained my intense physical fitness program. Unlike a lot of footballers who turn to fat as soon as their sporting life ends, I was as fit in my late 30s and 40s as I was in my 20s. Each day I'd run six-10 kilometres, pump iron and swim in my pool or in the surf. I continued to play touch football every weekend, and turned my hand to golf, though without much success. If you are fit you can cope better with stress and pressure and work harder for longer, so I made a point of getting all the exercise I could. One morning back in 1967, just three years after I'd started at Channel 7, I went for a morning swim at South Steyne before heading off for a typically long day at the studio. There, in the most mountainous seas seen at the beach in years, my fitness saved my life.

I love body-surfing when the waves are running big. This day the surf was huge, so I strapped on my flippers and swam out to catch some rides. After a while I realised that to stay out there would be lunacy. Even with a lifetime's experience in all kinds of surf, conditions were just too dangerous. Beach inspector Max Whitehead thought so too, and promptly closed the beach. While I was sitting on the sand, gasping for air after my long swim back to shore, I noticed a group of young swimmers practising for their bronze medallion and it was clear that they were in serious trouble. Four or five of them were trying to drag in a line, at the end of which, 70 metres offshore, was the belt man, a lifesaver in his 30s. This fellow was caught in the pounding waves and kept disappearing from view. The youngsters on the beach had no idea what they were doing and kept pulling the lifesaver in the belt under the water. As usual, acting before I considered the consequences, I took off down the beach and told them, "Hold it, you're drowning your belt man. I'll be first linesman and pull myself out along the line and try to bring him in."

A vicious rip powered me fast through the turbulent seas. I kept hold of the line, but when I was nearing its end I saw it went straight down under the water. I dived deep and saw the guy in the belt was all tangled up in seaweed. He was still struggling but had been under a long time and I knew that he was just about gone. Somehow I freed him from the weeds, brought him to the surface and disengaged him from the belt. But my troubles were just beginning. By now we were 80 metres out to sea and the waves were crashing down on me and the unconscious lifesaver whose limp body I was desperately trying to keep from slipping back under the water. It was all I could do to keep myself afloat, let alone support this fellow, who was a dead weight. To complicate things further, the youngsters pulling us in didn't really have a clue what to do, which is pull on the reel until the wave comes, then give the bloke in the belt a bit of slack so he can go underneath the wave, then start pulling again when the wave has passed by. This requires timing and knowledge and these kids were novices and had neither. I just hung on to the line and the unconscious lifesaver for dear life as the waves pounded down on top of us.

When at last I reached shore, I was totally exhausted. A less fit bloke would have drowned out there for certain. We carried the lifesaver to the surf club casualty room where I performed mouth-to-mouth resuscitation. There must have been a gallon and a half of water in his lungs. The poor fellow kept vomiting black bile into my mouth and for days after I would spit and spit, trying to rid my mouth of the horrible taste that remained. Then the ambulance arrived and medicos gave the victim shock treatment in an attempt to revive him, but it was clear that he was brain dead, so they let him slip away. Strangely enough, Channel 9, my rival network, filmed the whole rescue and its aftermath. They had sent a team to South Steyne to shoot the huge seas for the evening news and they caught the whole drama. They gave me a little clip of 16mm film showing me clinging to the stricken man and later making the most ungodly retching noise as I gave him mouth to mouth.

As sports director at Channel 7, the responsibility for Olympic Games coverage was mine. Although my involvement in 1964 was confined to organising a telethon, I packed my bags and jetted off to Mexico City for the Games of '68. That was the Olympics where most of the athletes had trouble breathing in the high altitude and our champion long distance runner Ron Clarke collapsed in the 10,000 metres and almost died. The Games of course were as spectacular and exciting as they always are, but Mexico City was a hole, a squalid place full of poverty and disease.

I came down with the dreaded Montezuma's Curse midway through the Games. It's a virus that gets in your bowel and gives you the runs so bad that you need to go to the toilet 20 or 30 times a day. Everything you eat or drink passes straight through. It was an appalling and humiliating condition to have, but the show had to go on. In spite of the fact that I felt sick all the time, had lost eight kilos and was forced to grow a beard to cover a bad skin infection on my face, I took my place at the commentary position every day. Sometimes I just couldn't help it, I'd soil my pants while doing an interview, but I had to disregard my discomfort and press on. What a disaster. I would wait until everybody had left the stadium before I would get up to go, my briefcase strategically held to conceal my stained trousers. In Mexico City, professionalism took on a whole new meaning for me.

There was disaster of an altogether more violent kind at the tragic Munich Olympic Games of 1972. I'd just finished interviewing our great swimming champion Shane Gould when Norman "Nugget" May and I caught a cab in search of a few steins of beer. Two hundred metres down the road we heard what sounded like fireworks exploding. "What the hell's going on?" we wondered. Suddenly we heard a voice crying out, "They're killing the Jews! They're killing the Jews!" Arab terrorists had just stormed the Israeli athlete's quarters and were mowing them down with machine guns. Pandemonium broke out in the street with people panicking and rushing in all directions. The German authorities then moved in and cleared the area. We abandoned our plan to go out and get drunk and hurried back to the safety of our hotel to watch the day's horrifying events unfold on television. The Games continued, but to my mind they should have been cancelled on the spot.

My memories of Munich are not all bad. One night my hotel roommate Nugget May and I did manage to sink some beer. We batted on for many hours in some Munich cellar until Nugget decided he'd had enough and returned to our hotel and bed. A few hours later I staggered back, located the room and found Nugget under the covers but seemingly wide awake. For half an hour I regaled him with my adventures of the evening until I realised the conversation was all one way. "Nugget?" I said, "Nugget, are you listening to me?" For a moment I watched him lying there, breathing evenly and staring at the ceiling. Then the penny dropped. Nugget has a false eye, which he had neglected to take out. Behind its glassy glare the veteran sportscaster was sleeping like a baby, happily oblivious to every word I'd said.

Another time there was a commotion outside our hotel as one very prominent Australian broadcaster was pursued by the madame of a local brothel. She was noisily, and embarrassingly, demanding money from him. But he was not intimidated and steadfastly refused to hand over a cent. "No way," the Australian protested in earshot of us all, "if I don't come, I don't pay!" He looked a sight, with his pants folded over his arm and carrying his shoes, but he was adamant.

The pressures of being away on assignment, not to mention the long hours I spent at the studio six days a week, can create pressures at home. Happily, I am married to a saint, who over the years has kept the home fires burning while I've been out busy being a TV star, who's listened to my rantings and ravings, calmed me down and reminded me that all that really matters in life is a loving and happy home. I have such a home now, and I had it back in those difficult years of the '60s and '70s when I was trying to establish myself in television. By then Joan and I had built a beautiful house on our land in Balgowlah, the land I'd bought with my first rugby league pay cheque back in 1951. Our family was growing. Kirk now had a brother, Greg, who was born in 1956. Both boys were growing up sturdy and athletic and I hoped they would follow the sporting life. Kirk was a big lump of a boy and was a promising rugby forward. Also, I was indulging my love of dogs. I owned a few from 1955-on and, just as they do today, they had the run of the house.

Our home was my fortress, a refuge from the problems of a life lived largely in the public eye. Usually I could come home from work, lock the door and forget the hassles of television land. But there were inevitable intrusions. The way I was on TV, controversial, domineering and aggressive, caused me a few problems in my private life. Among the many letters I'd receive each week would invariably be a few from nut cases and cranks, some obscene, some merely abusive. The vicious ones were never signed. I made a point of answering all the genuine correspondence personally, and throwing the whackos' mail out with the rubbish.

If somebody comes up in the street and says, "Excuse me, Rex, can I have an autograph?" I'll always oblige. I will even be civil to blokes who approach me in a shopping centre or at the beach and say, "Rex, you remember me, don't you? You broke my nose in a rugby match back in '47." There have been hundreds of these. If even half of them had been telling the truth I would have been the nastiest bastard in football history. But I draw the line at aggressive people who barge in on me when I'm eating out with Joan or friends, who rudely invade my privacy just because they have so often had me in their living room. These people will always find their rudeness returned in spades. Occasionally I cop a mouthful from some coward in a passing car and more than once I've had my life threatened by some idiot who's been angered by something I've said. Threats and abuse are never pleasant, but they come with the territory of being in the public eye. They'll never stop me from speaking my mind.

16

FURORES, FIASCOS AND FORWARD PROGRESS

The apple was big, green and hard — and it hurt like blazes when it smashed into the side of my face. The grand final of 1977 had just been decided and I was farewelling viewers from the Sydney Cricket Ground — "Well, ladies and gentlemen, that was it, 197 . . ." when *bang* the apple hit me smack in the head. I was stunned and reeled out of my chair at the commentary position. I thought I'd been shot. When I show friends the incident on video today they always fall down laughing. Even I can raise a smile. But, believe me, it was no laughing matter then. If I'd caught the gutless wonder who threw the fruit I would have given him lots of time in a hospital bed to regret his stupidity. But, of course, the coward hurled the apple from the safety of the huge crowd filing out of the ground and with me perched 40ft up in the air in scaffolding there was little danger of him being apprehended.

A person in the public eye, and especially one with strong opinions, is always going to be a target. I have spent my 27-year media career dishing it out, I make no bones about that, but I have copped plenty, too. Books have been written making fun of my way with words, gross and outlandish puppets called Rex Phonebooth and Rocks Messup have been unleashed on TV and radio audiences, vindictive journalists and media people have mounted smear campaigns against me, I've received death threats and my home and family have been put under siege. It all seemed so much simpler back in my football days when I'd thump someone, he'd thump me back and that was the end of the matter.

I'm not whingeing. If you live by the sword you're going to get stabbed in the back. I have a way of alienating 50 percent of the people every time I open my mouth to talk about sport, politics, whatever. Many people can't stand me, I know that and I'm comfortable with the fact, but they switch me on because they know I will say *something*. Like the guests on Controversy Corner, no one leaves empty-handed. Viewers and listeners know that I will have an opinion that will make them react. And something is better than nothing at all, which is exactly what too many media commentators serve up. These blokes, bland and without opinions, please nobody and they offend nobody. To my mind, they have no right taking up air space.

Probably the longest-running knock of all is that Mossop mangles the language. I plead guilty. I was a footballer who, because of my down-to-earth qualities, because I was a bit rough around the edges, because I was myself, became a TV personality. I was hired by Channel 7 because I was a man who had played football at the very highest level and understood the game, and who, in my own way, could bring the excitement of sport into people's living rooms. I could have recited "the rain in Spain" until the brown cows came home, but it wouldn't have been me. I love words and I can think fast, but in the heat of the moment when you're calling the game live, of course things are going to get scrambled occasionally — I'll use the wrong word, commit a "tautology" — that's using two or three words where one will do, or I'll let fly with a "bloody", a "Christ", a "bastard" or a "hell". I can live with these minor crimes, so long as the atmosphere and colour of a game beams through to viewers loud and clear. To me that is all that has ever mattered.

Once I became notorious for tautology, people started listening for it and I believe the whole thing got blown out of proportion. I hasten to add that my notoriety did my ratings no harm at all. Anyway, here's a challenge. Next time you're tuned in to a radio or TV commentary, make a note of the number of times the caller gets tangled up, uses the wrong words or doesn't finish a sentence. But none of this matters a damn so long as the commentary is accurate and entertaining. The perfect call has not been made and I doubt that it ever will be.

Blokes with nothing better to do than nit-pick over tautology have lambasted me for saying "Pearce is making forward progress" or "Kenny bursts into the vacant gap" when a great forward charges through a ruck or a brilliant back breaks into the clear. At these times I have wondered whether viewers would prefer to tune in to a word-perfect product of some elocution school who knows nothing about rugby league but a lot about English, someone who is as wrong as often as he is dull. Most viewers, I believe, would prefer to listen to a bloke who knows what he's talking about and is not too embarrassed to get a little excited.

Those who make a living listing others' mistakes have had a field day with me, filling books and articles with examples of the way I sometimes crash tackle the language. I've heard all the atrocities I'm supposed to have uttered: "I don't want to sound incredulous but I can't believe it", "a verbal tonguelashing", "tiny, diminutive,little Mark Shulman", "If I keep getting Boyd and O'Grady mixed up, it's because they look alike, especially around the head", "He seems to be favouring a groin injury at the top of his leg", "I've had to switch my mental thinking", "You'd have to be Mephistopheles to work that one out", "What are you looking for? Utopia? Perfection?", "I saw Manly visibly wilt". Yes, I've said most of these at some time or another, and I'm happy to live with having said them so long as those critics who breathlessly report them to the newspapers spell my name right. However, I'm pretty certain at least a few of the examples above are products of the wishful thinking of people like the playwrite Alex Buzo who for years conducted his Australian Indoor Tautology Pennant in the now-defunct *National Times*. This bloke would list "classic examples of tautology" perpetrated by the likes of myself, Nugget May, Bob

Hawke, Mike Gibson and others and each year name a winner of these "tautological stakes". It was usually me. Buzo collected all the pieces in a book entitled *Tautology Too*. Tautology? For years I thought it was the study of dead tortoises.

I was in a lift with Buzo once. He recognised me immediately, but I had no idea the little fellow in such close proximity was my tormentor from *The National Times*. He tells how he was not game to introduce himself to me for fear that I might belt him. For God's sake! In fact, in one Tautology Stakes a relative of his almost took the prize when she warned Buzo about singling me out for ridicule too often: "You'd better be careful of Rex Mossop," cautioned the relative, "he's such a big giant!"

Buzo and I were brought face to face by *60 Minutes'* Jeff McMullen early in 1991 when the program did a profile of me. It was all light-hearted. The idea was for Buzo to confront me with some of the things I'm supposed to have said and I'd defend myself. Unfortunately for *Sixty Minutes*, Buzo seemed intimidated by the confrontation and was as flat as old beer. He just couldn't go on with it. His articles and books might have been funny, but in person he was a non-event. I did my best to stir him up, but this great meeting of the minds didn't get off the ground. The camera crew shot about 800 feet of film, but could only use 10 seconds of it on the finished show. I had to laugh when the *Sixty Minutes* producer introduced us and Alex's first remarks to me were tautological!

Next, a word about "Flabbergasted", the expression so synonymous with Rex Mossop that a few years ago Channel 7 had sweatshirts promoting *Seven's Big League* printed with my face on the front and "Flabbergasted!" emblazoned across the back. It's a word that used to be used much more than it is today, but it's a good, strong way of saying "shocked" or "astounded", which I often am when it comes to sport, especially these days. I knew that media stars such as Jack Davey, Bob Dyer and Brian Henderson were well known for certain catchphrases. Davey would say "Hi-ho everybody", Dyer "Happy lathering customers!" and Henderson signs off the news each night with

"The way it is". And Ita Buttrose and Ron Casey have their lisps. Anyway, I thought I would make "Flabbergasted" my trademark. Over the years, with a little help from Mike Carlton's Rocks Messup, it has stuck.

People often ask me whether I get offended by the caricatures of me on the Mike Carlton and Doug Mulray radio shows. Of course I don't. I'll admit that the snorting, thick-necked bruiser puppet version of me that appeared on the TV version of Carlton's *Friday News Review* had me thinking, "Gees, I know I'm no oil painting, but surely I'm not as bad as that!" So I asked my wife Joan what she thought and she said she reckoned whoever made the puppet was being kind to me! Mike Carlton and Doug Mulray are top talents with a wonderful sense of humour. If we can't laugh at ourselves occasionally we'll all go insane. And it's not as if I'm in bad company when they send me up: Bob Hawke, Paul Keating, George Bush, Maggie Thatcher have all had the treatment. Nobody bothers to send you up if you're a nonentity.

When Triple M's Doug Mulray recently released a record, he asked me to make a guest appearance in the music video. The song was called *You Are Soul*, which of course when sung sounds like a common term of abuse. My role was to come on at the end and make all kinds of threats: "I'll get you one of these nights, Mulray! When I get my hands on you, you'll be sorry . . ." that kind of thing, all in fun. After the taping I went home and waited for my cheque to arrive in the mail. I reckon my splendid performance was worth at least $1000. I'm glad I didn't hold my breath waiting for the money to arrive! So consider this a warning, Mulray, when I get my hands on you . . . only joking!

If criticism is constructive or meant in fun, I have no problems with it. As an old showman like me knows, there is nothing like a little harmless sensation and controversy to keep the ratings high, and controversy has been a constant sidekick throughout my career.

Journalists from a variety of newspapers and magazines have been to my house down the years to interview me and write profiles. Many of these reporters have arrived at my house with pre-conceived notions about me and no matter what we talk about in the interview, no matter the hospitality they are shown in our home, almost invariably they portray me as a muscleheaded, chauvinistic, bombastic, intolerant, right-wing, biffo-advocating bastard. Well, to all you scribes, you got it wrong. I'm no musclehead!

Seriously, I have made blunders over the years and the press has always been quick to remind me of them. But some of the mistakes that have appeared in these reporters' articles about me you wouldn't believe. Facts about my career have been ludicrously wrong. One reporter wrote that I was in the habit of summoning my wife Joan with a dog whistle, another had Joan's name as "Janet". Talk about people in glass houses.

Most of these wrong-headed and sloppy profiles have caused me no lasting damage, but personal and professional attacks motivated by hatred, jealousy, ignorance or sheer mischief is another matter. I believe there are people in this town whose attacks on me down the years have overstepped the mark that divides constructive criticism and personal abuse. These people have distressed my family and damaged my reputation. As I grow older I find myself mellowing a little, but I will never forgive them for what they have done.

There is no doubt I have been a godsend to all those newspaper editors over the years keen to fill their pages with a bit of sensation. My most celebrated headline must be "Rex Arrests Nude Bather!" I'd been campaigning for months against a State Labor Government decision to turn Reef Beach at the bottom of my street into a nudist beach. All my life Reef Beach had been a peaceful, private spot for families to swim and picnic and here in one scratch of a politician's pen, it had become a haven for perverts and deviates. When my neighbour rang and told me there was a naked man parading up our street that summer morning in 1976, I snapped. I stormed out into the road, caught up with this gibbering dope who was trying to reach his car where friends waited with his clothes, and held him fast by the shoulder while neighbours called the police. He was shaking like a jelly and begging me to let him put his clothes back on, but I made him stand there in the street desperately trying to cover his genitals with a clump of leaves until the law arrived and dragged him away. I meant what I said at the time, the Government had no right shoving male genitals down people's throats, and that's exactly what they were doing by letting these creeps loose in public places.

One of the first times I made the papers for reasons other than my football prowess was back in 1969 when my son Kirk set free his blue cattle dog Cobber from the back of the local dogcatcher's van. Cobber had tagged along when the boys and their friends went swimming at Forty Baskets Beach, near our house. Somehow Cobber became separated from the boys and was dognapped by the local dogcatcher and locked away in the poochs' paddy wagon. Kirk, who was then 16, broke into the wagon, freed his pet and let out all the other dogs in the van for good measure.

The dogcatcher, a neighbourhood nuisance known to all as "Pat The Rat", recognised Kirk and notified Manly Police who sent a sergeant and two constables around to our house to question my son. Local aldermen overturned a motion that a reprimand be punishment enough for Kirk, and he was charged with wilful damage to council property, obstructing a council servant in the execution of his duty and breaching a regulation prohibiting dogs on beaches.

I hired a good solicitor who made mincemeat of the dogcatcher when he got him in the witness stand. First he made Pat The Rat admit that Cobber may not even have been in the prohibited area, then demanded to know just how experienced a dogcatcher this bloke was. Pat The Rat boasted to the court that in a distinguished World War II fighting career he had carried a gun for Australia overseas and was a long-serving guard. Our man had done a bit of homework on this poor fellow and was able to expose him as a liar: he'd never fired a weapon in anger, never fought overseas and the only thing he'd ever guarded was the Manly gas works during a coal strike. The magistrate had heard enough. Glaring at Pat The Rat he said, "Sir, your statements here today reveal you as a man incapable of telling the truth. It seems to me you have a mental problem and we must disregard all your evidence. I award the case to the Mossop family, plus costs."

That wasn't the end of Pat The Rat. For years we had a running battle with him. If we had a picnic at Reef Beach, there he'd be complaining about our barbecue. If we were playing touch football at the local oval, he'd wait until the ball was kicked in his direction, then try to confiscate it. He had a death wish, but he was too pathetic to take seriously. He became a terrible pisspot. Many times I saw him swerving all over the road in his car in an alcoholic stupor. Once I watched alarmed as he tumbled dead-drunk down a steep rock footpath in the area. Over he went, head over bloody heels, 20 metres to the rocks below. I raced over to see if he was alright — I was sure he'd be a goner after such a fall — but being so drunk he'd landed limply and done no damage. When he came to, he picked himself up and weaved his way home.

Another mini-sensation that kept newspaper readers amused was when Darrell Bampton, the South Sydney skipper in '78, was caught with his pants down by the *Seven's Big League* cameras. The practice then was for a camera team to film pre-match interviews in the rival teams' dressing rooms. Believe it or not, but there were a few footballers at the time who got a kick out of performing a quick flash and exposing themselves to the huge viewing audience while the cameras were rolling. There was one Cronulla player who was always trying this trick on. So the film crew learned to be careful how they set up their shots and the editors were instructed to examine every frame before it was broadcast, But the system broke down that day at Redfern Oval. In the Souths dressing room, Darrell Bampton changed into his playing gear, not realising that the cameras were recording an interview with another player close by, and that night a full-frontal view of him was broadcast into loungerooms all over the state. It was a terrible mistake and Bampton was rightly furious. In banner headlines he threatened legal action. Channel Seven management said they regretted any embarrassment Bampton suffered and made a public apology to the player.

I caused another furore when I announced that Cronulla and Australian second row star Greg Pierce was "too nice a bloke" to captain Australia. He subsequently went on to captain Australia in a Test against France and be vice captain to Bob Fulton on the 1978 Kangaroo tour. Pierce, who, incidentally, did a good job each time, was a super-clean player who to my knowledge never threw a punch in his life, and my remarks were just a way of saying that in my view strong-arm tactics should be a part of any forward's armoury when the need arose, as it always did in a Test match.

I also found myself in hot water the night I unwittingly insulted Lester Piggott, the champion English jockey. It happened this way. Lester has a terrible speech impediment but, not being a racing man, I wasn't aware of his affliction. On the Channel Seven news one night in 1985 we ran footage of him stumbling through a speech at some function in Britain. As soon as it ended I blurted out the throwaway line: "Well, I don't think Lester has a future as an after-dinner speaker." I was accused of being insensitive and crude and told that I should have known better. Sydney jockey Ron Quinton said my off-the-cuff comment was in "appalling taste" and he was probably right, but I honestly meant no harm. And I still believe Lester has no future as an after-dinner speaker.

I can honestly say I've been responsible for jamming more TV station switchboards over the years than possibly any other commentator in television history. Outraged viewers rang the station in droves to complain when I slammed Merv Hughes, the kissing cricketer. I couldn't believe it when this bloke, a national hero at the time, would rush up and plant a big smacker on the face of some unfortunate teammate who'd just taken a wicket. I slammed his antics as unmanly. My stance on Aussie rules, a pussycat's game, has also won me no friends south of the border. I can't stand the code, with its scrambling and sloppy handling and its lack of any real body contact.

Once I gave a bit of verbal biffo on the evening news to the bikie community after another weekend of rioting at Mount Panorama motor races. Next morning I drove into the station carpark and the attendant told me there was a big bloke in leathers waiting for me — and, he warned, "he looks mean". I picked the bloke out immediately, a young fellow clad head to toe in leather with a death's head painted on the back of his jacket, chains, tattoos, a bushy beard, about 100 kilos. Yes, he was the bikie, alright.

Following the normal Mossop practice, I led with my chin. "Do you have a problem?" I testily enquired. He said he did. He reckoned my words on the news last night had tarnished all bikies and it was only a few who had gotten out of control at Bathurst. "Don't be so bloody stupid," I told him. "I wasn't criticising you personally. If you were one of the idiots who did your cause so much harm at Bathurst, then I *was* criticising you and you're welcome to take a poke at me right here and now if you're game. But if you weren't, we're wasting each other's time continuing this conversation." At that, he said "G'day", revved up his bike and rode off. I was a little glad he did. I was well into my 50s when this incident occurred and he was young and strong. He would have given me a run for my money.

Happily, the bikie was harmless, just a fierce-looking bloke with a point of view. Most people who have taken issue with things I've said are reasonable people with an opinion they're entitled to — even when it's wrong! However, there is a lunatic fringe out there and you never know when someone who threatens you or your family is serious or not. One night I said something inflammatory, I can't even remember what, on the *Mossop Report* segment of Channel TEN's *Eyewitness News*. After the report a viewer rang the station and said he was going to shoot me. Channel TEN security took the threat seriously and, in spite of my protests that they were overreacting — people who are going to kill you usually don't warn you first — TEN hired a couple of heavies from Mayne Nickless to follow me around for a couple of days. "Minders For The Moose" said the *Sydney Morning Herald's* report of the furore.

The papers had a field day with me only last year when, in a Channel TEN Cup pre-season game I made scathing comments about young St George prop Shane Kelly. From where I was commentating, Kelly was having a very quiet match and when he was replaced with injury I ventured that he must have been suffering from sunstroke. Unbeknown to me Kelly had suffered kidney damage, which was affecting his performance. But I had no knowledge of that, the club had not passed that information on, and it is my job to call it as I see it. I saw Kelly contributing little on the field and I said so. It was my *job* to say so. My criticism provoked a torrent of abuse and a public demand for an apology from St George secretary Geoff Carr. I wasted no time answering back with a press statement: "I watched Kelly for six or seven minutes before he went off and he didn't get out of a trot. All I want to say is I watch football and footballers with an objective point of view and it comes out in the commentary. How was I to know the player was hurt? I'm watching my old club Manly go around tonight and if I feel something needs to be said, I'll say it. I won't be told what to say about anyone. That's the only comment I wish to make on the matter." There was no apology.

Nor did I say I was sorry to my beloved Sea Eagles later that season after I slammed them mercilessly for what I felt was a sub-standard performance in a loss to Canterbury. The new Manly coach Graham Lowe came out in *The Daily Mirror* and said my comments were an insult to his players. He said I was being totally unfair and that he wouldn't stand back and tolerate "such garbage". He accused me of "hurting" the Manly players. My reply, also published in the *Mirror*, was this: "Some people don't like me criticising Manly. My suggestion that they played a sub-standard game against Canterbury bruised a few people's feelings. To them, all I can say is that I'll call it as I see it and I'm not going to be worried in the least by negative comments from anybody. I'm afraid that's the way it's going to be."

This year, 1991, I gave it to Newcastle, blasting them for what I considered to be their dull and unadventurous play. I said that the Knights' forwards would not last into the second round if they persisted with their barging play. My forthright views earned me the ire of Newcastle coach Allan McMahon and club supporter Jack Newton, the former golfing champion. Newton and I had a damn good barney on the Controversy Corner segment of 2GB's Saturday football broadcast when I told him he might know plenty about golf, but his knowledge of rugby league was negligible. Weeks later McMahon quit, after his own players criticised the stodgy, one-man-out style of league they were being forced to play game after game, a style that was no longer even winning them matches. The man who heard the players' grievances and made them known to Newcastle management was none other than my critic Jack Newton. I believe my criticism was vindicated, but that did not stop many people in the game from publicly ridiculing my stance.

Such controversies are all part of the cut and thrust of being a public figure with public opinions. I admit I relish them and certainly have never lost a moment's sleep over them. People read newspaper headlines like these breathlessly one day and wrap their fish in them the next. But headlines of a more vicious, sinister sort at one time almost tore me and my family apart.

17

A FAMILY
BESIEGED

It's no secret that both my sons, Kirk and Greg, at one stage of their lives had problems with the law. The problems that almost destroyed them — and their mother and father — in the 1980s are behind them now. Today they're husky men, working hard and doing the very best they can with the cards they've been dealt and Joan and I appreciate what a struggle it's been for them both to come through, but their rehabilitation has been made so much more difficult by the headline treatment they received in the Sydney press at the time of their troubles.

I have no doubt that the big banner headlines their misdeeds received had more to do with the fact that their Dad was a well-known TV star than with the enormity of their crimes. If my name was Brown and I worked for Manly Council, my sons' run-ins with the police would not have been news. These press jackals, in one monster front page splash after another, cashed in on the Mossops' misfortune to sell more of their grimy rags.

As any parents would be, Joan and I were devastated when our boys got into trouble. They'd grown up strong and healthy: both were fine surfers, Kirk had played second row in the Manly rugby union first grade side and Greg was a first-rate snow skier who worked as an instructor in Australia and America. They then went off the rails, as so many other kids have done. Both my sons have paid dearly for their weakness. It was the worst time of Joan's and my life.

The constant prying of the media — the late night phone calls and the early morning ringing of the front doorbell by reporters — followed by huge front page exposes nearly hounded us to the brink. But the love and support we gave each other saw us through the long crisis and we presented a strong and united front to a world we were sure really had it in for us. While everything seemed to be falling in a heap around us and people gossiped and whispered about us behind our backs, we held our heads high and knuckled down to work as usual. My composure broke on just three occasions throughout that long nightmare.

The first was when a group of us from Channel 7 were invited to lunch by the directors of John Fairfax and Sons at their head office in Broadway, Sydney. Fairfax at the time owned Channel 7. *The Sydney Morning Herald* had come out that day with a big photo of me over a story about one of my sons being arrested. All the way from Channel 7 to Broadway I seethed about the vicious campaign I believed the press was waging against me. I decided I couldn't remain silent and no matter how embarrassing it may be to my TV colleagues I was going to tell these newspapermen exactly what I thought of them. In the dining room I was introduced to a fellow from the *Herald* and I straight away launched into him. I told him that what he had done to me and my son was a disgrace. I told him that *he* was a disgrace. When I blow my stack I am a sight to behold and I let this bloke and his newspaper have both barrels that day. My workmates tried to pacify me but I would not be silenced. When I had finished with the director I left the room and the building. To share a meal with those people after the pain they had caused me would have been hypocritical. I believe today that my blast set the battlelines between myself and Fairfax. For the rest of my TV career the organisation's papers got stuck into me every chance they got.

The second time I lost control was when I became involved in a slanging match with a psychiatrist who told me Kirk was being self-destructive in an effort to embarrass me because all his life I had overpowered and dominated him and had been reluctant to let him be independent. This fellow brought me undone. I knew I had been far from the perfect father — I *was* stern, just as my father had been with me, and there were times when I tried to do their thinking for them — but to blame me for all their problems was ridiculous. One thing I *had* taught my sons was that we are all responsible for our own actions in this world.

They don't hand out an instruction manual when you have children. There's no guide to being a good parent. All you can do is what you believe is right based on your own experience and hope for the best. Dad was a disciplinarian and I had never caused him a moment's trouble, but my own boys rebelled against my brand of strictness. I admit I was guilty of trying to make my sons carbon copies of myself. I was keen that they be sportsmen and when other Dads were playing and laughing with their children I'd have Kirk and Greg down at the park putting them through passing, kicking and tackling drills and making them do it until they got it right. I know I made mistakes, but Joan and I did our best.

I tried to understand, but I was profoundly disappointed in Kirk when he gave rugby away just when his career was getting started, at the end of the 1974 season when he was only 21. The Queensland coach Bob Templeton had been monitoring Kirk's progress through the ranks at Manly — I didn't get to see him play too often because of my commentating duties with Channel 7 — and told me he was a real goer who took after his father and he would soon be making rep teams. Overjoyed at this news, I grabbed Kirk and said, "Son, this summer we'll do a lot of weightlifting and long stamina runs together to build you up." But he replied, "Oh look, Dad, I've decided I don't like football, I hate training. I'm giving the game away." That hurt.

I can't put my finger on the reason, but all through their growing-up years I found it hard to loosen up with my boys and treat them as mates. That has never been the case with my grandchildren. Both Greg and Kirk have kids of their own now and it is these wonderful children, Rachel, James, Rebecca, Jessica and Nathan, that are bringing my sons and me closer at last.

The third time the pressure got to me during this difficult period when our private life seemed to be everybody else's business was at Leichhardt Oval while I was calling a game for Channel 7. It had been a rough week, the lowpoint being when my face was plastered all over the the front page of *The Sun* below the headline "Tragedy Of A TV Star's Family". I was calling the first half action when a big, long-haired fellow walked past the commentary box and sneered something derogatory about one of my sons. He'd picked the wrong bloke at the wrong time. That day my nerves were at breaking point. I had the microphone in one hand, but with the other I reached out of the box, grabbed this bastard by the hair and belted him. After I'd landed a dozen such blows, he struggled free and fled to the back of the Latchem Robinson stand to lick his wounds. But I wasn't finished with him. As soon as the whistle blew for halftime in the game I flew out the back door of the broadcasting position and up to where I knew the bloke was. I then proceeded to belt him backwards and forwards along the aisle. I kept backhanding him until a policeman and an off-duty touch judge persuaded me to put him down. I then returned to the microphone and continued my call as if nothing had happened. A year or so later the fellow came up to me at a league match, extended his hand and apologised for being such a galoot.

18

CHANGING CHANNELS

By the early '80s, *Seven's Big League* was an integral part of Sunday nights for many hundreds of football fans across New South Wales. It was a slick, seamlessly-edited replay of that afternoon's match of the day that went to air at 6.30pm. I selected the match, produced the show, hosted it and called the action. From the day it kicked off in 1976 until the New South Wales Rugby League blew fulltime on the program at the end of the 1982 season, *Big League* was a wonderful ratings success for Channel Seven. I believe it set the standard for TV rugby league telecasts: the multi-camera coverage, the colourful expert commentary, the post-match interviews. We pioneered all that. Proof of the *Big League's* popularity was that right through the seven years of its existence would regularly receive hundreds of letters a week from fans in the winter months. With the help of my wonderful assistant Anne Claxton I made a point of answering every one.

I always refused to work with a co-commentator, but Barry Ross, schoolteacher, sporting journalist and a good bloke, helped out with statistics and kept an eye on backplay from his vantage point on the sideline. Barry was another personality whom viewers loved to hate and was cruelly known as "Yes, Rex" because of his no-nonsense, deadpan comments. The guy was in a no-win situation, having to play second-banana to a bad-tempered old know-all like yours truly, but he was a terrific help to me and was a factor in *Big League's* success.

Barry came to Channel 7 back in 1978, when he succeeded my long-time statistical sidekick Bill Kerr. He had a spot on

Sports World where he would do two minutes or so of stand-up commentary then present a "Skill Award" to the player who had thrown the best pass or made the best tackle or kick in last week's match of the day — but his TV career got off to the worst possible start. Barry was keen to make an impressive TV debut, so before he fronted the cameras for the first time he sat down and memorised two pages of script word for word. Of course, when he went before the cameras he froze. For what seemed an eternity he stood there live on TV, eyes staring panic-stricken, mouth gaping but with no sounds coming out. I saw what was happening and strode on camera. I put my arm around Barry's shoulders and addressed the viewers. "Ladies and gentlemen," I said, "this is Barry Ross's first time on live TV. Few of you out there would appreciate how difficult it is. Give him another chance." All at once, Barry relaxed and finished his spot like an old pro. We worked together until 1983 when Barry Ross left TV after he was accused of receiving a secret commission in return for mentioning a particular sport on *Sports World.* To my mind, he was innocent of the charge and I believed he was entitled to greater support from Channel 7 management than he received.

Over the years Channel 7 had built a cosy relationship with the New South Wales Rugby League. *Seven's Big League* was good for the game, and the game was good for the station. Even so, I often thought that Seven management took the valuable league TV rights for granted, and were a little condescending to what was then, still is, and always will be, the premier winter sport in the State. There were some people in influential positions at Seven who regarded rugby league as a necessary evil. I could never be accused of that and as sports director gave the game my devoted attention. Because I loved rugby league so much I was happy to present the code as "The Greatest Game Of All" at every opportunity and I was always exhorting viewers to go out to the games. Many of my outspoken opinions — particularly on the benefits of biffo — embarrassed League bosses from time to time, but generally we had a good working relationship and I would think nothing of doing them small favours such as supplying copies of match videotapes when the League required them. So it rocked me to my socks when, just three weeks after our big rating 1982 grand final broadcast, Channel TEN snatched the league TV rights out from under Seven's nose.

I don't believe Channel 7 tried hard enough to keep the league when the rights for seasons 1983-'85 came up for grabs. We'd done a fine job bringing the game to the public since 1964 and I'm sure if we had even been competitive with the other networks the league would have remained with Seven. But an apathetic Seven management went to league chief Kevin Humphreys and said, "Here's our offer, here's all we think the league rights are worth. Take it or leave it." Humphreys left it. We were blown out of the water by Channel TEN which bid $7 million for the right to replay the Sunday match of the day for the next three years. Ray Warren would be the caller.

At first I was shattered. Commentating on rugby league was my career, and there I was at 54, a league caller without portfolio. The big switch caused a furore in the press and reporters lurked around my home, hoping for what they hoped would be a furious reaction from me. Somehow I managed a stony-faced "no comment". I was glad I kept my cool, because none of them could have printed my real thoughts on the matter. I showed no such restraint when I confronted Seven management and blasted them for their foolishness.

Eventually I simmered down and thought rationally about the situation. I had had a number of offers to leave, but decided to stay at the station. After all, Seven had paid my wages for 18 years and loyalty is a big part of the Mossop Code. And anyway, I was still sports director, and there was *Sports World* to host and produce each Sunday, and my *Mossop Report* spot on the news, and, I thought, you never know what might come up.

What came up was soccer. Seven thought they could fill the yawning gap left when they lost the league by televising international soccer matches featuring the Socceroos. I would head a commentary team with Johnny Warren. I threw myself into the new challenge. I already held a soccer referee's ticket, having become interested in the game while in England, but in the months before the first telecast I boned up anew on the rules. I would be prepared to bet that not one of the viewing audience tuned in to those telecasts guessed that their enthusiastic head commentator was secretly tearing his now-greying hair out, champing at the bit to have another crack at calling his No.1 sporting love — rugby league. I continued to work long and hard at Channel 7, but I must be truthful and say that for those next three years at the station, years without league, my heart wasn't in my work.

During this time I'd rejected a number of offers from radio stations in NSW and Queensland to do weekend rugby league calls. I missed league, but radio was a new medium for me, and my duties at Seven were many. But finally, after a hell of a lot of deliberation, I signed a $60,000 one-year contract with 2UE to call Saturday and Sunday matches for them in the 1986 season as well as take part in a Saturday morning panel discussion and record editorial comments to be broadcast at drive-time during the week. Channel 7 had no problem with that when I assured them that my radio duties would not interfere with my TV commitments, but there was no doubt that I was going to have my work cut out for me.

I was shocked by how bad my first radio broadcasts sounded. I was making the mistake of doing a TV commentary full of those long pauses that a TV caller makes when he knows the viewer can see for himself what's taking place and description is redundant. A radio commentator, however, always has to paint the full picture, tell who made the run, how far he ran, who tackled him, where on the field the movement came to a halt. I adapted quickly however and beefed up my call to meet the demands of radio.

Otherwise it was Mossop as usual. In an interview with my old Controversy Corner panellist Alan Clarkson, I said, "I'm looking forward to the challenge of radio and I can promise those who bring the game of rugby league into disrepute a very rough time. I am going to be me. I can't change and I won't change. I intend to hit straight from the shoulder as usual and I won't be pulling any punches. If people thought I was tough on those guilty of bad behaviour, people like John McEnroe, they haven't heard anything yet. I am not a new chum to radio because I have worked on most stations in Sydney over the last 20 years on talk-back segments. I will be as profesional as I can be and even my toughest critics will have to agree that I know the game. I have a feel for it. As for winning ratings, that's something I am not into. I will simply do my best."

I may not have been into ratings, but the management of 2UE, John Brennan and company, certainly were. Then, as now, there was cut-throat competition between the networks to be top dog. Advertisers like to be where most of the listeners are and commercials are the life blood of radio, as they are of TV. I was vying for No.1 spot with 2GB's Peter Peters and Greg Hartley. I knew that the law of the jungle often applied in television, but nothing prepared me for the attacks of my radio rivals. I have never minded constructive criticism of my commentaries but when those attacks become personal it's like waving a red rag in front of a moose.

I'd known Peters as a journalist on *The Sun* and as a tradesmanlike player with Parramatta and Manly. He'd also done a stint on Channel 7. Hartley was a former referee who had embroiled himself in controversy in his whistle-blowing days. Obviously seeing the new kid on the block as a serious threat to their top-rating stature, Peters weighed in early with the newspaper pronouncement: "Rex's best asset is his looks and you can't see them on radio." Peters bagged me continually that radio year and in years to come, often stooping to unpleasant personal attacks. To me, this was garbage. My father always said never to dignify cheap shots with a response, so I didn't get involved in a demeaning slanging match.

2GB won the ratings war that year, but what gave them the edge was their management's decision to give listeners a continuous call, that is, the full 80-minute match uninterrupted by commercials. 2UE was not prepared, at that stage, to forsake their advertising dollars. The customers didn't want the action broken into by sponsors' messages so they tuned in to 2GB. These days, 2UE has realised its mistake and wouldn't dream of offering listeners anything but a continuous description of play.

I enjoyed radio, but it was only ever a Clayton's solution to my great dilemma: that I was a TV league commentator without a game to call. The year before, 1985, Channel TEN had put out a tentative feeler to me. "Would you be interested in talking about a change of channels?" I told them I would not. I desperately wanted to call TV league but leaving Seven would have been too radical a step for the company man I then was and, besides, TEN already had the very competent, if safe, Ray Warren calling their matches. But the offers persisted and Joan and I began to take them a little more seriously. Perhaps, just perhaps, there was life after Channel 7.

The first formal meeting between myself and senior TEN management was in March, 1986. Again I rejected their bid. Six weeks later another offer was made, an offer so good I listened intently. More meetings followed. Finally TEN chief George Brown put a solid proposal to me. I would be sole-commentator of the premiership match of the day on Sunday night, of *Monday Night Football* and the midweek knockout match, and present a sports segment on the evening news. If TEN won the rights to televise the 1988 Olympic Games in Seoul I would be the host. In return I would be paid *four* times my present Channel 7 salary. My contract would last seven years. The high-powered negotiations were always conducted in out-of-the-way places, such as on my boat in Middle Harbour. I hated these clandestine meetings, but I was learning fast to put my family and myself before company loyalty, and if Seven or the staff at TEN learned I was being courted so enthusiastically the whole deal could have been blown. After five months of meetings with the TEN executives, much soul-searching and long heart-to-hearts with Joan, I agreed to change guernseys.

People who know me today as the type of man who appreciates the value of a buck and who wouldn't blow his nose without a contract won't believe this, but I worked all those years at Seven without a written agreement. When I joined I shook hands with Harry Chester and that was that for the next two decades or so, in spite of the fact that Seven paid me a comparatively low salary and worked me into the ground. I remember times when I'd summon the courage to ask management for a raise of $5,000 or $10,000 and gladly accept when they'd offer me $1000.I was just an easy-going sporting man who loved his job. So with no contract the only ties I had to the place were emotional ones. It was merely a case of writing my resignation, handing it in to general manager Ted Thomas, then serving one month's notice.

Ted Thomas couldn't believe it when I finally convinced him that I was determined to leave. He offered me more money to stay but, as usual with Seven, it was too little, too late. "I'm sorry Ted, but I've made up my mind. One month's notice and then I'm off."

Leaving a place where you have worked for 23 years is always difficult, but Channel Seven management made it easier for me. I returned to my office, determined to be the complete professional and work my butt off for the station in the four weeks I had left there. Next day a memo arrived on my desk. It was from Thomas's secretary. She said Mr Thomas had asked her to relay to me that I should clean out my desk and leave the premises tomorrow. A second blow came in the form of a letter delivered to my home. On the outside was my name and my address. Inside was my superannuation cheque — no covering letter, no message of thanks for 23 years' faithful service — just a cheque with my name on it. There was no farewell party, no speeches, no chance to have a final get-together with my colleagues.

The one light moment came when *The Daily Telegraph* ran a Zanetti cartoon depicting my farewell ceremony. Two Channel 7 workers are presenting me with a huge Oxford Dictionary as a parting gift. One says: "Rex, we thought we'd give you a going away present you could use . . ." I reply: "Just what I've always wanted — a paperweight!"

I don't mind admitting I was bloody hurt when Channel Seven spat the dummy. I thought this was a shoddy way to treat someone who had been a loyal and hardworking employee for almost a quarter of a century. As I drove out of the carpark for the last time I remembered my early stumbling efforts on *Sports Action*, the fun we had with the Commonwealth Bank Passing Competition, the banter and mateship of Controversy Corner. I recalled flying by the seat of my pants on *The Club Show*, being beastly to those wonderful girls on *Beauty and the Beast*, 23 years of highs and lows, of Olympic Games, grand finals and Kangaroo tours, the praise and the criticism . . . the whole damn thing.

Joan, as usual, was the Rock of Gibraltar through the whole trying period of my departure. We discussed the pros and cons of my changing channels for months. She's an old-fashioned girl and had a soft spot for Channel Seven, but she knew I'd given the station my all for most of my working life and any debt I might have owed to the station had been paid in full a long time ago. She supported my move every step of the way.

I left Seven in August, 1986, and was due to start work at TEN in October when I would travel to England to cover that year's Kangaroo tour. In the meantime I relaxed, swimming, running and lifting weights. I wanted to be in fighting form for my new challenge. Joan put me on the Pritikin Diet and I lost eight kilos.

The big switch caused more drama than *Dallas*. Article after article appeared in the press. Many people were glad that the cranky old bloke they'd grown up with on TV would be calling the football again. Such goodwill was not universal. The sportscaster I'd be replacing at TEN, Ray Warren, was bitter about his axing. We had always been friendly to each other and I made it clear there was nothing personal in my taking his job. Channel TEN management had approached me, after all. They thought I would rate better than Ray, it was as simple as that. Warren himself had displaced me as No.1 TV league caller when Seven lost the league rights to TEN four years before but even though I was deeply disappointed at the time I took the blow on the chin and refrained from personal attacks. You never let the bastards know when they've hurt you.

Ray Warren was quoted ad nauseum in the press saying how he'd been kicked in the guts by Channel TEN when he lost his job. "I'm completely devastated — it's not my job, it's my life!" he told journalists. "Maybe I should have been a tautologist and more controversial. I should have made a citizen's arrest." From my point of view, TEN's move was purely a business decision and I was disappointed by Ray's attitude. I felt no guilt at all at taking his position. We're all big boys and TV is a tough business.

19

STRICKEN AND
SACKED

I t was good to be back in the north of England, and especially good to be calling rugby league again. I settled into my role as TEN's chief commentator for the '86 Kangaroo Test series as if I'd never been away from the commentary box. My return to the microphone had been anticipated with a fair bit of hype and I don't think I let anybody down as I relayed the excitement of the '86 Tests from wet and freezing Manchester, Leeds and Wigan to the viewers back home.

As usual, Joan and I were treated royally in the Old Dart. We looked up many old friends and had wonderful times reminiscing about those halcyon days at Leigh more than 30 years before when we were newlyweds with a brand new baby, skimping and saving but as happy as we have ever been in our lives. Leigh looked down at heel in '86, unemployment was high and you only had to look at the people — their worn clothes and grim, pale faces — to know they were doing it tough. But just like in the dark decade that followed World War II, days of food ration ing and clothes queues, their spirits ran high. No matter how broke the league followers of this mighty little football town may be, they can always afford to shout an old Aussie player a pint in one of their cosy pubs. They reckon this gives them the right to reminisce with you about the old days — they have a wonderful knowledge and feeling for the traditions of the game — and to take you down a peg or two with that splendid dry sense of hum our of theirs.

I threw myself into my work, determined to make up for lost time and to re-establish myself as the No.1 TV commentator in the game. I laid firm ground rules at TEN: no co-commentator, no instructions over the headset from the director, nobody in the box with me. I had heard that previous callers at TEN had been hamstrung by a stream of instructions from directors, telling them what to do and say, when to get excited, when to tone it down. The poor bloke doing the call couldn't have known whether he was coming or going. There was no way that was going to happen with me. I had no problems with Graeme Hughes, a former Canterbury second rower now employed as a sportscaster at TEN, making a few comments at the start and end of the broadcast as well as adding a little colour during the game, but as for calling the action, it was to be Mossop flying solo.

The series, of course, was a walkover for Wally Lewis's Kangaroos who completed their tour undefeated, but the series had its moments, particularly in the Third Test when the British gave a hint that they were gradually lifting their game and would be competitive by the time the next Roos arrived four years later. Although few of the Poms would have made any of the great English teams of the '50s and '60s, I was impressed by a rock-hard, uncompromising front rower named Kevin Ward who was probably Great Britain's best player of the series. When Manly snapped him up for the 1987 season I knew they'd bought wisely. The big Pom was the rock on which the Sea Eagles based their premiership-winning campaign that year.

The camera work of the British crews was not up to the high technical and creative standards of the Australian operators. The blokes our director Alan Catt had to work with were part-timers, unused to covering rugby league, and league is a demanding, highly specialised game to telecast. Nevertheless, the broadcasts were first rate and I felt I had made a good fist of the commentary duties after having been out of action for four years. I had positive feedback from Channel TEN hierarchy, the production crew and the public back home who stayed up in large numbers to watch the late night live telecasts.

Many of the players, too, told me they were glad to have me

back calling the games, but that didn't stop them from belting me when we played touch football, as we often did on that Kangaroo tour. I enjoy a good relationship with players — possibly because they know that, unlike many outspoken commentators, I have competed at the highest level and know the game. Even so, while most footballers are terrific blokes and excellent company, I have always considered it a mistake to get too close to them. Problems can arise when you go out drinking with a bloke on Saturday and then blast him on Sunday.

I arrived back in Australia raring to go. Monday, January 19, 1987 was my first day at Channel TEN. One difference between Channel 7 and my new stable hit home immediately. That first day people came from everywhere to wish me luck. Office boys, technical staff, on-air personalities, all told me they were glad to have me aboard. They made me realise how much I was regarded as just part of the furniture at Seven.

There was the odd hiccup. After being made up for my first appearance on *Eyewitness News*, I lost my way to the studio and had to ask directions, making it onto the set only minutes before my segment. Then, when I finally appeared on-camera, I got a bit excited during a story on rugby league and dropped a "bloody hell". In spite of both words being in the dictionary, the switchboard at TEN lit up with calls from irate viewers. Twenty eight people were offended enough to send the station letters complaining about my earthy language. "Well" I thought, after a message from station management telling me they were glad to have me, but could I please try to control my swearing, "it's business as usual."

After experiencing the frugal ways of Channel 7 for so long I was amazed to see the way the TEN people spent money like there was no tomorrow. My office there was palatial; at Seven I had a pigeonhole. Compared to what my old masters had paid me, I was earning a fortune at TEN. Even so, my salary was chickenfeed when stacked up against the money a lot of people at the station were getting, and many of these were programming and publicity people. It was nice to live so high on the hog, but Blind Freddie could see the network was heading for financial disaster. Camaraderie among the staffers ran high, but in the executive corridors trouble was in the air. Just a fortnight after I arrived at the station, general manager George Brown, the man who had hired me, departed. He was replaced by Ian Gow, a sales whiz from Channel 9. The station boss was Frank Lowie, a man who had made a fortune in shopping centre development.

Unlike Channel 9, which has topped the ratings for years on a policy of selecting the right on-air personalities and leaving them in their job long enough for viewers to get to know and like their style — Brian Henderson is the prime example — Channel TEN seemed to believe that the key to ratings success was to chop and change staff and spend a fortune on new sets and costly publicity campaigns.

For my money, TEN executives set too much faith in the power of razzamatazz, of style over substance. I fell out repeatedly with executives over their insistence on polluting the football telecasts with such American-style gimmicks as dancing girls, appearances by the station's soap opera stars, and, most of all, Wacka the Emu.

Wacka was a product of the TEN publicity department. A bloke would climb into this ridiculous emu suit and cavort around the sidelines during *Monday Night Football*. I had nothing against the poor bastard in the suit, but the whole idea of the emu ran deeply against my grain. Australia is not America, rugby league is not gridiron which thrives on cheap novelties. I knew the publicity machine was trying to widen the code's appeal and so boost ratings, but rugby league has survived for more than 80 years because it is a great game. It has never needed tawdry gimmicks or childish stunts, that only cheapen the code. I swear that if I'd had a shotgun with me in the commentary box I would have shot stupid bloody Wacka stone dead. And I'd dispense the same medicine to that dopey, shapeless Sea Eagle that hogs the limelight when Manly play at Brookvale. In fact the whole nonsensical rabble of rubber-foam rabbits, tigers, panthers, sharks, knights and broncos should all be wrapped up together in a giant sack and dropped over the nearest cliff.

Why can't people realise that all the marching girls, dancers, pop stars, monster flags and people in animal suits only *detract* from the drama of rugby league. How much more stirring is it just to see the two teams run on to that wide, green field in a big match without all the showbiz hype? I know that I can barely contain myself when the sides that have made it to the biggest game of the year burst onto the field on grand final day. Why should they have to play second fiddle to some TV warbler or an over-sized koala bear in a digger's hat! English teams today are not quite what they used to be, but to me there has never been a more ominous sight in sport, no spectacle more guaranteed to raise the hairs on the back of my neck, than when the Great Britain team does its slow walk onto the field. I believe a great injustice was committed on grand final day, 1990, when the pre-match entertainment was allowed to continue until 20 past three. In the dressing room were two football teams who had been primed to reach their physical and emotional peak at exactly 3pm that afternoon. I know that both the Canberra and Penrith sides were climbing the walls in fury and frustration.

From our first broadcast of 1987 *The Big Game*, which went to air at 6.30 on Sunday nights, wiped the floor with the best programs the opposition channels could pit against us. For years, *Sixty Minutes* had thrashed all comers to be the No.1 show on TV, but we beat it with our first two-hour telecast, a top of the table clash between Balmain and Parramatta at Parramatta Stadium.

"Moose Call Boots A Ratings Goal" announced *The Daily Telegraph*. "Let a moose loose among the TV ratings and anything can happen," said the paper. "Rex Mossop's return to the commentary box for his first big league game under Channel TEN colours was a huge success, booting *Sixty Minutes* into touch for the first time in years." The football telecast was instrumental in my new station winning the overall ratings survey and ending Channel 9's winning run of 10 consecutive surveys.

I was delighted, but not surprised. I knew we had the right mix: a good director in Alan Catt, a fine crew, and young Graeme Hughes in a subordinate role doing the "colour" — that is, describing the atmosphere, the weather, the crowd — as a complement to my call.

Hughes and I got together early and decided we could give the show a bit of bite if we occasionally took a swipe at each other. I told him if he disagreed with anything I said he should come out on air and say so. It's a common ploy with broadcasters to add a little showmanship to a commentary by staging minor disagreements. I believe Hughes took my invitation too far and became overly-aggro. Things reached boiling point between us one afternoon during a match at Parramatta Stadium. There is a difference between a disagreement, which viewers enjoy, and a heated argument, which they don't. At Parramatta that day, Hughes argued on and on with me over a rule interpretation. In my view, he was wrong, but he continued on and I had to say to him in the end, "OK, Graeme, we'll just have to agree to disagree." People tune in to enjoy a football match, not to cringe as two blokes wearing microphones go at each other hammer and tong. Surely there's enough action on the field. For my money Graeme Hughes overstepped the mark. From that point on, ours was a rocky relationship for real.

Good working conditions and a lot of nice people made for a happy time at TEN, although there was never any love lost between me and management who I thought went out of their way to keep their distance. Perhaps they found me a bit difficult. I believed my broadcasts were being hurt by too many long ad breaks, and I said so, and I copped flak from the powers-that-be when viewers saw me throw my papers in the air in anger after learning I may have to be in Seoul for the Olympics at the same time as the '88 league finals series. There was also the occasion when, after announcing some Australian rules news on *The Mossop Report*, I added jokingly — ". . . if anyone out there is interested." Someone *was* interested. A station executive took exception and hauled me over the coals. "What you have to understand," he said, "is that our station has certain financial affiliations with the VFL and we will not stand by and let you jeopardise our association." When it was my turn I pointed out to him that apart from my love of rugby league I had *no* ties to any sporting body and then told him what I'd been repeating to management for the past quarter of a century: that nobody was going to tell me what to do or say.

I believed I was on safe ground — wrongly as it turned out — so long as I was doing what I had been employed to do: make a success of TEN's league coverage. The Sunday night replay and the Monday night game contined to rate spectacularly, I had never been paid so well in my life, answering my fan mail was becoming a full-time job, and God was in his heaven. Then one night in Newcastle the wheels fell off.

In the weeks preceding I had been working terribly long hours and one of my sons had again found himself in serious trouble with the law. I was tired and I was distressed, but I did not feel that my health was under threat. I was as fit as ever and getting plenty of professional satisfaction from my work. Then one afternoon Joan and I drove to Newcastle to broadcast a midweek Panasonic Cup game. When we got close to Newcastle city I became unusually agitated and was having trouble finding the right route to the ground. Suddenly I lost control and began shouting and screaming. I can be aggressive in traffic, but this time I went over the top. Joan ordered me to pull over. I sat there a mess in the passenger's seat as Joan asked directions to the ground and drove us into the carpark with plenty of time to spare.

I took my place in the outside broadcast van to record my opening comments but I couldn't concentrate on what I was supposed to be saying. I have always prided myself on being able to do these comments in one take, but this time I kept stumbling over my words. It took me four times to get it right. I kept apologising to the crew, but they told me not to worry. Something was haywire in my head.

The players ran onto the field and the game got underway,

but when I tried to call the play, it all came out wrong. Today I have no real recollection of the nightmare, but people told me I just sat there gazing at the action, saying little, and when I did say something it had nothing to do with what was happening on the field. An alarmed director and crew helped me out of the commentary box and sportscaster David Fordham picked up my call. Everything was a whirl. I knew something was not right, but didn't know what. One of the TEN staffers drove me straight home to Balgowlah with Joan sitting cramped in the back of our little two-seater sports car. Once in bed, I fell into a deep sleep.

Next day Joan insisted I have a cat-scan. The doctor x-rayed the inside of my head then gave me the news. I had suffered a stroke. I was horrified. Fitness and health had been the cornerstones of my whole life and any sickness or injury I'd ever suffered had always been sport-related. Yet here was an illness I had no control over. Suddenly I felt very mortal.

Until now, nobody outside my immediate family has ever known that I suffered a stroke that night. A minor stroke, sure, that over the years has responded to treatment, but a stroke nevertheless that paralysed my brain and sent me right off the air.

All my football career I had played down injury, never letting on when I was hurt. Just as the St George forwards hit me all the harder once they knew my cheekbone was broken back in '59, I knew that my present adversaries, those detractors in the media who delighted in highlighting the tiniest mistakes in my commentary — would have really gone to town on me if they felt I was off my game. So I decided not to give them any ammunition. I released a statement saying I was suffering from a middle-ear infection and it was that which turned my call of the Panasonic Cup game into a disaster. By inventing a relatively minor illness I thought I could keep the ghouls at bay. But no, as soon as they learned I had a medical problem, my critics closed in on me like jackals on a wounded moose.

Suddenly it was open season. There was a crescendo of criticism about my commentary in the press, on radio and on rival TV networks as old rivals settled scores and newcomers leapt in to kick me while I was down. I believe that many of these attacks were the work of jealous and bitter minds. Certainly, apart from the night I'd suffered my stroke, I had done nothing for fair-minded critics to get up in arms about. But my opponents tried to say that I'd been making disastrous calls for years. Occasionally I'd be guilty of a little tautology and at times I might mix up two players, but I'd back my knowledge of the game and my ability to describe it against anybody.

The Fairfax press led the mud-slingers. *The Sun-Herald* ran a street poll asking people what they thought of me, and printed all the negative replies. That paper and *The Sydney Morning Herald* gave plenty of space to the verbal assaults of 2GB's Peter Peters, and *The Sun-Herald's* David Hickie weighed in with what I thought was a nasty below-the-belt attack. Questioning why TEN had hired me in the first place, Hickie continued: "One could be excused for thinking the likely candidate for any plum commentator's spot ought to possess at least a majority of the following: broken nose, cauliflower ears, gruff manner, penchant for yelling, known desire for blood and guts, Australian blazer and, above all, an aversion to grammar."

As usual, I did not dignify any of these moose-baiters with a response, but by God, I was hurt. Nobody wants to hear that they're not doing a good job, that they're getting too old — especially someone who takes as much pride in his work as me. I had been one of the most professional people in TV for 24 years and now I was being berated as unprofessional and past my prime. I was disappointed but not unduly concerned when Channel TEN management failed to support me publicly and defend their ratings winner in the press. I assumed that my bosses at the station had too much sense to take any notice of the jackals. Looking back, I should have known better.

The public took no pleasure in the vendetta against me. My broadcasts continued as top-raters through all the furore and many viewers took the time to send me letters of encouragement. To all those people who wrote to me during that period telling me they still loved me and to keep my chin up, I say "thank you". Your kind words helped.

The only way I could repay my fans and keep my self-respect was to put my head down and prove my tormentors wrong. It would have been easy for me to say to my detractors, "Look, you blokes are out of order. I've had a stroke, I've had crippling family problems, that's why I called David Boyle Les Boyd in last Saturday's telecast. Just be a bit understanding and give me a few weeks to recuperate and I'll be back on top of things." It would have been easy, but it would not have been the Mossop way. I soldiered on.

Turbulent 1987 ended well for me when my Sea Eagles won the comp. Once more, I carefully concealed my elation as I described the men in maroon and white doing their victory lap. Like Manly, I had overcome some huge obstacles to finish the year a winner. In my first season at TEN I'd consistently won the ratings after being away from the game for four years, I'd beaten a stroke, and I was feeling on top of the world, in the right frame of mind to tackle 1988. I knew damn well I had enemies at the station and in the media, but the new year promised to be a big one for me. I planned to consolidate the good ratings my broadcasts were getting and as well as a big league season to cover that featured a tour by the improving Great Britain team, TEN had the TV rights to the Seoul Olympic Games and I would be heavily involved in that. In fact, things were too good to be true.

At the end of January, just weeks before the '88 rugby league season got underway, Channel TEN lined me up and hit me with a bellringer. Without warning they kicked me out of the commentary chair and replaced me with Graeme Hughes and veteran sportscaster Ian Maurice. Billy Anderson would be the so-called "sideline commentator". TEN sports director John Davies tried to placate me with the title of "executive producer" and "presenter" and said I could introduce and close the program and make expert comments throughout Hughes and

Maurice's co-call. Management told me I had their full support. I wasn't so sure of that.

My station had blithely ignored my good ratings and my popularity and shuffled me upstairs, I believe, as a knee-jerk reaction to continued criticism of me in the press. There was definitely a clique of people at TEN who wanted me cut down to size, and those pygmies who bore it up me week in and week out in the papers, on TV and on the radio, gave them the excuse they wanted. Fortunately, my contract was iron-clad, otherwise I would have been out on the street, I have no doubt about that.

I kept a stiff upper lip and told reporters I was excited about my new post and was looking forward to the challenge. The reality was that I was furious at the way I had been treated, but I would buckle down and make the best fist of what I knew even then would be an unworkable situation. All my commentating career I had believed that the most effective commentary was a solo-call, just one bloke describing the action and delivering opinions in a straightforward and entertaining fashion. Viewers obviously thought so, too. But now I was forced to compete with *three* others. It was a battle to get a word in edgeways, and the commentary became ragged and fragmented. Often viewers did not even know who was speaking. The mental picture people watching the telecasts at home must have had was of four big blokes crammed into a tiny commentary box and all talking over the top of each other. Chaos.

Everybody knows that if something is not broken, you don't fix it, but this ridiculous revamp of the football broadcast was just another example of Channel TEN's knee-jerk-reaction style of management. A dip in the ratings, a little criticism in the press and there would be a dreadful over-reaction: mass sackings and changes in the on-air lineup, a new musical theme, a new set, a costly new publicity campaign. Often all that was needed was for the program to be left alone long enough for viewers to grow comfortable with it, or perhaps given a little fine-tuning, but these blokes would have performed brain surgery with an axe. In the three years I was there, three separate organisations had a go at running the station. The Frank Lowie mob was succeeded by Steve Cosser and his Broadcom team who were in turn ousted by a bankers' consortium headed by Gary Rice. Much of this period was marked by turmoil and instability as the station desperately tried to escape the financial mess it found itself in.

It is accepted TV wisdom that whichever station has the highest-rating news presentation keeps many of those viewers for the rest of the evening's programs. I believe the chiefs at TEN were obsessed with Brian Henderson's domination at Channel 9 and in their frantic efforts to come up with a combination of newsreaders that could topple Hendo, destroyed the credibility of their program completely. I know that enormous pressure was put on me to come up with a *Mossop Report* segment on the *Eyewitness News* every night that would win my 10-minute time-spot. I made the point at the time that no matter how good my report was, it couldn't work when viewers had lost patience with the continual chopping and changing of the rest of the news team and deserted to the opposition. The wise men at TEN, many of whom had it in for me anyway, didn't listen. I have lost count of the people who have presented the news on TEN since 1987: Katrina Lee, Steve Liebmann, Geraldine Doogue, Ron Wilson, Eric Walters, John Mangos, Katrina Lee again, and more. It's a bit like the Queensland-NSW State of Origin set-up. Queensland sticks with its tried and true players through defeat and victory; NSW selectors wield the hatchet at the drop of a hat. And we all know which State is the Origin champ.

My confidence was badly shaken when they took my microphone away from me, but there was no way I was going to let them off the hook by resigning. My contract stated plainly that I must be paid my salary for seven years and, by God, for what they were putting me through, I was going to get every cent that was coming to me. If they wanted me gone, they would have to sack me and pay me out.

Management aside, there were some very special people at

TEN, all trying to get by in an atmosphere of back-stabbing, crisis and paranoia. Steve Liebmann was a good mate to me, and so was Geraldine Doogue — two fine professionals. I have a photograph that was taken at a 60th birthday party Channel TEN staff threw for me of Steve helping me blow out the candles on a big cake. My girl-Friday Debbie Thomas was a tower of strength there too. I was lucky to have had two wonderful secretaries in my TV career. There was Debbie and before her the marvellous Anne Claxton. I know I had a reputation as an ill-tempered ogre at both Seven and TEN, but the fact that these two wonderful people stuck by me for so long may just be a hint that my bark is worse than my bite.

The Tuesday after the 1988 grand final I arrived in Seoul to call the Olympic Games. The security was unbelievable as the city swelled to bursting with hundreds of thousands of visitors. Seoul was a seething, overcrowded city. I have never seen traffic jams like it, queues of stationary cars stretching back four and five kilometres. The Channel TEN contingent was not, however, doing it tough. After forking out $30-$40 million to buy the TV rights for the great event and sending a technical and on-air cast of thousands to the place, the station heavies arrived in their private jets and booked themselves a floor in the best hotel in town where they luxuriated for the duration of the Games. Hardly what you would expect from people running a station balanced precariously on the edge of a financial precipice.

My main task there was to call the boxing. The set-up was for me to base myself in an underground studio and watch the fights on a monitor. They were being beamed in live from the stadium some distance away. I would then record a commentary, and the pictures and my words would be broadcast in Australia later that day. I made one mistake when I called a boxer by the wrong name. I'm not excusing myself, but it was a fairly understandable blunder made while working under difficult conditions. Although only boxing aficionados would have known the difference between the two foreign fighters, news of my blue reached my enemies in the press who gleefully ripped in to me. I know for a fact that someone in a position of power at TEN leaked the news of my blunder to a hostile journalist in an effort to embarrass me.

A month or so later, I was replaced as reader of the sports report on *Eyewitness News* by Ian Maurice. I was told at the time that my rough-hewn, up-front style was putting a lot of younger viewers off. Letters and phone calls of complaint from the public poured into TEN, but the decision was not reversed.

I took my Christmas holidays that year on the north Coast of NSW. One day I was white-water rafting near Coffs Harbour when I fell heavily, injuring my knee. It was an painful experience and I had to return home for an operation. What hurt more than my injured knee, however, was the front-page headline of *The Sydney Morning Herald* that was published the day I went under the knife. "Mossop Sacked, But No-one Will Tell Him" claimed the former Wests and St George coach Roy Masters, who was now a journalist on the *Herald*. According to Masters' report, "Rex Mossop, the grand old man of TV sport, has been sacked from Channel TEN and no-one has the courage to tell him. 'The Moose' is on holidays, unaware that his five-year (sic) contract has been terminated."

I contacted the station at once and demanded to know what in God's name was going on. Management assured me there was no truth in Masters' report and, to their credit, came out and said so in the press. The station chiefs wrote me a letter guaranteeing me that my position was not under threat and then directed TEN legal people to seek a public retraction of the story and an apology from the *Herald*. One month later a small article appeared on one of the inside sports pages of the paper — note that the original story had been given front-page prominence — admitting that the Masters article was "incorrect". "During 1988," the piece continued, "Rex Mossop's role was changed from that of 'match caller' to presenter and executive producer of Rugby League for Channel TEN and he will continue in that role in 1989. *The Sydney Morning Herald* apologises unreservedly for the embarrassment caused to Channel TEN, its executives and Rex Mossop for the inaccurate report and regrets that it did not carefully check the facts prior to publication."

The day after his original article was published, Masters tracked me down at the Harbord hospital where doctors had just operated on my knee. He gained entry to my private room where he found me flat on my back, still woozy from the effects of the anaesthetic. I have only a vague recollection of him being there, and none of giving him an interview, but I do remember abusing Masters and his photographer mate and roaring at them to get the hell out of my room and allowing me some privacy. In the article that appeared in the *Herald* next day, Masters quoted me as saying, "I've not been sacked. I have an iron-clad salary situation for the next four years." However, he said that his story had been right but that a wave of public outrage at my dismissal may have caused TEN management to reverse their decision.

I have no time for Masters as a journalist, just as I had no time for him as a coach. I believe he was a poor coach and think the way he brought out the aggression in his teams with his face-slapping routines and incited open warfare between the so-called wealthy teams, the "Silvertails", and his Western Suburbs "Fibros" was complete garbage.

Management's guarantee gave me no relief. The bagging by the media and the lack of support from the station bosses continued all through 1989 and '90. I knew things were nearing crisis-point at the end of the 1990 league season when I received a memo from sports director John Davies listing a number of mistakes I had made during the commentaries that year and demanding an explanation for them. I wrote back immediately. In my letter I admitted I was far from perfect, but pointed out that since I had been at the station I had enjoyed considerable ratings success and that the bags of fan mail I received each week were testimony to my popularity with viewers. There was no such thing as a perfect call — Hughes, Maurice, Anderson and the rest made their share, too — but a Mossop mistake was always magnified out of all proportion.

THE MOOSE THAT ROARED

A good example of this can be found in an article written by journalist Ray Chesterton in the May 21, 1989, edition of *The Sunday Telegraph*. His piece was headlined: "The Noose Ready For The Moose". He predicted that I was soon to be sacked by TEN, but added that "In many ways a lot of people will be sorry to see Mossop go. In his highly-stylised way he has been a basic, hard-working and integral part of rugby league commentary in this town for decades and no one could doubt his love of the game. But time, as it tends to do so relentlessly, has tackled Mossop into touch. I've never been one of Mossop's fans but I appreciate his appeal to others and I'm not going to slip in the knife now that his fortunes have turned . . ." Chesterton than proceeded to do exactly that, slip in the knife, by drawing attention to three minor aberrations I had made in recent commentaries. The following typifies the pettiness of his argument: ". . .Then there was (my comment that) 'Leeds' try doesn't alter the score' when the Parramatta fullback raced over in the final minutes. Of course Leeds' try altered the score: it went from 42-0 to 42-4, with a kick to come. Leeds' try might not have altered the situation but it altered the score, otherwise a lot of players are wasting their time each week trying to get to the goal line." Of course I meant to say "situation" and not "score", but mistakes like this are made countless times in every radio and TV call each weekend. Has Chesterton himself never blundered? I've never written to the press about the countless errors journalists make in their stories, even though reporters, unlike TV and radio broadcasters, have the luxury of the sub-editing process to help them get their facts right. So why single out Mossop?

It was in my contract that I would travel to England and France to head the 1990 Kangaroo tour coverage for TEN, and that Joan would accompany me. However just weeks before the team was due to depart, sports director John Davies told me the station was in such a financial mess management could not justify paying for Joan's ticket. "Well," I replied, "you've broken your part of the deal, so I'm going to break mine. I'm not going either." Financial belt-tightening was also the reason they gave for sacking Peter Sterling and David Morrow from the commentary team at the end of that year. Ian Maurice was long gone by then.

By the end of 1990, I knew I had no future at TEN. At one stage I seriously planned to depart in a blaze of glory by going on air as usual at the end of that night's league replay then saying, "Ladies and gentlemen, I hope you enjoyed the match. This is Rex Mossop signing off from Channel TEN for the very last time, but before I do I'd just like to pass on this message to all you critics who have wrecked my career: 'Get stuffed!'" What a last hurrah that would have been.

As it turned out, Channel TEN beat me to it. In February, 1991, I was called to the office of TEN chief executive Gary Rice. Waiting there were Rice and John Davies. Rice buttered me up by telling me what a great man I was and how good I'd been for the station. Then he told me he was going to terminate my contract. I stared at him, not saying a word. Joan had always counselled me to keep my cool if faced with a situation like this and, difficult as it was for me to do, I took her advice. Rice ploughed on, stressing there was nothing personal in the decision, but the station was in a bad way financially, the banks were closing in, and they'd been forced into a position where they'd lost the league rights to Channel 9 and were paying their great rival for the privilege of presenting *Friday Night Football* and the Sunday replay. I continued to stare at him. After an embarrassed pause, Rice indicated they were prepared to make a cash payment to me of $60,000 to pay out my contract, which still had three years to run. He knew, as I knew, that this was a ridiculously low amount. I then spoke for the first time. "You'll be hearing from my solicitor," I said. "Thank you very much." I left his office and walked out into the late summer sunshine, as devastated as any man would be who has just been sacked for the first time in his life.

20

REXURRECTION

I sat at home feeling sorry for myself for about a week. Then, like any old forward worth his salt who picks himself up and gets stuck in again after being dumped on his backside, I lowered my head Moose-style and charged headlong into the rest of my life.

I got over my self-pity quick smart, but don't think my anger subsided. I was angered and shocked at my dismissal and I am upset about it to this day. I will never get over how badly those people treated me nor understand how they could make a hash of the league, which was one of the few good things the station had going for it.

First they overdid the gimmickry, then they tampered with a successful format by relegating me to the role of presenter, turning me into little more than a support act to Hughes, Maurice and Anderson. This fragmented the presentation and, to my mind, damaged it seriously. As if this were not enough, certain executives over that period badly managed the station's finances. Their spendthrift policies delivered a once-thriving network into the hands of the receivers. When TEN reneged on their payment to the New South Wales Rugby League the League took the rights off TEN and negotiated a deal with Channel 9, who kept the State of Origin replay rights and sublet to TEN the rights to screen Winfield Cup games, the pre-season knockout and the Sevens tournament. Channel 7 would telecast the international games.

Although the network was on its knees, I had no qualms about holding out for what I considered to be a fair pay-out figure on my terminated contract. I made good my promise to put the matter into the hands of my solicitor and before long TEN backed down and paid me the figure I sought.

I could not believe the many, many letters of support I received from viewers who wanted me back behind a microphone. There's an old saying that you never appreciate what you have until you lose it, and for many viewers, league without the Moose, it seemed, was not quite the same. I might have been a dinosaur from the Dark Ages, I might have shouted and argued and made people mad, I might even have made mistakes, but I'd been doing all these things for a long, long time and when I disappeared from the screen, people missed me. In the street, on the beach and at league matches I'd be greeted continually by wellwishers asking me when I'd be back on TV. There was a great, warm groundswell of support for me and I'd be lying if I didn't admit that I was deeply moved.

Some very prominent people also made their feelings known. NSW and Australian League chief Ken Arthurson blasted TEN's decision to carry on without me. "I honestly think the station has made a mistake by getting rid of Mossop," he told the *Telegraph Mirror*. "He has been one of the outstanding rugby league commentators of all time and he still has plenty to offer. Channel TEN has had great success with the ratings and a lot of that has come from Rex's telecasts. People have always respected his knowledge of the game. He came in for a bit of criticism over the years but that was only because he was prepared to speak his own mind. A lot of people go ducking for cover . . . but Rex always told it as he saw it. I think the station may regret its decision."

Another dual rugby-rugby league international, Ray Price, demanded my immediate reinstatement. "Bring back Rex," he said. "The others waffle far too much. The current Channel TEN team don't seem to be able to make a decision in their call because they don't want to be controversial. There's two reasons for this — the financial position of the network and they are too chummy with the NSWRL . . . They're treating the public like idiots."

Price said the commentary of Graeme Hughes, Bill Anderson and Wayne Pearce lacked "colour and excitement". "The three there at the moment are absolutely boring. Rex did get his names muddled up but at least he put some colour into the game. Rex knew the basics of the game. He also knew how a game should run. League needs someone like Rex — someone with flair and personality."

In what seemed an immediate knee-jerk reaction to Price's plea for more controversy, TEN added Peter Peters to the *Friday Night Football* commentary team, but the experiment was short-lived.

Even 'Arold Parks, Scott Rigney's outspoken cartoon character in *Rugby League Week* begged Channel TEN to bring me back and lambasted the station's presentation. "Fair dinkum!" he raged, "The league coverage is like a 90-minute commercial for Macleans toothpaste. Sanitised, deodorised, pre-packaged rugby league for the '90s. Well, you can keep it Channel TEN. And put it in a place where footballs weren't designed to go!"

Rigney was only half joking when he pined for a return to the days "when Frank Hyde sang *Danny Boy* and gave away a Seiko watch. When Noel Kelly and Ferris Ashton used to hammer it out on Controversy Corner after the passing competition. When a brass band played at halftime of the grand final with not a Bob Abbott balloon or video clip of an aging pop star grandmother in sight. When the closest things we ever had to a sex symbol were John Donnelly and Les Boyd, and 'what we saw was what we got' without all the razzamatazz. When the game, and only the game, was 'simply the best' . . . the days of Rex."

Continued Rigney, "Quite frankly, to quote the great one himself, 'I'm flabbergasted!' The management at Channel TEN have done the rugby league viewing public a grave disservice. The Moose may be an endangered species, but please, let's not make him extinct!"

I noted with no satisfaction that with me removed from the scene the press turned their vindictive attention to my successors. *The Sun-Herald* lampooned Graeme Hughes for saying

"A converted try, maybe even just a try, could send us into sudden death", "All you Newcastle fans, they are storming home at the right end of the match" and "Oh what a finish . . . who wrote the script! . . . unbelievable." Bill Anderson copped it for "Those sorts of kicks are good only if they come off" and "Cameron Wade, he's had a memorable series all day". Junior Pearce received a dishonourable mention for "They've caused a few surprise shocks". The paper's sports column "The Eye" condemned the trio's presentation, singled out a few blunders the commentary team had committed and warned that "some League heavies down at Phillip Street are far from impressed with the Channel TEN effort so far."

As with my occasional gaffes, none of the above is a hanging offence. It's just a sad fact of life that some journalists are obsessed with the utterances of TV sports commentators, and the new boys at TEN will have to learn to live with it.

With my pay-out from Channel TEN and my other investments as security, I could have slipped easily into a comfortable retirement — but I had a point to prove. So when Radio 2GB's Jon Harker rang and asked was I available to join him and John McCoy on their Sunday football commentary team I leapt at the chance. The job grew. Soon I was doing the Saturday match as well, and the State of Origin, and the Australia-New Zealand Test series. I was also heard on GB's other sports shows and we even got a radio version of Controversy Corner going.

Sixty Minutes rang and said they wanted to do a profile of me and my career, and the ABC, of all people, got in touch and invited me to be a guest on Andrew Denton's popular sports satire show *Live And Sweaty*. While I was at the ABC studios I met Andrew's mum, a charming lady, who confided to me that her son would always eat his Sunday lunch on his lap while glued to Controversy Corner. So when Andrew decided to include a sports discussion segment on his program he naturally modelled it on my old show, and who better to be a regular panellist than the old bloke who started it all. Being on *Live And Sweaty* has won me a whole lot of new, younger fans. People tell me I'm a cult hero, but I wouldn't know about that. As for Andrew, he's one of the smartest, funniest blokes I've experienced. The only way I can compete with him is by clamping my hand over his mouth, hitting him on the head or throwing glasses of water over him!

I have the occasional guest speaking engagement and a 0055 comment telephone line, where the public can ring me up and have their ears belted with Mossop's opinions on the latest league controversies. I've signed up for a series of Toyota commercials, but with my busted old knees I won't be doing much leaping into the air. I have trouble even playing touch football on them these days. I just shovel the ball out and limp around the paddock like Quasimodo.

I also like to keep my eye on my property investments, which include some very nice land in NSW and Queensland I own in partnership with the tennis great Ken Rosewall and another friend. I owe thanks to an old mate named Sid Chambers who gave me plenty of good advice when I was young about the benefits of wise real estate investment. With these investments, writing this book, and the many other odds and ends that crop up regularly, I am busier than I have ever been. It's true that in my career a lot of people went out of their way to make life hard for me, but when I reflect on my life and see now where I've ended up, I reckon I beat the bastards in the end.

21

THE BEST THINGS IN LIFE

I used to believe the key to happiness was fame and fortune. Bitter experience helped me get my priorities right. It showed me that the cost of wealth and celebrity is high, and it's a price I'm not prepared to pay anymore. I'm a happy, mellow man today, one of the lucky ones. I've emerged from the media rat race still grasping tightly the same things that were dear to me the day I first walked through the doors of Channel 7 28 years ago. I'm older, wiser and I cart around plenty of scar tissue — physical and emotional — but I still have my wife, my health, my dogs and my sport. I live in the same house Joan and I built together back in the '50s and my best mates are blokes I grew up with on the beaches of Manly in the 1930s. These are the things that really matter. Mind you, there have been times in my life when I've come close to blowing the lot.

Joan and I have been lovers and friends now for nearly 50 years. This tough, funny and beautiful woman has been making my life very special for as long as I can remember. She's always had my measure. Through the triumphs and the tragedies she has kept a level head, deflating me when I am pompous, making me laugh when I am sad and giving me the courage to press on when I've felt like packing it in.

We met as teenagers. I was a local knockabout and she was the most sought-after beauty on the beach. For a few years we went steady then drifted away to play the field before linking up again. Just as I knew I would represent my country at football, I always believed Joan and I would share our lives.

I was attracted by her style, her intelligence, her sense of humour and, I have to admit it, her body. From the first day I laid eyes on Joan, poleaxed by a flash of garter high on a tanned leg as I pedalled my pushbike past on Manly Pier, I lusted after her. I lust after her today. Joan is as old as I am, 63, but even after bearing two children she has kept her trim teenage figure. She looks wonderful and I can't keep my hands off her. We're always kissing and holding hands and giving each other a playful pat on the bum. She tells me she has a few lines on her face but I've never seen them. All I see when I look at her is that cheeky face, so full of life, that knocked me head over heels one fateful day on the beach back in the late 1930s.

How she has put up with me for so long defies belief. She coped with being a footballer's wife for the first years of our marriage: the sprains and broken bones, the months spent apart when I was on tour, the late nights out drinking with teammates. Then for the next 28 years she was married to a workaholic TV personality whose life seemed to be lived as much in the public eye as in the privacy of our home. I did many things in those years that I am not proud of. People with a high public profile have to be very strong not to give in to the many temptations on offer and I wasn't always as strong as I should have been. For too many years I took Joan and our home life for granted. For a while there I nearly destroyed our marriage.

Then suddenly, about 13 years ago, lightning struck. I realised what a great woman my wife is. Through all the strife she's been at my side with her jokes and laughter and her great big hugs. I am a big, gruff guy who doesn't wear his heart on his sleeve, but I have no trouble telling Joan that I love her.

Not that we don't squabble. I reckon any couple who don't have the odd blue are probably dead. We have some beauties. It always starts with me losing my temper over something or other. I fly off the handle and give her all my best shots, but I quickly run out of steam. One big explosion and it's over and done with. Joan's different, she's a counterpuncher. She absorbs all my punishment then when I weaken she lets me have it with her quick wit and irrefutable logic. I'm afraid Joan wins most of our fights on points.

Joan made the most of the time I spent away from home either playing football or working late to become a first-rate artist. A prolific painter, she involves herself in art groups and is in the Royal Art Society. She does landscapes and still lifes, but I think her forte is painting portraits. She has a talent for capturing a likeness in her first few strokes. Over the years, Joan has threatened to paint me but I can't sit still long enough.

Dad and Mum and my brother Kirk are all gone now. I'm the last one remaining of that little family who left Five Dock for Balgowlah all those years ago. When Dad retired from Anthony Horderns he slowed down a little, but remained my No.1 supporter and rarely missed a game I played. He was a real character in the neighbourhood and was loved by his many, many friends. The ladies adored old Norman Mossop. They'd come up to him and say, "Hello, Norman," and give him a big kiss on the head. Unlike his son, he had a warm, outgoing personality and could mix easily in any circle.

I can still see him, a lovely old guy in his 70s taking his daily stroll from the old house in Condamine Street along the harbour foreshores into Manly where he'd pass a few hours with his mates at Manly Surf Club. After a while he'd retrace his steps, returning home to be with his memories. Like Mum and Kirk, his heart killed him.

One of the regrets of my life is that Dad died before I could repay him for all he'd done for me. I would like to have lavished on him a few of the luxuries he went without all his days. Although I was working at Channel 7 at the end of Dad's life I was not being paid highly and most of my money was eaten up providing for Joan and the boys. I wish I could have bought him a new house, taken him out on my boat or on a good, long holiday. I loved him, and I think he knew it, but I don't think I ever told him. I know I didn't always show it.

I will regret until my dying day that I found it so hard to show affection to my father and my sons, but this is a mistake I am not repeating with my grandchildren Rebecca, Rachel, Jessica, James and Nathan. They're all terrific kids and I can't see enough of them. For some reason known only to himself, young James calls me "King". He'll go to my place at the table and say, "The King always sits here." He's only seven or eight but he's a determined little terror and has the makings of a good sportsman. His league team won the comp in his first year of footy and James did alright without knowing a whole lot about what was going on. We usually have a few of the grandkids sleeping at our place on the weekends and Joan and I really enjoy having them around. It's almost like getting a second go at parenthood.

Thanks to the children, a lot of the old wounds that existed between me and my sons Kirk and Greg have healed. Ours is not a perfect relationship, but it's better than it used to be and improving all the time. I'm thankful that my boys have had the strength to put their problems far behind them and are now getting on with their lives.

For all the years I spent in TV, it says a lot about the industry that I made no great friends at either Seven or TEN. There were lots of terrific workmates whose company and companionship I enjoyed, but television is a cut-throat game and there is no shortage of jealous and petty people as adept at playing station politics as sticking a knife in your back. Too often in TV it's appearances that count. The publicity machine can turn an unknown into a celebrity overnight and it's not uncommon for a new star to get himself a new personality, new friends, new hair transplant, a new life, to go with his newfound fame.

That's never been the Mossop way. Call me most things, and I'll probably agree with you, but I was never a stuck-up celebrity.

My personality hasn't changed, the hair I've got is a little grey these days, but it will do me fine, and my best mates are blokes I've known for more than half a century. The other two Musketeers, Clarrie Davis and Warwick Ritchie, are both alive and kicking. We all creak a bit now, and our days of ripping off the slot machines at Manly Pier are hopefully over, but we're as

THE BEST THINGS IN LIFE

close as ever. A good wife and good friends keep all the bullshit in perspective.

I've been overwhelmed by the expressions of warmth from the public since I left TEN. I used to be the man everybody loved to hate, and I admit that my aggressive, unlovable ways had plenty to do with that. But these days I get the impression that people genuinely like me and miss me now that I'm not in their living rooms every winter Sunday night. Time was when people would yell abuse when they drove past me on the street. Nowadays they'll most likely shout, "Good on ya, Rex!" or "When are you coming back to TV?" Just recently Joan and I were having dinner in the dining room at Manly Leagues Club. Nearby was a table of about 20 women celebrating a 60th birthday. Somehow one of the women passed word to Joan that the birthday girl was a fan of mine and wouldn't it be marvellous if I could wish her a happy 60th. I waited about 20 minutes then crept up behind the woman, said "Happy birthday!" and gave her a kiss on the cheek. She shrieked and nearly fell off her chair — I'm not sure whether in fright or surprise. When Joan and I finished our meal and went to leave, the women all called out for us to join them. Joan laughed and grabbed my arm and said, "Not tonight, girls. He's mine and I'm taking him home!"

My dogs are a wonderful source of satisfaction. This lifetime love of animals has helped me remain sane, no doubt about it. For some reason I've always found it easier to relate to animals than most humans. I can't stand to see an animal hurt. For this reason I have always made it a practice to avoid stepping on ants, worms and so on. If I see a beetle or a bug on the ground I'll pick it up and put it out of harm's way. At home Joan and I operate what we call "The Bee Patrol" where we rescue bees that fall into our pool. I've lost count of the times I've got out of the car to shepherd snakes, lizards and possums off the road when I'm driving in the bush. Once I stopped the traffic on busy Victoria Road at Ryde after a dog was hit by a car. I came to a screeching halt in my lane so I would not run over the stricken dog and everybody behind me had to hit the brakes as well so as not to run up the back of me. Traffic was in chaos as I picked the dog up and carried it to the footpath. All of a sudden these busy drivers to whom a couple of minutes were more important than the life of a dog started blasting their horns and abusing me. I told them to go to hell as I tended the whimpering beast.

Another time I took my dogs to touch football with me. One of them got a little excited and ran onto the field, bounding around and nipping at the heels of the other players. One bloke took exception and aimed a kick at her. "Kick that dog, my friend," I said, "and I shall take great pleasure in kicking you." I meant it.

Our first dog was Grock. We bought him in 1955, soon after I returned from my stint playing league with Leigh. He was a full blood boxer. Then came Panzer, son of Grock, another full blood boxer. Then Sergeant and Cobber, small blue heeler cattle dogs, Sheba, a boxer bitch, Sam who was part-labrador and part-sheep dog, and Missy and Rocko, a suburban terrier. Missy, a pedigree boxer bitch, and Rocko are still with us today. Rocko, I'm afraid, is a bit of a lad and there are a suspicious number of little Rocko lookalikes in the district. He's spread his seed far and wide. Sam had to be put down only a month or so ago aged 16, Sheba died of heartworm, Cobber hanged himself at a kennel where we'd left him while we were holidaying in Fiji, Sergeant died of old age and Panzer was a ratbag so we gave him away.

Grock lives on in our memories. We got him as an eight-week-old puppy. He was the son of an American grand champion called Warlord of Mazerlane and was named, would you believe, Beresford Dandy of Blossomlea. Well, no dog of Rex Mossop was going to be called Beresford Dandy of Blossomlea, so I changed his name to Grock. Grock weighed 82lbs and was a big friendly, salivating dog. He was also ferocious and the most territorial dog I've ever known. Once he got tangled up with a white alsatian down at Manly and the two dogs went at each other for nearly an hour. I tried to separate them but was badly bitten for my trouble. Eventually they wore themselves out and the epic fight ended with us having to pull Grock's jaws away from the alsatian's throat.

Our dog was also a famous wanderer. On more than 50 occasions I was woken up at midnight or later by the harbinger at Manly Wharf who would say, "Sorry to bother you, Rex, but your dog's just been found at Circular Quay. They're putting him on the first ferry home. Can you come down and collect him?" I'll never know how, but in his lifetime Grock also found his way from Balgowlah to the Sydney Showground, to Woolloomooloo, and onto a tramp steamer docked at Walsh Bay.

Grock could be a real nuisance and once made me so angry that I knocked him out, as cold as a spud. At the risk of upsetting the RSPCA, here's how it happened. When my sons were very young — Kirk was five and Greg one and a half — Joan and I took them on a walk along the rocky headland at Forty Baskets Beach to Dad's place in Condamine Street. Grock came too. As we were walking along a bush path bordering a sheer drop down to the water, Grock saw another dog and started growling. I yelled at him to heel but he took no notice and hared off after the enemy. In his rush he barrelled into Kirk, knocking him flying in the direction of the precipice. I grabbed the boy just before he plummeted over. I was so enraged with Grock that when he finally returned I hauled off and hit him on the nose with a big right hook. Down he went, unconscious. We were all relieved when he came to his senses a few minutes later and we all continued our walk with no hard feelings.

Today, I take Missy and Rocko with me nearly everywhere I go. So if you're around Manly and Balgowlah and you see an old bloke in shorts and a floppy hat shambling along the road with two frisky hounds in tow, chances are it'll be me and my two mates.

Fortress Mossop has grown like Topsy over the years. We bought our block of land in Balgowlah for 1000 pounds in 1951. In 1957 we built a small weatherboard cottage on the land and made extensions as the need arose. It's now a spacious two-storey house. Many times in my life I've been so glad to come home, close that front door and lock the world away. There is lots of Joan and me in our house. You can see her artistic touch in the bedrooms and the lounge room, while the mark of the Moose is unmistakable in the family room. It's there I keep the mementoes of my football and TV career, my photographs, trophies, books, my TV and video set-up and my paperwork. Unlike other rooms of the house where you find flower patterns, chintz and frills, the family room furniture is of dark brown leather. A common touch throughout the house is paintings by Joan and my brother Kirk. There is a self-portrait of Kirk in the family room. He painted it in the last years of his life and looks a lot more severe in it than I remember him. The entertainment room opens onto my other workplace, the swimming pool, sauna and barbecue area.

I love the feeling of the sun on my body. When people ask me why I'm always so brown I tell them it's because all my skin cancers have joined together. In summer and winter I strip to a pair of swimming costumes, drag a banana chair out beside the pool and do my writing and make my phone calls in the sunshine. Only the bleakest day will drive me indoors. Beside my banana chair I keep an old set of weights which I lift as I work and I try to break up my day at the "office" by swimming a few laps.

I always start each day with a run, about three kilometres around the parks and bays of the district. I follow that with a swim in the surf or the pool. I try to make time to walk the dogs along the beach. Wearing nothing but my old shorts and my big floppy sun-hat I must look like some grizzled old beachcomber, and maybe that's what I am. Throughout the day I'll lift weights as the mood takes me. I've got a battered old set of dumbells that I've been hefting around for years and they reside permanently by the pool. In the late afternoon I'll have another jog. On weekends I might play touch football with some mates, even though my wrecked right knee makes running harder every day.

I first damaged the knee when a Canterbury player fell across it in a game at Belmore Oval. He twisted my leg right around and I can still hear the crunching sound my knee ligaments made. I missed the next game, but should have taken more time off to get my knee right. It was never the same again. In '78 I had it operated on but the surgeon tightened up the ligaments so much that I've never been able to extend my leg since.

My spinal injury, caused when big Jack Wilkinson dumped me in 1955, is still there, but no longer causes me any pain thanks to the surgical skill of Dr Skyrme Rees. I have a liitle arthritis in the knee and sometimes my hands ache, a legacy of 17 broken fingers. Many of these fractures were the work of Balmain players. The Tigers in my day loved to stand on your hands as you rose to play the ball. My cauliflower ears, broken nose and sundry other aches and pains remind me of my league and union years. I'm no special case, however. Most footballers are plagued for the rest of their lives by injuries sustained in their playing careers. Happily my stroke has left no lasting scars except occasionally I'll have a slight memory loss or forget my train of thought and go off on another tangent.

Most sports and games have come naturally to me, but there have been a couple I've never been able to master. I used to go down to the snow to ski when the kids were younger. They were excellent skiers and Greg became an instructor. The boys were both good surfers before they hit the slopes and took to the sport like veterans. I remember the first time I took them to Perisher. "OK," I said, "we'll go up to the top of the mountain then you both follow me down single file. We'll do our left turns very slowly, and then we'll turn right. In a few weeks you'll get the hang of it." Of course when we got to the top, Greg and Kirk said, "See you later, Dad!" and they took off hell for leather down the slope leaving their red-faced father in their wake.

Joan reckons I'm the funniest skier she's ever seen. I used to wear a headband to protect my cauliflower ears from the icy winds, and I'd always be falling down and swearing loudly. At the end of the day everyone would turn up at the chalet for drinks looking immaculate, and I'd stumble in, headband askew, sopping wet from all my falls and in a ropable mood.

Golf was another sport I could never get the hang of, not that

I didn't give it my best shot. I played the game without success for 25 years. At one stage I was so determined to master this frustrating, absorbing game that I paid for lessons and I'd go down to Manly Golf Club before work and and put in an hour belting practice balls to get my swing right. All I was doing was practising my mistakes.

About 10 years ago I realised that as long as I lived I would never correct my built-in slice and thought, "What the hell, I'd rather be swimming or sunbaking or boating." About then we bought a boat, and it's become a terrific part of our lives because going boating is something Joan and I enjoy and can do together. We love cruising Sydney Harbour and Middle Harbour in *The Moose*. It's a 40ft, twin-engine, V-shaped cruiser. I swim off the side while the grandkids fish and usually we'll drop anchor off one of those picturesque little beaches and have a picnic.

Both Joan and I have a thing about Italian food. She's an excellent cook, but there are any number of terrific little Italian BYOs in the area and we'd eat out about three times a week. I'm not into octopus or sardines, but I love the way Italian chefs cook prawns and lobster. I think God must have been an Italiano.

Joan and I are both film buffs and we've collected an extensive video library, divided up into movie classics, musicals, sport, current affairs and kids' shows for the grandchildren. We pull our favourites out once or twice a year and enjoy them together. My all-time-great movie is *The Quiet Man* starring John Wayne and directed by John Ford. It's funny and very Irish in an idealised way with lots of singing and downing Guinness stout in pubs and lush emerald green scenery. There's also a bit of biffo when John Wayne and Victor McLaglen turn on one of the best brawls ever filmed. We'll also watch anything by Woody Allen — a genius — or starring Errol Flynn or Humphrey Bogart.

I enjoy music, but not heavy metal. Andrew Denton always has a loud rock band appearing on *Live And Sweaty* and they play unbelievably loudly. I reckon they've done more damage to my poor old ears than 20 years of packing into scrums. I like a wide variety of music. I go more for the classics — piano concertos — and I marvel at the beautiful voices of Pavarotti, Domingo and Carrera on *The Three Tenors*. I'm a Sinatra fan and, unlike a lot of Frankie's critics, I'd be happy if he kept singing till his dying day. He obviously enjoys it so why shouldn't he keep it up? I agree his voice is not what it used to be but he's one of the true greats of entertainment. I also have time for the country singers John Denver and Willie Nelson.

I'm a reader but don't read as voraciously as I did in my early TV days when I saw reading as a way of increasing my word power. My preference for the past few years has been for biographies or books on World War Two. I'm a keen student of the conflict and must have read most of what's been written about it, including many books by German military men that have been translated into English. The Germans' Russian campaign — when millions upon millions died — holds particular fascination for me. The world really did go mad in that period.

If I said, "Come on, Joan, we're off to England . . . or Asia, or America" she'd have her bags packed and be calling the cab for the airport within the hour. Once I would have been as keen, but not any more. I've seen most of the world and my curiosity is satisfied. Travel today is too frustrating for me: long queues at airports, immigration hassles, language barriers, the traffic, trying to find a hotel, grappling with strange currencies. I can't handle it any more. We both plan to see a lot more of Australia over the next few years and may even live part of the year on our property on the beach up at Mackay.

On the walls of my entertainment room are many framed photographs. There is one of me riding a surfboard back in the early '40s. In another, Dad is helping me clean barnacles off the bottom of a boat. Yet another shows me being sent from the field after clashing with Mike Sullivan in the Great Britain-NSW game in 1958. Other football shots have me scoring a try in the First Test of that year, crunching an All Black in a tackle, and running with the ball in my hands and straining to set up a support, possibly Johnny Raper or Harry Wells, who is ranging up alongside. There is a picture of me wearing a check coat and turtleneck sweater, my trademark gear in the Channel 7 days. Steve Liebmann features in a shot taken at my 60th birthday party at Channel TEN. You can see me sitting in the commentary box in the stand at Hull, mouth wide open as I describe Kangaroo winger Eric Grothe, hair streaming behind him as he races down the sideline in a Test against the Poms. Elsewhere on the wall are photos of Joan, the boys, the grandchildren and my dynasty of dogs. Many of the most important times of my life are there, frozen in time. In the years to come I plan to make many additions to the Mossop gallery.

I have a few regrets about my life. I wish I'd been a better family man and a better husband to Joan in those hectic, workaholic TV years. I'm sorry I wasn't able to show more affection to Dad and my boys. I should have turned to rugby league earlier. I wish I'd never bought my brother Kirk those running shoes. And I probably shouldn't be such a penny-pincher. I'm generous with large amounts of money and am on every charity's mailing list, but I'm notoriously stingy with the small sums. That's what comes of being a Depression kid. No other regrets come to mind.

I admit it, I am mellowing, maybe even slowing down a little. I have learned at last what are the real priorities of life and I'm grateful now to have the time and good health to enjoy them. But before I go I have a warning for my traditional foes — to the wimps and weaklings, nude bathers, can throwers and loud-mouthed louts, to the poison pen journos and those who would turn rugby league into tiddlywinks. The warning is this: Beware! There's plenty of roar in the old Moose yet.

POSTSCRIPT

THE GAME
I LOVE

A part from my wife, the great love in my life has been rugby league. It's infuriated me, exasperated me, flabbergasted me — but I have never stopped loving this wonderful sport. It makes me angry when people try to change it, when they try to water it down by banning rugged play, or to Americanise it, or bring in rules that stifle creativity and take the guts out of the game. At its best, league provides more drama, excitement, courage, skill and power than any other sport..

Of the thousands of games I've seen, a few stand out as classics. In this category I'd put the First and Second Tests against England in 1958 and the First Test against the Poms in 1959, the World Cup match against the Englishmen in 1960 at Bradford, the Second Test against France in 1960 when we won 56-6, the Battle of Leeds — Australia versus England in the World Cup final of 1970, the Manly-Cronulla grand final of 1973 - as wild and dramatic a match as I have ever witnessed, and the Test series against Great Britain in 1982, '86 and '90. I also enjoy State of Origin and would give plenty to have had the chance to play in some of these terrific contests.

I'll finish my book by paying tribute to a few of the players who have made the game great for me over the years. Here is my choice of the six best players I have seen in my time as a player and commentator.

Johnny Raper: The best all-round player bar none. Chook had it all. He had magnificent ball skills and superb defence. He was a master of every facet of the game. And, as important as anything, he was durable.

Harry Bath: Ruthless, strong and skilful and a prolific goalkicker. Would have been one of the first men picked in Australian Test sides between 1950-57 had he not been playing in England. Like Raper, durable.

Reg Gasnier: The Prince of Centres, he had blinding acceleration, a mesmerising swerve, was fast over a distance and could sniff out tries when nothing seemed on. A steady defender.

Bob Fulton: The most tough-minded and competitive player I have ever known. Hated to lose. He was clever, elusive, had immense strength and was very, very fast. Although he often played centre, Bozo's best position was five eighth.

Brian Bevan: It was a pleasure to play against this remarkable athlete. Unwanted in Australia, he went to Warrington where he scored 796 tries in 15 seasons and became a hero. He was the best attacking player in the world — and the ugliest.

Vince Karalius: The hardest of all the hard men. For years he took my best shots without blinking. Demolished me on three separate occasions. A hard runner and spirited tackler who loved to win; never more so than when playing against Australians, whom he hated.

Honourable mentions must go to Clive Churchill, Graeme Langlands, Ken Irvine, Ian Moir, Eddie Lumsden, Harry Wells, Steve Rogers, Poppa Clay, Keith Holman, Peter Diversi, Roy Bull, Alex Murphy, Billy Smith, Ron Coote, Malcolm Reilly, Jack Rayner, Norm Provan, Arthur Beetson, John O'Neill and Brian McTigue.

I believe that only a handful of the players of the modern era could match it with these giants of earlier days. Wally Lewis, at his best, would be a star in any company, but I cringe at many of the things he's done that I believe have harmed the game's image. Peter Sterling, Brett Kenny, Gene Miles, Ellery Hanley, Mal Meninga, Michael O'Connor,Steve Rogers, Mick Cronin, Ben Elias, are all top rank players. But true greats of the code? I will reserve my judgement on that. Allan Langer and Mark Geyer have the potential to be anything, but both still have a lot to prove as far as I am concerned. Eric Grothe had everything a great winger should have, except durability, a key factor when assessing greatness in a rugby league player.

The wonderful thing about our game is that it keeps throwing up new stars, new skills and new controversies. Every game has the potential to be a classic encounter. I'll be a fan for the rest of my life. One day, a long time off I hope, the groundsman at Brookvale Oval will find an old bloke with cauliflower ears, big gnarled hands and a much-broken nose slumped over his microphone in the commentary box. It'll be a warm winter's afternoon with the Sunday sun shimmering off the sea nearby. The happy sounds of the Manly boys celebrating another victory will be drifting up from the dressing room below. I'll have a smile on my face.